The THINK
& GROW
RICH
ACTION
PACK

The THINK & GROW RICH ACTION PACK

NAPOLEON HILL

E. P. DUTTON · NEW YORK

Published in the United States by E. P. Dutton,
a division of Penguin Books USA Inc.,
2 Park Avenue, New York, N.Y. 10016.

Published simultaneously in Canada by
Fitzhenry and Whiteside,
Limited, Toronto.

Library of Congress Catalog Card Number: 75-38620

ISBN: 0-525-48349-7

3 5 7 9 10 8 6 4

Contents

Contents

A Word from the Publisher:

IT GIVES YOU A TESTED PLAN THAT MAKES MEN RICH. IT shows you exactly how to use it, and gets you started right now.

What is it that makes one man march forward all his life, accomplishing, earning, multiplying his wealth and his happiness—while another man never gets started?

What is it that gives one man great personal power, but leaves another ineffectual? What makes one man able to see his way through any problem, find his path over all the rough spots of life to the fulfillment of his dearest dreams—while another struggles, fails, ends nowhere?

Years ago, Napoleon Hill sat down with Andrew Carnegie, then one of the world's richest men, and caught his first glimpse of the great Secret. Hill was entrusted by Carnegie to find out

One of the World's Most Powerful Books Is in Your Hands.

---

how others used the Secret, to study their methods, and to work out a single method that could be given to the world as a Master Plan.

THINK AND GROW RICH reveals the Secret and gives the Plan. Since its publication in 1937, 42 editions have been bought as fast as they could be printed. The present edition is brought up to date with brand new special aids, including a chapter-by-chapter one-page "refresher course."

At last here is the one, sure way to overcome *all* obstacles, achieve *any* ambition, bring success as though provided from an ever-flowing river. This book is about to shake you with its life-transforming power. Soon you will know *why* certain people acquire great stores of money and happiness—because you will be one of those people.

Preface

IN EVERY CHAPTER OF THIS BOOK I MENTION THE MONEY-making secret that has made fortunes for hundreds of exceedingly wealthy men—men I have carefully analyzed over a long period of years.

The secret was brought to my attention by Andrew Carnegie more than half a century ago. The canny, lovable old Scotsman carelessly tossed it into my mind when I was but a boy. Then he sat back in his chair with a merry twinkle in his eyes and watched carefully to see if I had brains enough to understand the full significance of what he had said to me.

When he saw that I had grasped the idea, he asked if I would be willing to spend twenty years or more preparing myself to take it to the world, to men and women who, without the secret, might go through life as failures. I said I would and, with Mr. Carnegie's cooperation, I have kept my promise.

This book contains the secret, a secret put to practical test by thousands of people, in almost every walk of life. It was Mr. Carnegie's idea that the magic formula, which gave him a stupendous fortune, ought to be placed within reach of people who do not have time to investigate how men make money, and it was his hope that I might test and demonstrate the soundness of the formula through the experience of men and women in every calling. He believed the formula should be taught in all public schools and colleges, and expressed the opinion that if it were properly taught it would so revolutionize the entire education system that the time spent in school could be reduced to less than half.

True Stories Prove the Secret's Amazing Power

In the chapter on Faith, you will read the astounding story of the organization of the giant United States Steel Corporation, as it was conceived and carried out by one of the young men through whom Mr. Carnegie proved that his formula will work *for all who are ready for it*. This single application of the secret by Charles M. Schwab made him a huge fortune in both money and opportunity. Roughly speaking, this particular application of the formula was worth *six hundred million dollars*.

These facts—and they are facts well known to almost everyone who knew Mr. Carnegie—give you a fair idea of what the reading of this book may bring to you, provided you *know what you want*.

The secret was passed on to thousands of men and women who have used it for their personal benefit, as Mr. Carnegie planned that they should. Some have made fortunes with it. Others have used it successfully in creating harmony in their homes. A clergyman used it so effectively that it brought him an income of upwards of $75,000 a year.

Arthur Nash, a Cincinnati tailor, used his near-bankrupt business as a "guinea pig" on which to test the formula. The business came to life and made a fortune for its owners. It is still thriving, although Mr. Nash has gone. The experiment was so unique that newspapers and magazines gave it more than a million dollars' worth of laudatory publicity.

The secret was passed on to Stuart Austin Wier, of Dallas, Texas. He was ready for it—so ready that he gave up his profession and studied law. Did he succeed? That story is told, too.

While serving as advertising manager of the LaSalle Extension University when the university was little more than a name, I had the privilege of seeing J. G. Chapline, president of the university, use the formula so effectively that he made LaSalle one of the great extension schools of the country.

The secret to which I refer has been mentioned no fewer than a hundred times throughout this book. It has not been directly named, for it seems to work more successfully when it is merely uncovered and left in sight, where those who are ready and searching for it may pick it up. That is why Mr. Carnegie tossed it to me so quietly, without giving me its specific name.

The Secret Speaks to Those Who Listen

If you are ready to put it to use, you will recognize this secret at least once in every chapter. I wish I might feel privileged to tell you how you will know if you are ready, but that would deprive you of much of the benefit you will receive when you make the discovery in your own way.

If you have ever been discouraged, if you have had difficulties to surmount which took the very soul out of you, if you have tried and failed, if you were ever handicapped by illness or physical affliction, the story of my son's discovery and use of the Carnegie formula may prove to be the oasis in the Desert of Lost Hope for which you have been searching.

This secret was extensively used by President Woodrow Wilson during World War I. It was passed on to every soldier who fought in the war, carefully wrapped in the training he received before going to the front. President Wilson told me it was a strong factor in raising the funds needed for the war.

A peculiar thing about this secret is that those who once acquire it and use it find themselves literally swept on to success. If you doubt this, study the names of those who have used it wherever they have been mentioned; check their records for yourself, and be convinced.

There is no such thing as something for nothing!

The secret to which I refer cannot be had without a price, although the price is far less than its value. It cannot be had at any price by those who are not intentionally searching for it. It cannot be given away, it cannot be purchased for money, for the reason that it comes in two parts. One part is already in possession of those who are ready for it.

The secret serves equally well all who are ready for it. Education has nothing to do with it. Long before I was born, the secret had found its way into the possession of Thomas A. Edison, and he used it so intelligently that he became the world's leading inventor, although he had had but three months of schooling.

The secret was passed on to Edwin C. Barnes, a business associate of Mr. Edison. He used it so effectively that, although he was then making only $12,000 a year, he accumulated a great fortune and retired from active business while still a young man. You will find his story at the beginning of the first chapter. It should convince you that riches are not beyond your reach, that you can still be what you wish to be, that money, fame, recognition and happiness can be had by all who are ready and determined to have these blessings.

How do I know these things? You should have the answer before you finish this book. You may find it in the very first chapter, or on the last page.

While I was performing the twenty-year task of research, which I had undertaken at Mr. Carnegie's request, I analyzed hundreds of well-known men, many of whom admitted that they had accumulated their vast fortunes through the aid of the Carnegie secret; among these men were:

HENRY FORD

WILLIAM WRIGLEY JR.

JOHN WANAMAKER

JAMES J. HILL

GEORGE S. PARKER

E. M. STATLER

HENRY L. DOHERTY

CYRUS H. K. CURTIS

GEORGE EASTMAN

CHARLES M. SCHWAB

HARRIS F. WILLIAMS

DR. FRANK GUNSAULUS

DANIEL WILLARD

KING GILLETTE

RALPH A. WEEKS

JUDGE DANIEL T.
   WRIGHT

JOHN D. ROCKEFELLER

THOMAS A. EDISON

FRANK A. VANDERLIP

THEODORE ROOSEVELT

JOHN W. DAVIS

ELBERT HUBBARD

WILBUR WRIGHT

WILLIAM JENNINGS BRYAN

DR. DAVID STARR JORDAN

J. ODGEN ARMOUR

ARTHUR BRISBANE

WOODROW WILSON

WILLIAM HOWARD TAFT

LUTHER BURBANK

EDWARD W. BOK

FRANK A. MUNSEY

ELBERT H. GARY

CLARENCE DARROW

DR. ALEXANDER GRAHAM
   BELL

JOHN H. PATTERSON

JULIUS ROSENWALD

STUART AUSTIN WIER

F. W. WOOLWORTH   DR. FRANK CRANE
COL. ROBERT A.   GEORGE M. ALEXANDER
    DOLLAR   J. G. CHAPLINE
EDWARD A. FILENE   U.S. SEN. JENNINGS
EDWIN C. BARNES   RANDOLPH
ARTHUR NASH

These names represent but a small fraction of the hundreds
of well-known Americans whose achievements, financial and
otherwise, prove that those who understand and apply the
Carnegie secret reach high stations in life. I have never known
anyone who was inspired to use the secret who did not achieve
noteworthy success in his chosen calling. I have never known
any person to distinguish himself, or to accumulate riches of
any consequence, without possession of the secret. From these
two facts I draw the conclusion that the secret is more important, as a part of the knowledge essential for self-determina-
tion, than any which one receives through what is popularly
known as "education."

What is education, anyway? This has been answered in full
detail.

The Turning Point in Your Life

Somewhere, as you read, the secret to which I refer will
jump from the page and stand boldly before you, if you are
ready for it! When it appears, you will recognize it. Whether
you receive the sign in the first or the last chapter, stop for a
moment when it presents itself, and turn down a glass for that
occasion will mark the most important turning point of your
life.

Remember, too, as you go through the book, that it deals
with facts and not with fiction, its purpose being to convey a

great universal truth through which all who are ready may learn *what* to do and *how* to do it! They will also receive the needed stimulus to make a start.

As a final word of preparation, before you begin the first chapter, may I offer one brief suggestion which may provide a clue by which the Carnegie secret may be recognized? It is this—*all achievement, all earnèd riches, have their beginning in an idea!* If you are ready for the secret, you already possess one half of it; therefore, you will readily recognize the other half the moment it reaches your mind.

NAPOLEON HILL

Thoughts
Are Things

TRULY, "THOUGHTS ARE THINGS," AND POWERFUL THINGS at that when they are mixed with definiteness of purpose, persistence, and a burning desire for their translation into riches, or other material objects.

Some years ago Edwin C. Barnes discovered how true it is that men really do *think and grow rich*. His discovery did not come about at one sitting. It came little by little, beginning with a burning desire to become a business associate of the great Edison.

One of the chief characteristics of Barnes' desire was that it was *definite*. He wanted to work *with* Edison, not *for* him. Observe carefully the description of how he went about translating his desire into reality, and you will have a better understanding of the principles which lead to riches.

The power that signals success is the power of your mind.
How to make life say YES instead of NO to your plans and your ambitions.

When this desire or impulse of thought first flashed into his mind he was in no position to act upon it. Two difficulties stood in his way. He did not know Edison, and he could not pay his railroad fare to East Orange, New Jersey,

These difficulties were sufficient to have discouraged the majority of men from making any attempt to carry out the desire. But his was no ordinary desire!

Edison Looked Into His Face....

He presented himself at Mr. Edison's laboratory and announced he had come to go into business with the inventor. In speaking of the first meeting between Barnes and Edison, years later, Mr. Edison said:

"He stood there before me, looking like an ordinary tramp, *but there was something in the expression of his face which conveyed the impression that he was determined to get what he had come after.* I had learned, from years of experience with men, that when a man really desires a thing so deeply that he is willing to stake his entire future on a single turn of the wheel in order to get it, he is sure to win. I gave him the opportunity he asked for, *because I saw he had made up his mind to stand by until he succeeded.* Subsequent events proved that no mistake was made."

It could not have been the young man's appearance which got him his start in the Edison office, for that was definitely against him. It was what he *thought* that counted.

Barnes did not get his partnership with Edison on his first interview. He did get a chance to work in the Edison offices, at a very nominal wage.

Months went by. Apparently nothing happened to bring nearer the coveted goal which Barnes had set up in his mind as his *definite major purpose.* But something important was happening in Barnes' mind. He was constantly intensifying his desire to become the business associate of Edison.

Psychologists have correctly said that "when one is truly ready for a thing, it puts in its appearance." Barnes was ready for a business association with Edison; moreover, he was determined to remain ready until he got that which he was seeking.

He did not say to himself, "Ah well, what's the use? I guess I'll change my mind and try for a salesman's job." But he did say, "I came here to go into business with Edison, and I'll accomplish this end if it takes the remainder of my life." *He meant it!* What a different story men would have to tell if only they would adopt a definite purpose, and stand by that purpose until it had time to become an all-consuming obsession!

Maybe young Barnes did not know it at the time, but his bulldog determination, his persistence in standing back of a single desire was destined to mow down all opposition and bring him the opportunity he was seeking.

Opportunity Came by the Back Door

When the opportunity came, it appeared in a different form and from a different direction than Barnes had expected. That is one of the tricks of opportunity. It has a sly habit of slipping in by the back door, and often it comes disguised in the form of misfortune, or temporary defeat. Perhaps this is why so many fail to recognize opportunity.

Mr. Edison had just perfected a new office device, known at that time as the Edison Dictating Machine. His salesmen were not enthusiastic over the machine. They did not believe it could be sold without great effort.

Barnes knew he could sell the Edison Dictating Machine. He suggested this to Edison, and promptly got his chance. He did sell the machine. In fact, he sold it so successfully that Edison gave him a contract to distribute and market it all over the nation. Out of that business association Barnes made himself rich in money, but he did something infinitely greater. He proved that one really may *think and grow rich.*

How much actual cash that original desire of Barnes' was worth to him, I have no way of knowing. Perhaps it brought him two or three million dollars, but the amount, whatever it is, becomes insignificant when it is compared with the greater asset he acquired in the form of definite knowledge that *an intangible impulse of thought can be transmuted into material rewards* by the application of known principles.

Barnes literally *thought* himself into a partnership with the great Edison! He thought himself into a fortune. He had nothing to start with except the capacity to know what he wanted, and the determination to stand by that desire until he realized it.

The Man Who Quit Too Soon

One of the most common causes of failure is the habit of quitting when one is overtaken by *temporary defeat*. Every person is guilty of this mistake at one time or another.

An uncle of R. U. Darby was caught by the "gold fever" in the gold-rush days, and went west to dig and grow rich. He had never heard that *more gold has been mined from the thoughts of men than has ever been taken from the earth.* He staked a claim and went to work with pick and shovel.

After weeks of labor, he was rewarded by the discovery of the shining ore. He needed machinery to bring the ore to the surface. Quietly, he covered up the mine, retraced his footsteps to his home in Williamsburg, Maryland, and told his relatives and a few neighbors of the "strike." They got together money for the needed machinery and had it shipped. The uncle and Darby went back to work the mine.

The first car of ore was mined and shipped to a smelter. The returns proved they had one of the richest mines in Colorado! A few more cars of that ore would clear the debts. Then would come the big killing in profits.

Down went the drills! Up went the hopes of Darby and Uncle! Then something happened. The vein of gold ore disappeared! They had come to the end of the rainbow, and the pot of gold was no longer there. They drilled on, desperately trying to pick up the vein again—all to no avail.

Finally, they decided to *quit*.

They sold the machinery to a junk man for a few hundred

dollars, and took the train back home. The junk man called in a mining engineer to look at the mine and do a little calculating. The engineer advised that the project had failed because the owners were not familiar with "fault lines." His calculations showed that the vein would be found *just three feet from where the Darbys had stopped drilling!* That is exactly where it was found!

The junk man took millions of dollars in ore from the mine because he knew enough to seek expert counsel before giving up.

Success with One Step Beyond Defeat

Long afterward Mr. Darby recouped his loss many times over *when he made the discovery* that desire can be transmuted into gold. The discovery came after he went into the business of selling life insurance.

Remembering that he lost a huge fortune because he stopped three feet from gold Darby profited by the experience in his chosen work by the simple method of saying to himself, "I stopped three feet from gold, but I will never stop *because men say 'no'* when I ask them to buy insurance."

Darby became one of a small group of men who sell over a million dollars in life insurance annually. He owed his "stickability" to the lesson he learned from his "quitability" in the gold mining business.

Before success comes in any man's life he is sure to meet with much temporary defeat and, perhaps, some failure. When defeat overtakes a man, the easiest and most logical thing to do is to quit. That is exactly what the majority of men do.

More than five hundred of the most successful men this country has ever known told the author their greatest success came just one step *beyond* the point at which defeat had overtaken them. Failure is a trickster with a keen sense of irony and cunning. It takes great delight in tripping one when success is almost within reach.

The Child Who Mastered a Man

Shortly after Mr. Darby had received his degree from the "College of Hard Knocks" and had decided to profit by his experience in the gold mining business, he had the good fortune to be present on an occasion that proved to him that "No" does not necessarily mean no.

One afternoon he was helping his uncle grind wheat in an old-fashioned mill. The uncle operated a large farm on which a number of colored share-crop farmers lived. Quietly, the door was opened, and a small colored child, the daughter of a tenant, walked in and took her place near the door.

The uncle looked up, saw the child, and barked at her roughly, "What do you want?"

Meekly, the child replied, "My mammy say send her fifty cents."

"I'll not do it," the uncle retorted, "now you run on home."

"Yas sah," the child replied. *But she did not move.*

The uncle went ahead with his work, so busily engaged that he did not pay enough attention to the child to observe that she did not leave. When he looked up and saw her still standing there, he yelled at her, "I told you to go on home! Now go, or I'll take a switch to you."

The little girl said "Yas sah," *but she did not budge.*

The uncle dropped a sack of grain he was about to pour into the mill hopper, picked up a barrel stave, and started toward the child with an expression on his face that indicated trouble.

Darby held his breath. He was certain he was about to witness an assault. He knew his uncle had a fierce temper.

When the uncle reached the spot where the child was standing, she quickly stepped forward one step, looked up into his eyes, and screamed at the top of her shrill voice, "*My mammy's gotta have that fifty cents!*"

The uncle stopped, looked at her for a minute, then slowly laid the barrel stave on the floor, put his hand in his pocket, took out half a dollar, and gave it to her.

The child took the money and slowly backed toward the door, never taking her eyes off the man *whom she had just conquered.* After she had gone, the uncle sat down on a box and looked out the window into space for more than ten minutes. He was pondering, with awe, over the whipping he had just taken.

Mr. Darby too was doing some thinking. That was the first time in all his experience that he had seen a colored child deliberately *master* an adult white person. How did she do it? What happened to his uncle that caused him to lose his fierceness and become as docile as a lamb? What strange power did this child use that made her master of the situation? These and other similar questions flashed into Darby's mind, but he did not find the answer until years later, when he told me the story.

Strangely, the story of this unusual experience was told to the author in the old mill, on the very spot where the uncle took his whipping.

The "Yes" Behind the "No"

As we stood there in that musty old mill, Mr. Darby repeated the story of the unusual conquest and finished by asking, "What can you make of it? What strange power did that child use that so completely whipped my uncle?"

The answer to his question will be found in the principles

described in this book. The answer is full and complete. It contains details and instructions sufficient to enable anyone to understand and apply the same force which the little child accidentally stumbled upon.

Keep your mind alert, and you will observe exactly what strange power came to the rescue of the child. You will catch a glimpse of this power in the next chapter. Somewhere in the book you will find an idea that will quicken your receptive powers, and place at your command, for your own benefit, this same irresistible power. The awareness of this power may come to you in the first chapter, or it may flash into your mind in some subsequent chapter. It may come in the form of a single idea. Or, it may come in the nature of a plan or a purpose. Again, it may cause you to go back into your past experiences of failure or defeat and bring to the surface some lesson by which you can regain all that you lost through defeat.

After I had described to Mr. Darby the power unwittingly used by the little colored child, he quickly retraced his thirty years of experience as a life insurance salesman, and frankly acknowledged that his success in that field was due, in no small degree, to the lesson he had learned from the child.

Mr. Darby pointed out: "Every time a prospect tried to bow me out without buying, I saw that child standing there in the old mill, her big eyes glaring in defiance, and I said to myself: 'I've gotta make this sale.' The better portion of all sales I have made were made after people had said 'NO.'"

He recalled, too, his mistake in having stopped only three feet from gold. "But," he said, "that experience was a blessing in disguise. It taught me to *keep on keeping on*, no matter how hard the going may be, a lesson I needed to learn before I could succeed in anything."

Mr. Darby's experiences were commonplace and simple

enough, yet they held the answer to his destiny in life; therefore they were as important (to him) as life itself. He profited by these two dramatic experiences because *he analyzed them*, and found the lesson they taught. But what of the man who has neither the time, nor the inclination to study failure in search of knowledge that may lead to success? Where and how is he to learn the art of converting defeat into stepping stones to opportunity?

In answer to these questions, this book was written.

With One Sound Idea You Achieve Success

The answer called for a description of thirteen principles, but remember, as you read, the answer *you* may be seeking to the questions which have caused you to ponder over the strangeness of life may be found *in your own mind*, through some idea, plan, or purpose which may spring into your mind as you read.

One sound idea is all that one needs to achieve success. The principles described in this book contain ways and means of creating useful ideas.

Before we go any further in our approach to the description of these principles, we believe you are entitled to receive this important suggestion:

> *When riches begin to come they come so quickly, in such great abundance, that one wonders where they have been hiding during all those lean years.*

This is an astounding statement, and all the more so when we take into consideration the popular belief that riches come only to those who work hard and long.

When you begin to think and grow rich, you will observe that riches begin with a state of mind, with definiteness of purpose, with little or no hard work. You, and every other person, ought to be interested in knowing how to acquire that state of mind which will attract riches. I spent twenty-five years in research because I too wanted to know "how wealthy men become that way."

Observe very closely, as soon as you master the principles of this philosophy and begin to follow the instructions for applying those principles, your financial status will begin to improve, and everything you touch will begin to transmute itself into an asset for your benefit. Impossible? Not at all!

One of the main weaknesses of mankind is the average man's familiarity with the word "impossible." He knows all the rules which will not work. He knows all the things which cannot be done. This book was written for those who seek the rules which have made others successful, and are willing to *stake everything* on those rules.

Success comes to those who become success conscious.

Failure comes to those who indifferently allow themselves to become failure conscious.

The object of this book is to help all who seek it to learn the art of changing their minds from failure consciousness to success consciousness.

Another weakness found in altogether too many people is the habit of measuring everything, and everyone, by *their own* impressions and beliefs. Some persons who read this will believe that they cannot think and grow rich because their thought habits have been steeped in poverty, want, misery, failure, and defeat.

These unfortunate people remind me of a prominent Chinese, who came to America to be educated in American ways. He attended the University of Chicago. One day President Harper met this young Oriental on the campus, stopped to chat with him for a few minutes, and asked what had impressed him as being the most noticeable characteristic of the American people.

"Why," the student exclaimed, "the queer slant of your eyes. Your eyes are off slant!"

What do we say about the Chinese?

We refuse to believe that which we do not understand. We foolishly believe that our own limitations are the proper measure of limitations. Sure, the other fellow's eyes are "off slant," because they are not the same as our own.

"I Want It and I'll Have It"

When Henry Ford decided to produce his famous V-8 motor, he chose to build an engine with the entire eight cylinders cast in one block, and instructed his engineers to produce a design for the engine. The design was placed on paper, but the engineers agreed, to a man, that it was simply *impossible* to cast an eight-cylinder engine block in one piece.

Ford said, "Produce it anyway."

"But," they replied, "it's impossible!"

"Go ahead," Ford commanded, "and stay on the job until you succeed, no matter how much time is required."

The engineers went ahead. There was nothing else for them to do if they were to remain on the Ford staff. Six months went by, nothing happened. Another six months passed, and still nothing happened. The engineers tried every conceivable plan to carry out the orders, but the thing seemed out of the question; *"impossible!"*

At the end of the year Ford checked with his engineers, and again they informed him they had found no way to carry out his orders.

"Go right ahead," said Ford. "I want it, and I'll have it."

They went ahead, and then, as if by a stroke of magic, the secret was discovered.

The Ford determination had won once more!

This story may not be described with minute accuracy, but the sum and substance of it is correct. Deduce from it, you who wish to think and grow rich, the secret of the Ford millions, if you can. You'll not have to look very far.

Henry Ford was a success because he understood and *applied* the principles of success. One of these is desire, knowing what one wants. Remember this Ford story as you read, and pick out the lines in which the secret of his stupendous achievement has been described. If you can do this, if you can lay your finger on the particular group of principles which made Henry Ford rich, you can equal his achievements in almost any calling for which you are suited.

A Poet Saw the Truth

When Henley wrote the prophetic lines, "I am the master of my fate, I am the captain of my soul" he should have informed us that we are the masters of our fate, the captains of our souls, *because* we have the power to control our thoughts.

He should have told us that our brains become magnetized with the dominating thoughts which we hold in our minds and, by means with which no man is familiar, these "magnets" attract to us the forces, the people, the circumstances of life which harmonize with the nature of our *dominating* thoughts.

He should have told us that before we can accumulate riches in great abundance we must magnetize our minds with intense desire for riches, that we must become "money conscious" until the desire for money drives us to create definite plans for acquiring it.

But, being a poet and not a philosopher, Henley contented himself by stating a great truth in poetic form, leaving those who followed him to interpret the philosophical meaning of his lines.

Little by little the truth has unfolded itself, until it now appears certain that the principles described in this book hold the secret of mastery over our economic fate.

A Young Man Sees His Destiny

We are now ready to examine the first of these principles. Maintain a spirit of open-mindedness, and remember as you read, they are the invention of no one man. The principles have worked for many men. You can put them to work for your own enduring benefit.

You will find it easy, not hard, to do.

Some years ago, I delivered the commencement address at Salem College, Salem, West Virginia. I emphasized the principle described in the next chapter with so much intensity that one of the members of the graduating class definitely appropriated it and made it a part of his own philosophy. The young man became a congressman and an important factor in Franklin D. Roosevelt's administration. He wrote me a letter which so clearly stated his opinion of the principle outlined in the next chapter that I have chosen to publish his letter as an introduction to that chapter. It gives you an idea of the rewards to come:

My dear Napoleon:

My service as a member of Congress having given me an insight into the problems of men and women, I am writing to offer a suggestion which may become helpful to thousands of worthy people.

In 1922, you delivered the commencement address at Salem College, when I was a member of the graduating class. In that address, you planted in my mind an idea which has been responsible for the opportunity I now have to serve the people of my state, and will be responsible, in a very large measure, for whatever success I may have in the future.

I recall, as though it were yesterday, the marvelous description you gave of the method by which Henry Ford, with but little schooling, without a dollar, with no influential friends, rose to great heights. I made up my mind then, even before you had finished your speech, that I would make a place for myself, no matter how many difficulties I had to surmount.

Thousands of young people will finish their schooling this year, and within the next few years. Every one of them will be seeking just such a message of practical encouragement as the one I received from you. They will want to know where to turn, what to do, to get started in life. You can tell them, because you have helped to solve the problems of so many, many people.

There are thousands of people in America today who would like to know how they can convert ideas into money, people who must start at scratch, without finances, and recoup their losses. If anyone can help them, you can.

If you publish the book, I would like to own the first copy that comes from the press, personally autographed by you.

With best wishes, believe me,

Cordially yours,

JENNINGS RANDOLPH

Thirty-five years after I made that speech, it was my pleasure to return to Salem College in 1957 and deliver the baccalaureate sermon. At that time I received an honorary Doctor of Literature degree from Salem College.

Since that time in 1922, I have watched Jennings Randolph rise to become one of the nation's leading airlines executives, a great inspirational speaker and United States Senator from West Virginia.

POINTS TO PIN DOWN:

Like Edwin Barnes, a man may be poorly dressed and penniless, yet his burning desire can bring him the opportunity of his lifetime.

The longer you work in the right direction, the closer you are to success. Too many men give up when success is within their grasp. They leave it for someone else to capture.

***Purpose* is the touchstone of any accomplishment, large or small. A strong man can be defeated by a child who has a purpose. Shift your habits of thinking about the significance of your task and you can often accomplish the seemingly impossible.**

Like Henry Ford, you can transmit your own faith and persistence to others and get the "impossible" done well.

Whatever the mind of man can conceive and believe, it can achieve.

Step 1 Toward Riches:
Desire

WHEN EDWIN C. BARNES CLIMBED DOWN FROM THE freight train in East Orange, N.J., more than fifty years ago he may have resembled a tramp, but his *thoughts* were those of a king!

As he made his way from the railroad tracks to Thomas A. Edison's office, his mind was at work. He saw himself *standing in Edison's presence*. He heard himself asking Mr. Edison for an opportunity to carry out the one consuming obsession of his life, a burning desire to become the business associate of the great inventor.

Barnes' desire was not a *hope!* It was not a *wish!* It was a keen desire, which transcended everything else. It was definite.

A few years later Edwin C. Barnes again stood before Edison in the same office where he first met the inventor. This

Dreams come true when desire transforms them into concrete action. Ask life for great gifts and you encourage life to deliver them to you.

---

time his desire had been translated into reality. *He was in business with Edison.* The dominating dream of his life had become a reality.

Barnes succeeded because he chose a definite goal and placed all his energy, all his will power, all his effort, everything, back of that goal.

No Way to Retreat

Five years passed before the chance he had been seeking made its appearance. To everyone except himself he appeared only another cog in the Edison business wheel, but in his own mind he was the partner of Edison every minute of the time, from the very day that he first went to work there.

It is a remarkable illustration of the power of a definite

desire. Barnes won his goal because he wanted to be a business associate of Mr. Edison more than he wanted anything else. He created a plan by which to attain that purpose. But he burned all bridges behind him. He stood by his desire until it became the dominating obsession of his life—and—finally, a fact.

When he went to East Orange he did not say to himself, "I will try to induce Edison to give me a job of some sort." He said, "I will see Edison, and put him on notice that I have come to go into business with him."

He did not say, "I will keep my eyes open for another opportunity, in case I fail to get what I want in the Edison organization." He said, "There is but *one* thing in this world that I am determined to have, and that is a business association with Thomas A. Edison. I will burn all bridges behind me, and stake my entire future on my ability to get what I want."

He left himself no possible way of retreat. He had to win or perish!

That is all there is to the Barnes story of success!

He Burned His Boats

A long while ago, a great warrior faced a situation which made it necessary for him to make a decision which insured his success on the battlefield. He was about to send his armies against a powerful foe, whose men outnumbered his own. He loaded his soldiers into boats, sailed to the enemy's country, unloaded soldiers and equipment, then gave the order to burn the ships that had carried them. Addressing his men before the first battle, he said, "You see the boats going up in smoke.

That means that we cannot leave these shores alive unless we win! We now have no choice—*we win*—*or we perish!*"

They won.

Every person who wins in any undertaking must be willing to burn his ships and cut all sources of retreat. Only by so doing can one be sure of maintaining that state of mind known as a burning desire to win, essential to success.

The morning after the great Chicago fire, a group of merchants stood on State Street, looking at the smoking remains of what had been their stores. They went into a conference to decide if they would try to rebuild, or leave Chicago and start over in a more promising section of the country. They reached a decision—all except one—to leave Chicago.

The merchant who decided to stay and rebuild pointed a finger at the remains of his store and said, "Gentlemen, on that very spot I will build the world's greatest store, no matter how many times it may burn down."

That was almost a century ago. The store was built. It stands there today, a towering monument to the power of that state of mind known as a burning desire. The easy thing for Marshall Field to have done would have been exactly what his fellow merchants did. When the going was hard and the future looked dismal, they pulled up and went where the going seemed easier.

Mark well this difference between Marshall Field and the other merchants, because it is the same difference which distinguishes practically all who succeed from those who fail.

Every human being who reaches the age of understanding of the purpose of money wishes for it. *Wishing* will not bring riches. But *desiring* riches with a state of mind that becomes an obsession, then planning definite ways and means to acquire riches, and backing those plans with persistence which *does not recognize failure*, will bring riches.

Six Steps that Turn Desires into Gold

The method by which *desire* for riches can be transmuted into its financial equivalent consists of the following six definite, practical steps:

1. Fix in your mind the *exact* amount of money you desire. It is not sufficient merely to say "I want plenty of money." Be definite as to the amount. (There is a psychological reason for definiteness which will be described in a subsequent chapter.)
2. Determine exactly what you intend to *give* in return for the money you desire. (There is no such reality as "something for nothing.")
3. Establish a definite date when you intend to *possess* the money you desire.
4. Create a definite plan for carrying out your desire, and begin *at once*, whether you are ready or not, to put this plan into *action*.
5. Write out a clear, concise statement of the amount of money you intend to acquire, name the time limit for its acquisition, state what you intend to give in return for the money, and describe clearly the plan through which you intend to accumulate it.
6. Read your written statement aloud twice daily, once just before retiring at night, and once after arising in the morning. As you read—see and feel and believe yourself already in possession of the money.

It is important that you follow the instructions described in these six steps. It is especially important that you observe, and follow the instructions in the sixth paragraph. You may complain that it is impossible for you to "see yourself in possession of money" before you actually have it. Here is where a *burning desire* will come to your aid. If you truly *desire* money so keenly that your desire is an obsession, you will have no difficulty in convincing yourself that you will acquire it. The object is to want money, and to become so determined to have it that you *convince* yourself you will have it.

Principles Worth $100,000,000

To the uninitiated, who have not been schooled in the working principles of the human mind, these instructions may appear impractical. It may be helpful, to all who fail to recognize the soundness of the six steps, to know that the information they convey was received from Andrew Carnegie, who began as an ordinary laborer in the steel mills, but managed, despite his humble beginning, to make these principles yield him a fortune of considerably more than one hundred million dollars.

It may be of further help to know that the six steps here recommended were carefully scrutinized by the late Thomas A. Edison, who placed his stamp of approval upon them as being, not only the steps essential for the accumulation of money, but for the attainment of any goal.

The steps call for no "hard labor." They call for no sacrifice. They do not require one to become ridiculous, or credulous. To apply them calls for no great amount of education. But the successful application of these six steps does call for sufficient *imagination* to enable one to see and to understand that accumulation of money cannot be left to chance, good fortune, and luck. One must realize that all who have accumulated great fortunes first did a certain amount of dreaming, hoping, wishing, desiring, and planning *before* they acquired money.

You may as well know, right here, that you can never have riches in great quantities *unless* you can work yourself into a white heat of *desire* for money, and actually *believe* you will possess it.

Great Dreams Can Turn into Riches

We who are in this race for riches should be encouraged to know that this changed world in which we live is demanding new ideas, new ways of doing things, new leaders, new inventions, new methods of teaching, new methods of marketing, new books, new literature, new features for television, new ideas for moving pictures. Back of all this demand for new and better things, there is one quality which one must possess to win, and that is *definiteness of purpose*, the knowledge of what one wants, and a burning *desire* to possess it.

We who desire to accumulate riches should remember the real leaders of the world always have been men who harnessed and put into practical use the intangible, unseen forces of unborn opportunity, and have converted those forces (or impulses of thought) into skyscrapers, cities, factories, airplanes, automobiles, and every form of convenience that makes life more pleasant.

In planning to acquire your share of the riches, let no one influence you to scorn the dreamer. To win the big stakes in this changed world you must catch the spirit of the great pioneers of the past, whose dreams have given to civilization all that it has of value, the spirit which serves as the lifeblood of our own country—your opportunity and mine, to develop and market our talents.

If the thing you wish to do is right and *you believe in it*, go ahead and do it! Put your dream across, and never mind what "they" say if you meet with temporary defeat, for "they," perhaps, do not know that every failure brings with it the seed of an equivalent success.

Thomas Edison dreamed of a lamp that could be operated by electricity, began where he stood to put his dream into action, and despite more than *ten thousand failures,* he stood by that dream until he made it a physical reality. Practical dreamers *do not quit!*

Whelan dreamed of a chain of cigar stores, transformed his dream into action, and now the United Cigar Stores occupy some of the best corners in America.

The Wright brothers dreamed of a machine that would fly through the air. Now one may see evidence all over the world that they dreamed soundly.

Marconi dreamed of a system for harnessing the intangible forces of the ether. Evidence that he did not dream in vain may be found in every radio and television set in the world. It may interest you to know that Marconi's "friends" had him taken into custody and examined in a psychopathic hospital when he announced he had discovered a principle through which he could send messages through the air without the aid of wires or other direct physical means of communication. The dreamers of today fare better.

The world is filled with an abundance of opportunity which the dreamers of the past never knew.

They Put Desire Behind Their Dreams

A burning desire to be and to do is the starting point from which the dreamer must take off. Dreams are not born of indifference, laziness, or lack of ambition.

Remember that all who succeed in life get off to a bad

start, and pass through many heartbreaking struggles before they "arrive." The turning point in the lives of those who succeed usually comes at the moment of some crisis, through which they are introduced to their "other selves."

John Bunyan wrote *Pilgrim's Progress*, which is among the finest of all English books, after he had been confined in prison and sorely punished because of his views on the subject of religion.

O. Henry discovered the genius which slept within his brain after he had met with great misfortune and was confined in a prison cell in Columbus, Ohio. Being forced, through misfortune, to become acquainted with his "other self" and to use his imagination, he discovered himself to be a great author instead of a miserable criminal and outcast.

Charles Dickens began by pasting labels on blacking pots. The tragedy of his first love penetrated the depths of his soul and converted him into one of the world's truly great authors. That tragedy produced first *David Copperfield*, then a succession of other works that made this a richer and better world for all who read his books.

Helen Keller became deaf, dumb, and blind shortly after birth. Despite her greatest misfortune, she has written her name indelibly in the pages of the history of the great. Her entire life has served as evidence that *no one is ever defeated until defeat has been accepted as a reality*.

Robert Burns was an illiterate country lad. He was cursed by poverty, and grew up to be a drunkard in the bargain. The world was made better for his having lived because he clothed beautiful thoughts in poetry, and thereby plucked a thorn and planted a rose in its place.

Beethoven was deaf, Milton was blind, but their names will last as long as time endures because they dreamed and translated their dreams into organized thought.

There is a difference between wishing for a thing and being ready to receive it. No one is *ready* for a thing until he *believes* he can acquire it. The state of mind must be *belief*, not mere hope or wish. Open-mindedness is essential for belief. Closed minds do not inspire faith, courage, or belief.

Remember, no more effort is required to aim high in life, to demand abundance and prosperity, than is required to accept misery and poverty. A great poet has correctly stated this universal truth through these lines:

> I bargained with Life for a penny,
> And Life would pay no more,
> However I begged at evening
> When I counted my scanty store.

> For Life is a just employer,
> He gives you what you ask,
> But once you have set the wages,
> Why, you must bear the task.

> I worked for a menial's hire,
> Only to learn, dismayed,
> That any wage I had asked of Life,
> Life would have willingly paid.

Desire Performs the "Impossible"

As a fitting climax to this chapter, I wish to introduce one of the most unusual persons I have ever known. I first saw him a few minutes after he was born. He came into the world without any physical sign of ears, and the doctor admitted, when pressed for an opinion on the case, that the child might be deaf and mute for life.

I challenged the doctor's opinion. I had the right to do so; I was the child's father. I too reached a decision and rendered an opinion, but I expressed the opinion silently, in the secrecy of my own heart.

In my own mind I knew that my son would hear and speak. How? I was sure there must be a way, and I knew I would find it. I thought of the words of the immortal Emerson, "The whole course of things goes to teach us faith. We need only obey. There is guidance for each of us, and by lowly listening, we shall hear *the right word*."

The right word? *Desire!* More than anything else, I desired that my son should not be a deaf mute. From that desire I never receded, not for a second.

What could I do about it? Somehow I would find a way to transplant into that child's mind my own burning desire for ways and means of conveying sound to his brain without the aid of ears.

As soon as the child was old enough to cooperate I would fill his mind so completely with a burning desire to hear that nature would, by methods of her own, translate it into physical reality.

All this thinking took place in my own mind, but I spoke of it to no one. Every day I renewed the pledge I had made to myself that my son should not be a deaf mute.

As he grew older and began to take notice of things around him, we observed that he had a slight degree of hearing. When he reached the age when children usually begin talking he made no attempt to speak, but we could tell by his actions that he could hear certain sounds slightly. That was all I wanted to know! I was convinced that if he could hear, even slightly, he might develop still greater hearing capacity. Then something happened which gave me hope. It came from an entirely unexpected source.

We Find a Way

We bought a phonograph. When the child heard the music for the first time he went into ecstasies, and promptly appropriated the machine. On one occasion he played a record over and over for almost two hours, standing in front of the phonograph *with his teeth clamped on the edge of the case*. The significance of this self-formed habit of his did not become clear to us until years afterward, for we had not heard of the principle of "bone conduction" of sound at that time.

Shortly after he appropriated the phonograph, I discovered that he could hear me quite clearly when I spoke with my lips touching his mastoid bone, at the base of the skull.

Having determined that he could hear the sound of my voice plainly, I began immediately to transfer to his mind the desire to hear and speak. I soon discovered that the child enjoyed bedtime stories, so I went to work creating stories designed to develop in him self-reliance, imagination, and a *keen desire to hear and to be normal*.

There was one story in particular, which I emphasized by giving it some new and dramatic coloring each time it was told. It was designed to plant in his mind the thought that his affliction was not a liability, but an asset of great value. Despite the fact that all the philosophy I had examined clearly indicated that every adversity brings with it the seed of an equivalent advantage, I must confess that I had not the slightest idea *how* this affliction could ever become an asset.

Nothing Could Stop Him

As I analyze the experience in retrospect, I can see now that my son's *faith in me* had much to do with the astounding results. He did not question anything I told him. I sold him the idea that he had a distinct *advantage* over his older brother, and that this advantage would reflect itself in many ways. For example, the teachers in school would observe that he had no ears and, because of this, they would show him special attention and treat him with extraordinary kindness. They always did. I sold him the idea too that when he became old enough to sell newspapers (his older brother had already become a newspaper merchant) he would have a big advantage over his brother, for the reason that people would pay him extra money for his wares, because they could see that he was a bright, industrious boy, despite the fact he had no ears.

When he was about seven he showed the first evidence that our method of "programming" his mind was bearing fruit. For several months he begged for the privilege of selling newspapers, but his mother would not give the project her consent.

Finally he took matters in his own hands. One afternoon, when he was left at home with the servants, he climbed through the kitchen window, shinnied to the ground, and set out on his own. He borrowed six cents in capital from the neighborhood shoemaker, invested it in papers, sold out, reinvested, and kept repeating until late in the evening. After balancing his accounts and paying back the six cents he had borrowed from his banker, he had a net profit of forty-two cents. When we got home that night we found him in bed asleep, with the money tightly clenched in his hand.

His mother opened his hand, removed the coins, and cried. Of all things! Crying over her son's first victory seemed so inappropriate. My reaction was the reverse. I laughed heartily, for I knew that my endeavor to plant in the child's mind an attitude of faith in himself had been successful.

His mother saw, in his first business venture, a little deaf boy who had gone out in the streets and risked his life to earn money. I saw a brave, ambitious, self-reliant little businessman whose stock in himself had been increased a hundred percent because he had gone into business on his own initiative, and had won. The transaction pleased me, because I knew that he had given evidence of resourcefulness that would go with him all through life.

A Breakthrough in Hearing

The little deaf boy went through the grades, high school, and college without being able to hear his teachers, except when they shouted loudly at close range. He did not go to a school for the deaf. We would not permit him to learn the sign language. We were determined that he should live a normal life and associate with normal children, and we stood by that decision although it cost us many heated debates with school officials.

While he was in high school he tried an electrical hearing aid, but it was of no value to him.

During his last week in college, something happened which marked the most important turning point of his life. Through what seemed to be mere chance, he came into possession of another electrical hearing device, which was sent to him on trial. He was slow about testing it, due to his disappointment with a similar device. Finally he picked up the instrument and more or less carelessly placed it on his head, hooked up the battery, and lo! as if by a stroke of magic his lifelong desire for normal hearing became a reality! For the first time in his life he heard practically as well as any person with normal hearing.

Overjoyed because of the changed world which had been brought to him through his hearing device, he rushed to the telephone, called his mother, and heard her voice perfectly. The next day he plainly heard the voices of his professors in class for the first time in his life! For the first time in his life he could converse freely with other people, without the necessity of their having to speak loudly. Truly, he had come into possession of a changed world.

Desire had commenced to pay dividends, but the victory was not yet complete. The boy still had to find a definite and practical way to convert his handicap into an *equivalent asset*.

The "Deaf" Boy Helps Others

Hardly realizing the significance of what had already been accomplished, but intoxicated with the joy of his newly discovered world of sound, he wrote a letter to the manufacturer of the hearing aid enthusiastically describing his experience. Something in his letter caused the company to invite him to New York. When he arrived he was escorted through the factory, and while talking with the chief engineer, telling him about his changed world, a hunch, an idea, or an inspiration —call it what you wish—flashed into his mind. It was *this impulse of thought* which converted his affliction into an asset, destined to pay dividends in both money and happiness to thousands for all time to come.

The sum and substance of that impulse of thought was this: it occurred to him that he might be of help to the millions of deafened people who go through life without the benefit of hearing devices if he could find a way to tell them the story of his changed world.

For an entire month he carried on an intensive research, during which he analyzed the entire marketing system of the manufacturer of the hearing device, and created ways and means of communicating with the hard of hearing all over the world for the purpose of sharing with them his newly-discovered changed world. When this was done, he put in writing a two-year plan based upon his findings. When he presented the plan to the company, he was instantly given a position for the purpose of carrying out his ambition.

Little did he dream, when he went to work, that he was destined to bring hope and practical relief to thousands of deafened people who, without his help, would have been doomed forever to deafness.

There is no doubt in my mind that Blair would have been a deaf mute all his life if his mother and I had not managed to shape his mind as we did.

When I planted in his mind the desire to hear and talk, and live as a normal person, there went with that impulse some strange influence which caused nature to become bridge builder, and span the gulf of silence between his brain and the outer world.

Truly, a burning desire has devious ways of transmuting itself into its physical equivalent. Blair desired normal hearing; now he has it! He was born with a handicap which might easily have sent one with a less defined desire to the street with a bundle of pencils and a tin cup.

The little "white lie" I planted in his mind when he was a child, by leading him to believe his affliction would become a great asset, has justified itself. Verily there is nothing, right or wrong, which belief, plus burning desire, cannot make real. These qualities are free to everyone.

Desire Works Magic for a Singer

One short paragraph in a news dispatch concerning Mme. Schumann-Heink gives the clue to this unusual woman's stupendous success as a singer. I quote the paragraph, because the clue it contains is none other than desire.

Early in her career, Mme. Schumann-Heink visited the director of the Vienna Court Opera, to have him test her voice. But he did not test it. After taking one look at the awkward and poorly dressed girl, he exclaimed, none too gently, "With such a face, and with no personality at all, how can you ever expect to succeed in opera? My good child, give up the idea. Buy a sewing machine, and go to work. *You can never be a singer.*"

Never is a long time! The director of the Vienna Court Opera knew much about the technique of singing. He knew little about the power of desire when it assumes the proportion of an obsession. If he had known more of that power, he would not have made the mistake of condemning genius without giving it an opportunity.

Several years ago, one of my business associates became ill. He became worse as time went on, and finally was taken to the hospital for an operation. The doctor warned me that there was little if any chance of my ever seeing him alive again. But that was the doctor's opinion. It was not the opinion of the patient. Just before he was wheeled away, he whispered feebly, "Do not be disturbed, Chief, I will be out of here in a few days." The attending nurse looked at me with pity. But the patient did come through safely. After it was all over, his physician said, "Nothing but his own desire to live saved him. He never would have pulled through if he had not refused to accept the possibility of death."

I believe in the power of desire backed by faith because I have seen this power lift men from lowly beginnings to places of power and wealth; I have seen it rob the grave of its victims; I have seen it serve as the medium by which men staged a comeback after having been defeated in a hundred different ways; I have seen it provide my own son with a normal, happy, successful life, despite Nature's having sent him into the world without ears.

How can one harness and use the power of desire? This has

been answered through this and the subsequent chapters of this book.

Through some strange and powerful principle of "mental chemistry" which she has never divulged, Nature wraps up in the impulse of strong desire, "that something" which recognizes no such word as "impossible," and accepts no such reality as failure.

POINTS TO PIN DOWN:

When *desire* focuses great forces toward your victory, you do not need any way to retreat; victory is certain.

Six definite steps, shown here, turn desire into gold. For Andrew Carnegie, these principles were worth $100,000,000.

Desire builds new victory out of temporary defeat. It was desire that built one of the world's greatest department stores literally upon ashes.

A boy without ears learned to hear. A woman with "no chance" became a great opera singer. A sick man whom the doctors expected to die pulled through safely. Desire was the force that aided these people with some strange but natural "mental chemistry."

There are no limitations to the mind except those we acknowledge.

Step 2 Toward Riches: Faith

FAITH IS THE HEAD CHEMIST OF THE MIND. WHEN FAITH IS blended with thought, the subconscious mind instantly picks up the vibration, translates it into its spiritual equivalent, and transmits it to Infinite Intelligence, as in the case of prayer.

The emotions of faith, love, and sex are the most powerful of all the major positive emotions. When the three are blended, they have the effect of "coloring" thought in such a way that it instantly reaches the subconscious mind, where it is changed into its spiritual equivalent, the only form that induces a response from Infinite Intelligence.

Faith Waits for You to Find It

There comes, now, a statement which will give a better understanding of the importance the principle of autosugges-

Directed faith makes every thought crackle with power. You can rise to limitless heights, impelled by the lifting force of your mighty new self-confidence.

tion assumes in the transmutation of desire into its physical, or monetary equivalent; namely, faith is a state of mind which may be induced, or created, by affirmation or repeated instructions to the subconscious mind, through the principle of autosuggestion.

As an illustration, consider the purpose for which you are, presumably, reading this book. The object is, naturally, to acquire the ability to transmute the intangible thought impulse of desire into its physical counterpart, money. By following the instructions laid down in the chapter on autosuggestion, and those on the subconscious mind, summarized in that chapter, you may convince the subconscious mind that you *believe* you will receive that for which you ask, and it will act upon that belief, which your subconscious mind passes back to you in the form of "faith," followed by definite plans for procuring that which you desire.

Faith is a state of mind which you may develop at will, after you have mastered the thirteen principles, because it is a state of mind which develops voluntarily, through application and use of these principles.

Repetition of affirmation of orders to your subconscious mind is the only known method of voluntary development of the emotion of faith.

Perhaps the meaning may be made clearer through the following explanation as to the way men sometimes become criminals. Stated in the words of a famous criminologist, "When men first come into contact with crime, they abhor it. If they remain in contact with crime for a time, they become accustomed to it, and endure it. If they remain in contact with it long enough, they finally embrace it, and become influenced by it."

This is the equivalent of saying that any impulse of thought which is repeatedly passed on to the subconscious mind is, finally, accepted and acted upon by the subconscious mind, which proceeds to translate that impulse into its physical equivalent by the most practical procedure available.

In connection with this, consider again the statement *all thoughts which have been emotionalized* (given feeling) *and mixed with faith begin immediately to translate themselves into their physical equivalent or counterpart.*

The emotions, or the "feeling" portion of thoughts, are the factors which give thoughts vitality, life, and action. The emotions of faith, love, and sex, when mixed with any thought impulse, give it greater action than any of these emotions can do singly.

Not only thought impulses which have been mixed with faith, but those which have been mixed with any of the positive emotions, or any of the negative emotions, may reach and influence the subconscious mind.

No Such Thing as Bad Luck

From this statement, you will understand that the subconscious mind will translate into its physical equivalent a thought impulse of a negative or destructive nature just as readily as it will act upon thought impulses of a positive or constructive nature. This accounts for the strange phenomenon which so many millions of people experience, referred to as "misfortune" or "bad luck."

There are millions of people who believe themselves "doomed" to poverty and failure because of some strange force over which they believe they have no control. They are the creators of their own "misfortunes" because of this negative belief, which is picked up by the subconscious mind, and translated into its physical equivalent.

This is an appropriate place at which to suggest again that you may benefit by passing on to your subconscious mind any desire which you wish translated into its physical or monetary equivalent in a state of expectancy or belief that the transmutation will actually take place. Your belief, or faith, is the element which determines the action of your subconscious mind. There is nothing to hinder you from "deceiving" your subconscious mind when giving it instructions through autosuggestion, as I deceived my son's subconscious mind.

To make this "deceit" more realistic, conduct yourself just as you would if you were already in possession of the material thing which you are demanding when you call upon your subconscious mind.

The subconscious mind will transmute into its physical equivalent, by the most direct and practical media available, any order which is given to it in a state of belief, or faith that the order will be carried out.

Surely, enough has been stated to give a starting point from which one may, through experiment and practice, acquire the ability to mix faith with any order given to the subconscious mind. Perfection will come through practice. It *cannot* come by merely *reading* instructions.

It is essential for you to encourage the *positive emotions* as dominating forces of your mind, and discourage—and *eliminate* negative emotions.

A mind dominated by positive emotions becomes a favorable abode for the state of mind known as faith. A mind so dominated may, at will, give the subconscious mind instructions, which it will accept and act upon immediately.

Faith Gives Power to Thought

All down the ages, the religionists have admonished struggling humanity to "have faith" in this, that, and the other dogma or creed, but they have failed to tell people *how* to have faith. They have not stated that "faith is a state of mind that may be induced by self-suggestion."

In language which any normal human being can understand, we will describe all that is known about the principle through which faith may be developed where it does not already exist.

Have faith in yourself; faith in the Infinite.

Faith is the "eternal elixir" which gives life, power, and action to the impulse of thought!

Faith is the starting point of all accumulation of riches!

Faith is the basis of all "miracles," and all mysteries which cannot be analyzed by the rules of science!

Faith is the only known antidote for failure!

Faith is the element, the "chemical" which, when mixed with prayer, gives one direct communication with Infinite Intelligence.

Faith is the element which transforms the ordinary vibration of thought, created by the finite mind of man, into the spiritual equivalent.

Faith is the only agency through which the cosmic force of Infinite Intelligence can be harnessed and used by man.

Thoughts that Dominate Your Mind

The proof is simple and easily demonstrated. It is wrapped up in the principle of autosuggestion. Let us center our attention, therefore, upon the subject of self-suggestion, and find out what it is, and what it is capable of achieving.

It is a well-known fact that one comes, finally, to believe whatever one repeats to one's self, *whether the statement be true or false.* If a man repeats a lie over and over, he will eventually accept the lie as truth. Moreover, he will believe it to be the truth. Every man is what he is because of the dominating thoughts which he permits to occupy his mind. Thoughts which a man deliberately places in his own mind, and encourages with sympathy, and with which he mixes any one or more of the emotions, constitute the motivating forces which direct and control his every movement, act, and deed!

Thoughts that are mixed with any of the feelings of emotions constitute a "magnetic" force, which attracts other similar or related thoughts.

A thought thus "magnetized" with emotion may be compared to a seed which, when planted in fertile soil, germinates, grows, and multiplies itself over and over again, until that which was originally one small seed becomes countless millions of seeds of the same brand!

The human mind is constantly attracting vibrations which harmonize with that which dominates the mind. Any thought, idea, plan, or purpose which one *holds* in one's mind attracts a host of its relatives, adds these "relatives" to its own force, and grows until it becomes the dominating, motivating master of the individual in whose mind it has been housed.

Now, let us go back to the starting point, and become informed as to how the original seed of an idea, plan, or purpose may be planted in the mind. The information is easily conveyed: any idea, plan, or purpose may be placed in the mind *through repetition of thought*. This is why you are asked to write out a statement of your major purpose, or definite chief aim, commit it to memory, and repeat it, in audible words, day after day, until these vibrations of sound have reached your subconscious mind.

Resolve to throw off the influences of any unfortunate environment, and to build your own life to order. Taking inventory of mental assets and liabilities, you may discover that your greatest weakness is lack of self-confidence. This handicap can be surmounted, and timidity translated into courage, through the aid of the principle of autosuggestion. The application of this principle may be made through a simple arrangement of positive thought impulses stated in writing, memorized, and repeated until they become a part of the working equipment of the subconscious faculty of your mind.

Five Steps to Self-confidence

1. I know that I have the ability to achieve the object of my definite purpose in life; therefore, *I demand* of myself persistent, continuous action toward its

attainment, and I here and now promise to render such action.

2. I realize the dominating thoughts of my mind will eventually reproduce themselves in outward, physical action, and gradually transform themselves into physical reality; therefore, I will concentrate my thoughts for thirty minutes daily, upon the task of thinking of the person I intend to become, thereby creating in my mind a clear mental picture.

3. I know through the principle of autosuggestion, any desire that I persistently hold in my mind will eventually seek expression through some practical means of attaining the object back of it; therefore I will devote ten minutes daily to demanding of myself the development of *self-confidence*.

4. I have clearly written down a description of my *definite chief aim* in life, and I will never stop trying, until I shall have developed sufficient self-confidence for its attainment.

5. I fully realize that no wealth or position can long endure unless built upon truth and justice; therefore I will engage in no transaction which does not benefit all whom it affects. I will succeed by attracting to myself the forces I wish to use, and the co-operation of other people. I will induce others to serve me, because of my willingness to serve others. I will eliminate hatred, envy, jealousy, selfishness, and cynicism by developing love for all humanity, because I know that a negative attitude toward others can never bring me success. I will cause others to believe in me because I will believe in them and in myself. I will sign my name to this formula, commit it to memory, and repeat it aloud once a day,

with full faith that it will gradually influence my thoughts and actions so that I will become a self-reliant, and successful person.

Back of this formula is a law of nature which no man has yet been able to explain. The name by which one calls this law is of little importance. The important fact about it is—it WORKS for the glory and success of mankind, IF it is used constructively. On the other hand, if used destructively, it will destroy just as readily. In this statement may be found a very significant truth, namely, that those who go down in defeat, and end their lives in poverty, misery, and distress, do so because of negative application of the principle of autosuggestion. The cause may be found in the fact that all impulses of thought have a tendency to clothe themselves in their physical equivalent.

You Can Think Yourself into Disaster

The subconscious mind makes no distinction between constructive and destructive thought impulses. It works with the material we feed it, through our thought impulses. The subconscious mind will translate into reality a thought driven by fear just as readily as it will translate into reality a thought driven by courage, or faith.

Just as electricity will turn the wheels of industry, and render useful service if used constructively or snuff out life if wrongly used, so will the law of autosuggestion lead you to peace and prosperity, or down into the valley of misery, failure, and death, according to your degree of understanding and application of it.

If you fill your mind with fear, doubt, and unbelief in your ability to connect with and use the forces of Infinite Intelligence, the law of autosuggestion will take this spirit of un-belief and use it as a pattern by which your subconscious mind will translate it into its physical equivalent.

Like the wind which carries one ship east and another west, the law of autosuggestion will lift you up or pull you down according to the way you set your sails of *thought*.

The law of autosuggestion, through which any person may rise to altitudes of achievement which stagger the imagination, is well described in the following verse:

If you *think* you are beaten, you are.
If you *think* you dare not, you don't.
If you like to win, but you *think* you can't,
It is almost certain you won't.

If you *think* you'll lose, you're lost,
For out of the world we find,
Success begins with a fellow's will—
It's all in the *state of mind*.

If you *think* you are outclassed, you are,
You've got to *think* high to rise,
You've got to *be sure of yourself* before
You can ever win a prize.

Life's battles don't always go
To the stronger or faster man,
But soon or late the man who wins
Is the man WHO THINKS HE CAN!

Observe the words which have been emphasized, and you will catch the deep meaning which the poet had in mind.

The Great Experience of Love

Somewhere in your make-up there lies *sleeping* the seed of achievement which, if aroused and put into action, would carry you to heights such as you may never have hoped to attain.

Just as a master musician may cause the most beautiful strains of music to pour forth from the strings of a violin, so may you arouse the genius which lies asleep in your brain, and cause it to drive you upward to whatever goal you may wish to achieve.

Abraham Lincoln was a failure at everything he tried, until he was well past the age of forty. He was a Mr. Nobody from Nowhere, until a great experience came into his life, aroused the sleeping genius within his heart and brain, and gave the world one of its really great men. That "experience" was mixed with the emotions of sorrow and love. It came to him through Ann Rutledge, the only woman whom he ever truly loved.

It is a known fact that the emotion of love is closely akin to the state of mind known as faith, and this for the reason that love comes very near to translating one's thought impulses into their spiritual equivalent. During his work of research the author discovered, from the analysis of the lifework and achievement of hundreds of men of outstanding accomplishment, that there was the influence of a woman's love back of nearly every one of them.

If you wish evidence of the power of faith, study the achievements of men and women who have employed it. At the head of the list comes the Nazarene. The basis of Christianity is faith, no matter how many people may have perverted or misinterpreted the meaning of this great force.

The sum and substance of the teachings and the achievements of Christ, which may have been interpreted as "miracles," were nothing more nor less than faith. If there are any such phenomena as "miracles" they are produced only through the state of mind known as faith!

Let us consider the power of faith, as demonstrated by a man who was well known to all of civilization, Mahatma Gandhi of India. In this man the world had one of the most astounding examples known to civilization of the possibilities of faith. Gandhi wielded more potential power than any man living in his time, and this despite the fact that he had none of the orthodox tools of power, such as money, battleships, soldiers and materials of warfare. Gandhi had no money, no home, he did not own a suit of clothes, but he did have power. How did he come by that power?

He created it out of his understanding of the principle of faith, and through his ability to transplant that faith into the minds of two hundred million people.

Gandhi accomplished the astounding feat of influencing two hundred million minds to coalesce and move in unison, as a single mind.

What other force on earth, except faith, could do as much?

You Give Before You Get

Because of the need for faith and cooperation in operating business and industry, it will be both interesting and profitable to analyze an event which provides an excellent understanding of the method by which industrialists and businessmen accumulate great fortunes by *giving* before they try to *get*.

The event chosen for this illustration dates back to 1900, when the United States Steel Corporation was being formed. As you read the story, keep in mind these fundamental facts and you will understand how *ideas* have been converted into huge fortunes.

If you are one of those who have often wondered how great fortunes are accumulated, this story of the creation of the United States Steel Corporation will be enlightening. If you have any doubt that men can think and grow rich, this story should dispel that doubt, because you can plainly see in the story of United States Steel the application of a major portion of the principles described in this book.

This astounding description of the power of an idea was dramatically told by John Lowell, in the *New York World-Telegram*, through whose courtesy it is reprinted here:

A PRETTY AFTER-DINNER SPEECH FOR A BILLION DOLLARS

When, on the evening of December 12, 1900, some eighty of the nation's financial nobility gathered in the banquet hall of the University Club on Fifth Avenue to do honor to a young man from out of the West, not half a dozen of the guests realized they were to witness the most significant episode in American industrial history.

J. Edward Simmons and Charles Stewart Smith, their hearts full of gratitude for the lavish hospitality bestowed on them by Charles M. Schwab during a recent visit to Pittsburgh, had arranged the dinner to introduce the thirty-eight-year-old steel man to eastern banking society. But they didn't expect him to stampede the convention. They warned him, in fact, that the bosoms within New York's stuffed shirts would not be responsive to oratory, and that, if he didn't want to bore the Stillmans and Harrimans and Vanderbilts, he had better limit himself to fifteen or twenty minutes of polite vaporings and let it go at that.

Even John Pierpont Morgan, sitting on the right hand of Schwab as became his imperial dignity, intended to grace the banquet table with his presence only briefly. And so far as the press and public were concerned, the whole affair was of so little moment that no mention of it found its way into print the next day.

So the two hosts and their distinguished guests ate their way through the usual seven or eight courses. There was little conversation and what there was of it was restrained. Few of the bankers and brokers had met Schwab, whose career had flowered along the banks of the Monongahela, and none knew him well. But before the evening was over, they—and with them Money Master Morgan—were to be swept off their feet, and a billion-dollar baby, the United States Steel Corporation, was to be conceived.

It is perhaps unfortunate, for the sake of history, that no record of Charlie Schwab's speech at the dinner ever was made.

It is probable, however, that it was a "homely" speech, somewhat ungrammatical (for the niceties of language never bothered Schwab), full of epigram and threaded with wit. But aside from that it had a galvanic force and effect upon the five billions of estimated capital that was represented by the diners. After it was over and the gathering was still under its spell, although Schwab had talked for ninety minutes, Morgan led the orator to a recessed window where, dangling their legs from the high, uncomfortable seat, they talked for an hour more.

The magic of the Schwab personality had been turned on, full force, but what was more important and lasting was the full-fledged, clear-cut program he laid down for the aggrandizement of Steel. Many other men had tried to interest Morgan in slapping together a steel trust after the pattern of the biscuit, wire and hoop, sugar, rubber, whisky, oil or chewing gum combinations. John W. Gates, the gambler, had urged it, but Morgan distrusted him. The Moore boys, Bill and Jim, Chicago stock jobbers who had glued together a match trust and a cracker corporation, had urged it and failed. Elbert H. Gary, the sanctimonious country lawyer, wanted to foster it, but he wasn't big enough to be impressive. Until Schwab's eloquence took J. P. Morgan to the heights from which he could visualize the solid results of the most daring financial undertaking ever conceived, the project was regarded as a delirious dream of easy-money crackpots.

The financial magnetism that began, a generation ago, to attract thousands of small and sometimes inefficiently managed companies into large and competition-crushing combinations had become operative in the steel world through the devices of that jovial business pirate, John W. Gates. Gates already had formed the American Steel and Wire Company out of a chain of small concerns, and together with Morgan had created the Federal Steel Company.

But by the side of Andrew Carnegie's gigantic vertical trust, a trust owned and operated by fifty-three partners, those other combinations were picayune. They might combine to their heart's content but the whole lot of them couldn't make a dent in the Carnegie organization, and Morgan knew it.

The eccentric old Scot knew it, too. From the magnificent heights of Skibo Castle he had viewed, first with amusement and then with resentment, the attempts of Morgan's smaller companies to cut into his business. When the attempts became too bold, Carnegie's temper was translated into anger and retaliation. He decided to dupli-

cate every mill owned by his rivals. Hitherto, he hadn't
been interested in wire, pipe, hoops, or sheet. Instead, he
was content to sell such companies the raw steel and let
them work it into whatever shape they wanted. Now, with
Schwab as his chief and able lieutenant, he planned to drive
his enemies to the wall.

So it was that in the speech of Charles M. Schwab,
Morgan saw the answer to his problem of combination.
A trust without Carnegie—giant of them all—would be
no trust at all, a plum pudding, as one writer said, without
the plums.

Schwab's speech on the night of December 12, 1900,
undoubtedly carried the inference, though not the pledge,
that the vast Carnegie enterprise could be brought under
the Morgan tent. He talked of the world future for steel, of
reorganization for efficiency, of specialization, of the scrap-
ping of unsuccessful mills and concentration of effort on
the flourishing properties, of economies in the ore traffic,
of economies in overhead and adminstrative departments,
of capturing foreign markets.

More than that, he told the buccaneers among them
wherein lay the errors of their customary piracy. Their purposes, he inferred, had been to create monopolies, raise
prices, and pay themselves fat dividends out of privilege.
Schwab condemned the system in his heartiest manner.
The shortsightedness of such a policy, he told his hearers,
lay in the fact that it restricted the market in an era when
everything cried for expansion. By cheapening the cost of
steel, he argued, an ever-expanding market would be
created; more uses for steel would be devised, and a goodly
portion of the world trade could be captured. Actually,
though he did not know it, Schwab was an apostle of modern mass production.

So the dinner at the University Club came to an end. Morgan went home, to think about Schwab's rosy predictions. Schwab went back to Pittsburgh to run the steel business for "Wee Andra Carnegie," while Gary and the rest went back to their stock tickers, to fiddle around in anticipation of the next move.

It was not long coming. It took Morgan about one week to digest the feast of reason Schwab had placed before him. When he had assured himself that no financial indigestion was to result, he sent for Schwab—and found that young man rather coy. Mr. Carnegie, Schwab indicated, might not like it if he found his trusted company president had been flirting with the Emperor of Wall Street, the Street upon which Carnegie was resolved never to tread. Then it was suggested by John W. Gates, the go-between, that if Schwab "happened" to be in the Bellevue Hotel in Philadelphia, J. P. Morgan might also "happen" to be there. When Schwab arrived, however, Morgan was inconveniently ill at his New York home, and so, on the elder man's pressing invitation, Schwab went to New York and presented himself at the door of the financier's library.

Now certain economic historians have professed the belief that from the beginning to the end of the drama, the stage was set by Andrew Carnegie—that the dinner to Schwab, the famous speech, the Sunday night conference between Schwab and the Money King, were events arranged by the canny Scot. The truth is exactly the opposite. When Schwab was called in to consummate the deal, he didn't even know whether "the little boss," as Andrew was called, would so much as listen to an offer to sell, particularly to a group of men whom Andrew regarded as being endowed with something less than holiness. But Schwab did take into the conference with him, in his own handwriting, six sheets of copper-plate figures, representing to his mind the physical worth and the potential earning capacity of every steel company he regarded as an essential star in the new metal firmament.

Four men pondered over those figures all night. The chief, of course, was Morgan, steadfast in his belief in the divine right of money. With him was his aristocratic partner, Robert Bacon, a scholar and a gentleman. The third was John W. Gates whom Morgan scorned as a gambler and used as a tool. The fourth was Schwab, who knew more about the processes of making and selling steel than any whole group of men then living. Throughout that conference, the Pittsburgher's figures were never questioned. If he said a company was worth so much, then it was worth that much and no more. He was insistent, too, upon including in the combination only those concerns he nominated. He had conceived a corporation in which there would be no duplication, not even to satisfy the greed of friends who wanted to unload their companies upon the broad Morgan shoulders.

When dawn came, Morgan rose and straightened his back. Only one question remained.

"Do you think you can persuade Andrew Carnegie to sell?" he asked.

"I can try," said Schwab.

"If you can get him to sell, I will undertake the matter," said Morgan.

So far so good. But would Carnegie sell? How much would he demand? (Schwab thought about $320,000,000.) What would he take payment in? Common or preferred stocks? Bonds? Cash? Nobody could raise a third of a billion dollars in cash.

There was a golf game in January on the frost-cracking

heath of the St. Andrew's links in Westchester, with Andrew bundled up in sweaters against the cold, and Charlie talking volubly, as usual, to keep his spirits up. But no word of business was mentioned until the pair sat down in the cozy warmth of the Carnegie cottage nearby. Then, with the same persuasiveness that had hypnotized eighty millionaires at the University Club, Schwab poured out the glittering promises of retirement in comfort, of untold millions to satisfy the old man's social caprices. Carnegie capitulated, wrote a figure on a slip of paper, handed it to Schwab and said, "All right, that's what we'll sell for."

The figure was approximately $400,000,000, and was reached by taking the $320,000,000 mentioned by Schwab as a basic figure, and adding to it $80,000,000 to represent the increased capital value over the previous two years.

Later, on the deck of a trans-Atlantic liner, the Scotsman said ruefully to Morgan, "I wish I had asked you for $100,000,000 more."

"If you had asked for it, you'd have gotten it," Morgan told him cheerfully.

There was an uproar, of course. A British correspondent cabled that the foreign steel world was "appalled" by the gigantic combination. President Hadley of Yale declared that unless trusts were regulated the country might expect "an emperor in Washington within the next twenty-five years." But that able stock manipulator, Keene, went at his work by shoving the new stock at the public so vigorously that all the excess water—estimated by some at nearly $600,000,000—was absorbed in a twinkling. So Carnegie had his millions, and the Morgan syndicate had $62,000,-000 for all its "trouble," and all the "boys," from Gates to Gary, had their millions.

The thirty-eight-year-old Schwab had his reward. He was made president of the new corporation and remained in control until 1930.

Riches Begin Inside the Man

The dramatic story of big business which you have just finished is a perfect illustration of the method by which desire can be transmuted into its physical equivalent!

That giant organization was created in the mind of one man. The plan by which the organization was provided with the steel mills that gave it financial stability was created in the mind of the same man. His faith, his desire, his imagination, his persistence were the real ingredients that went into United States Steel. The steel mills and mechanical equipment acquired by the corporation, after it had been brought into legal existence, were incidental, but careful analysis will disclose the fact that the appraised value of the properties acquired by the corporation increased in value by an estimated six hundred million dollars, by the mere transaction which consolidated them under one management.

In other words, Charles M. Schwab's idea, plus the faith with which he conveyed it to the minds of J. P. Morgan and the others, was marketed for a profit of approximately $600,-000,000. Not an insignificant sum for a single idea!

The United States Steel Corporation prospered, and became one of the richest and most powerful corporations in America, employing thousands of people, developing new uses for steel, and opening new markets, thus proving that the $600,000,000 in profit which the Schwab idea produced was earned.

Riches begin in the form of thought!

The amount is limited only by the person in whose mind

the thought is put into motion. Faith removes limitations! Remember this when you are ready to bargain with life for whatever it is that you ask as your price for having passed this way.

POINTS TO PIN DOWN:

Faith is indispensable for success. Faith is induced and strengthened by instructions you give to your subconscious mind.

Here are five steps to self-confidence, all of them easily within your present power. Now you see how you can think yourself into disaster, or think yourself into victory and happiness—as the result of the very same circumstances.

Men like Lincoln and Gandhi show us how thoughts can carry a "magnetism" which attracts related thoughts, make millions of minds work as one mind.

It is essential to give before you get. Rich men had to learn this before piratical business could be turned into business that works *with* and *for* the public, yet is still profitable.

Both poverty and riches are the offspring of faith.

Step 3 Toward Riches: Autosuggestion

AUTOSUGGESTION IS A TERM WHICH APPLIES TO ALL suggestions and all self-administered stimuli which reach one's mind through the five senses. Stated in another way, auto-suggestion is self-suggestion. It is the agency of communication between that part of the mind where conscious thought takes place and that which serves as the seat of action for the subconscious mind.

Through the dominating thoughts which one *permits* to remain in the conscious mind (whether these thoughts be negative or positive is immaterial) the principle of auto-suggestion voluntarily reaches the subconscious mind and influences it with these thoughts.

Nature has so built man that he has absolute control over

For amazing results, get the deepest part of your mind to go to work for you. Back this with emotion power and the combination is terrific.

---

the material which reaches his subconscious mind through his five senses although this is not meant to be construed as a statement that man always exercises this control. In the great majority of instances he does not exercise it, which explains why so many people go through life in poverty.

Recall what has been said about the subconscious mind resembling a fertile garden spot, in which weeds will grow in abundance if the seeds of more desirable crops are not sown therein. Autosuggestion is the agency of control through which an individual may voluntarily feed his subconscious mind on thoughts of a creative nature or, by neglect, permit thoughts of a destructive nature to find their way into this rich garden of the mind.

The Money Power of Emotion

You were instructed, in the last of the six steps described in the chapter on desire, to read aloud twice daily the written statement of your desire for money, and to see and feel yourself already in possession of the money! By following these instructions, you communicate the object of your desire directly to your subconscious mind in a spirit of absolute faith. Through repetition of this procedure, you voluntarily create thought habits which are favorable to your efforts to transmute desire into its monetary equivalent.

Go back to the six steps described in the chapter on Desire, and read them again, carefully, before going further. Then (when you come to it) read very carefully the four instructions for the organization of your "Master Mind" group, described in the chapter on Organized Planning. By comparing these two sets of instructions with that which has been stated on autosuggestion, you, of course, will see that the instructions involve the application of the principle of autosuggestion.

Remember, therefore, when reading aloud the statement of your desire (through which you are endeavoring to develop a "money consciousness"), that the mere reading of the words is of no consequence—unless you mix emotion, or feeling with your words. Your subconscious mind recognizes and acts only upon thoughts which have been well mixed with emotion or feeling.

This is a fact of such importance as to warrant repetition in practically every chapter, because the lack of understanding of this is the main reason the majority of people who try to apply the principle of autosuggestion get no desirable results.

Plain, unemotional words do not influence the subconscious

mind. You will get no appreciable results until you learn to reach your subconscious mind with thoughts or spoken words which have been well emotionalized with belief.

Do not become discouraged if you cannot control and direct your emotions the first time you try to do so. Remember, there is no such possibility as something for nothing. You cannot cheat, even if you desire to do so. The price of ability to influence your subconscious mind is everlasting persistence in applying the principles described here. You cannot develop the desired ability for a lower price. You, and you alone, must decide whether or not the reward for which you are striving (the "money consciousness") is worth the price you must pay for it in effort.

Your ability to use the principle of autosuggestion will depend, very largely, upon your capacity to concentrate upon a given desire until that desire becomes a burning obsession.

See Yourself Making Money

When you begin to carry out the instructions in connection with the six steps described in the second chapter, it will be necessary for you to make use of the principle of concentration.

Let us here offer suggestions for the effective use of concentration. When you begin to carry out the first of the six steps, which instructs you to "fix in your own mind the exact amount of money you desire," hold your thoughts on that amount of money by concentration, or fixation of attention, with your eyes closed until you can actually see the physical appearance of the money. Do this at least once each day. As you go through these exercises, follow the instructions given in the chapter on faith, and see yourself actually in possession of the money!

Here is a most significant fact—the subconscious mind takes any orders given it in a spirit of absolute faith and acts upon those orders, although the orders often have to be presented *over and over again,* through repetition, before they are interpreted by the subconscious mind. Following the preceding statement, consider the possibility of playing a perfectly legitimate "trick" on your subconscious mind, by making it believe, *because you believe it,* that you must have the amount of money you are visualizing, that this money is already awaiting your claim, that the subconscious mind must hand over to you practical plans for acquiring the money which is yours.

Hand over the thought suggested in the preceding paragraph to your imagination, and see what your imagination can, or will do, to create practical plans for the accumulation of money through transmutation of your desire.

Inspiration Will Guide You

Do not wait for a definite plan through which you intend to exchange services or merchandise in return for the money you are visualizing, but begin at once to see yourself in possession of the money, demanding and expecting meanwhile that your subconscious mind will hand over the plan or plans you need. Be on the alert for these plans, and when they appear, put them into action immediately. When the plans appear they will probably "flash" into your mind through the sixth sense in the form of an "inspiration." Treat it with respect, and act upon it as soon as you receive it.

In the fourth of the six steps, you were instructed to "Create a definite plan for carrying out your desire, and begin at once to put this plan into action." You should follow this instruction in the manner described in the preceding paragraph. Do not trust to your "reason" when creating your plan for accumulating money through the transmutation of desire. Your reasoning faculty may be lazy, and, if you depend entirely upon it to serve you it may disappoint you.

When visualizing the money you intend to accumulate (with closed eyes), *see yourself rendering the service, or delivering the merchandise you intend to give in return for this money. This is important!*

Now Your Subconscious Mind Goes to Work

The instructions given in connection with the six steps in the second chapter will now be summarized, and blended with the principles covered by this chapter, as follows:

1. Go into some quiet spot (preferably in bed at night) where you will not be disturbed or interrupted, close your eyes, and repeat aloud (so you may hear your own words) the written statement of the amount of money you intend to accumulate, the time limit for its accumulation, and a description of the service or merchandise you intend to give in return for the money. As you carry out these instructions, see yourself already in possession of the money.

    For example, suppose that you intend to accumulate $50,000 by the first of January, five years hence, that you intend to give personal services in return for the money, in the capacity of a salesman. Your written statement of your purpose should be similar to the following:

    "By the first day of January, 19.., I will have in my possession $50,000, which will come to me in various amounts from time to time during the interim.

"In return for this money I will give the most efficient service of which I am capable, rendering the fullest possible quantity, and the best possible quality of service in the capacity of salesman of ......
...... (describe the service or merchandise you intend to sell).

"I believe that I will have this money in my possession. My faith is so strong that I can now see this money before my eyes. I can touch it with my hands. It is now awaiting transfer to me at the time, and in the proportion that I deliver the service I intend to render in return for it. I am awaiting a plan by which to accumulate this money, and I will follow that plan, when it is received."

2. Repeat this program night and morning until you can see (in your imagination) the money you intend to accumulate.

3. Place a written copy of your statement where you can see it night and morning, and read it just before retiring, and upon arising until it has been memorized.

Remember, as you carry out these instructions, that you are applying the principle of autosuggestion for the purpose of giving orders to your subconscious mind. Remember also that your subconscious mind will act only upon instructions which are emotionalized and handed over to it with "feeling." Faith is the strongest and most productive of the emotions. Follow the instructions given in the chapter on Faith.

These instructions may, at first, seem abstract. Do not let this disturb you. Follow the instructions, no matter how abstract or impractical they may at first appear to be. The time will soon come, if you do as you have been instructed *in spirit as well as in act,* when a whole new universe of power will unfold to you.

Why You Are Master of Your Destiny

Skepticism in connection with all new ideas is characteristic of all human beings. But if you follow the instructions outlined, your skepticism will soon be replaced by belief, and this, in turn, will soon become crystallized into absolute faith.

Many philosophers have made the statement that man is the master of his own *earthly* destiny, but most of them have failed to say *why* he is the master. The reason that man may be the master of his own earthly status, and especially his financial status, is thoroughly explained in this chapter. *Man may become the master of himself, and of his environment, because he has the power to influence his own subconscious mind.*

The actual performance of transmuting desire into money involves the use of autosuggestion as an agency by which one may reach and influence the subconscious mind. The other principles are simply tools with which to apply autosuggestion. Keep this thought in mind, and you will, at all times, be conscious of the important part the principle of autosuggestion is to play in your efforts to accumulate money through the methods described in this book.

After you have read the entire book, come back to this chapter, and follow in spirit and in action this instruction:

Read the entire chapter aloud once every night until you become thoroughly convinced that the principle of autosuggestion is sound, that it will accomplish for you all that has been claimed for it. As you read, underscore with a pencil every sentence which impresses you favorably.

Follow the foregoing instruction to the letter, and it will open the way for a complete understanding and mastery of the principles of success.

POINTS TO PIN DOWN:

You have a Sixth Sense—but you need only your five ordinary senses to control the thoughts that reach your subconscious mind. Once you do this, the subconscious drive toward prosperity leaves no room for poverty.

When your emotions help you actually to see and feel money in your hands, money can come from sources never before available. Set your goal as a definite amount and make it big. Set a time limit as well.

When your subconscious gives you a plan, start immediately to work the plan. Inspiration is precious and must be used at once. "Waiting for the right time" can defeat you.

Three simple procedures make you master of Autosuggestion. Follow instructions to the letter and you can be master of your destiny.

Every adversity carries with it the seeds of a greater benefit.

Step 4 Toward Riches: Specialized Knowledge

THERE ARE TWO KINDS OF KNOWLEDGE. ONE IS GENERAL, the other is specialized. General knowledge, no matter how great in quantity or variety it may be, is of but little use in the accumulation of money. The faculties of the great universities possess, in the aggregate, practically every form of general knowledge known to civilization. *Most of the professors have but little money*. They specialize on *teaching* knowledge, but they do not specialize on the organization or the *use* of knowledge.

Knowledge will not attract money, unless it is organized and intelligently directed, through practical *plans of action*, to the definite end of accumulation of money. Lack of understanding of this fact has been the source of confusion to millions of people who falsely believe that "knowledge is power."

Your education is what you make it, and you can find the knowledge that takes you where you want to go. You don't start at the bottom when you follow this simple plan.

It is nothing of the sort! Knowledge is only *potential* power. It becomes power only when and if it is organized into definite plans of action and directed to a definite end.

This "missing link" in all systems of education may be found in the failure of educational institutions to teach their students how to organize and use knowledge after they acquire it.

Many people make the mistake of assuming that because Henry Ford had but little "schooling" he was not a man of "education." Those who make this mistake do not understand the real meaning of the word "educate." That word is derived from the Latin word "educo," meaning to educe, to draw out, to develop from within.

An educated man is not, necessarily, one who has an

abundance of general or specialized knowledge. An educated
man is one who has so developed the faculties of his mind
that he may acquire anything he wants, or its equivalent, without violating the rights of others.

"Ignorant" Enough to Make a Fortune

During the first World War, a Chicago newspaper published certain editorials in which, among other statements,
Henry Ford was called "an ignorant pacifist." Mr. Ford objected to the statements, and brought suit against the paper
for libeling him. When the suit was tried in the courts, the
attorneys for the paper pleaded justification, and placed Mr.
Ford on the witness stand for the purpose of proving to the
jury that he was ignorant. The attorneys asked Mr. Ford a
great variety of questions, all of them intended to prove that
while he might possess considerable specialized knowledge
pertaining to the manufacture of automobiles, he was, in the
main, ignorant.

Mr. Ford was plied with such questions as the following:
"Who was Benedict Arnold?" and "How many soldiers did
the British send over to America to put down the Rebellion
of 1776?" In answer to the last question, Mr. Ford replied,
"I do not know the exact number of soldiers the British sent
over, but I have heard that it was a considerably larger
number than ever went back."

Finally Mr. Ford became tired of this line of questioning,
and in reply to a particularly offensive question, he leaned
over, pointed his finger at the lawyer who had asked the question and said, "If I should really want to answer the foolish
question you have just asked, or any of the other questions
you have been asking me, let me remind you that I have a
row of electric push-buttons on my desk, and by pushing the

right button, I can summon to my aid men who can answer any question I desire to ask concerning the business to which I am devoting most of my efforts. Now, will you kindly tell me, why I should clutter up my mind with general knowledge, for the purpose of being able to answer questions, when I have men around me who can supply any knowledge I require?"

There certainly was good logic to that reply.

That answer floored the lawyer. Every person in the courtroom realized it was the answer, not of an ignorant man, but of a man of education. Any man is educated who knows where to get knowledge when he needs it, and how to organize that knowledge into definite plans of action. Through the assistance of his "Master Mind" group, Henry Ford had at his command all the specialized knowledge he needed to enable him to become one of the wealthiest men in America. *It was not essential that he have this knowledge in his own mind.*

Knowledge Is Easy to Acquire

Before you can be sure of your ability to transmute desire into its monetary equivalent, you will require specialized knowledge of the service or merchandise which you intend to offer in return for fortune. Perhaps you may need much more specialized knowledge than you have the ability or the inclination to acquire, and if this should be true, you may bridge your weakness through the aid of your "Master Mind" group.

The accumulation of great fortunes calls for power and power is acquired through highly organized and intelligently directed specialized knowledge, but that knowledge does not, necessarily, have to be in the possession of the man who accumulates the fortune.

The preceding paragraph should give hope and encouragement to the man with ambition to accumulate a fortune, who has not possessed himself of the necessary "education" to supply such specialized knowledge as he may require. Men sometimes go through life suffering from "inferiority complexes" because they are not men of "education." The man who can organize and direct a "Master Mind" group of men who possess knowledge useful in the accumulation of money is just as much a man of education as any man in the group.

Thomas A. Edison had only three months of "schooling" during his entire life. He did not lack education; neither did he die poor.

Henry Ford had less than a sixth grade schooling but he managed to do pretty well by himself, financially.

Specialized knowledge is among the most plentiful, and the cheapest forms of service which may be had! If you doubt this, consult the payroll of any university.

Where to Find Knowledge

First of all, decide the sort of specialized knowledge you require, and the purpose for which it is needed. To a large extent your major purpose in life, the goal toward which you are working, will help determine what knowledge you need. With this question settled, your next move requires that you have accurate information concerning dependable sources of knowledge. The more important of these are:

1. One's own experience and education.
2. Experience and education available through co-operation of others (Master-Mind Alliance).
3. Colleges and universities.
4. Public libraries (through books and periodicals in

which may be found all the knowledge organized by civilization).

5. Special training courses (through night schools and home study schools in particular).

As knowledge is acquired it must be organized and put into use, for a definite purpose, through practical plans. Knowledge has no value except that which can be gained from its application toward some worthy end.

If you contemplate taking additional schooling, first determine the purpose for which you want the knowledge you are seeking, then learn where this particular sort of knowledge can be obtained.

Successful men, in all callings, never stop acquiring specialized knowledge related to their major purpose, business, or profession. Those who are not successful usually make the mistake of believing that the knowledge-acquiring period ends when one finishes school. The truth is that schooling does little more than to put one in the way of learning how to acquire practical knowledge.

The order of the day is *specialization!* This truth was emphasized by Robert P. Moore (formerly director of placements at Columbia University) in a news story:

SPECIALISTS MOST SOUGHT

Particularly sought after by employing companies are candidates who have specialized in some field—business-school graduates with training in accounting and statistics, engineers of all varieties, journalists, architects, chemists, and also outstanding leaders and activity men of the senior class.

The man who has been active on the campus, whose

personality is such that he gets along with all kinds of
people and who has done an adequate job with his studies
has a most decided edge over the strictly academic student.
Some of these, because of their all-around qualifications,
have received several offers of positions, a few of them as
many as six.

One of the largest industrial companies, the leader in its
field, in writing to Mr. Moore concerning prospective
seniors at the college, said:

"We are interested primarily in finding men who can
make exceptional progress in management work. For this
reason we emphasize qualities of character, intelligence
and personality far more than specific educational background."

"APPRENTICESHIP" PROPOSED

Proposing a system of "apprenticing" students in offices,
stores and industrial occupations during the summer vaca-
tion, Mr. Moore asserted that after the first two or three
years of college, every student should be asked "to choose
a definite future course and to call a halt if he has been
merely pleasantly drifting without purpose through an un-
specialized academic curriculum.

"Colleges and universities must face the practical consideration that all professions and occupations now demand
specialists," he said, urging that educational institutions
accept more direct responsibility for vocational guidance.

One of the most reliable and practical sources of knowledge available to those who need specialized schooling are
the night schools operated in most large cities. The correspondence schools give specialized training anywhere the
U. S. mails go, on all subjects that can be taught by the ex-

tension method. One advantage of home study training is the flexibility of the study program which permits one to study during spare time. Another advantage of home study training (if the school is carefully chosen) is the fact that most courses offered by home study schools carry with them generous privileges of consultation which can be of priceless value to those needing specialized knowledge. No matter where you live, you can share the benefits.

Study and Self-discipline

Anything acquired without effort and without cost is generally unappreciated, often discredited; perhaps this is why we get so little from our marvelous opportunity in public schools. The *self-discipline* one receives from a definite program of specialized study makes up to some extent for the wasted opportunity when knowledge was available without cost. Correspondence schools are highly organized business institutions. Their tuition fees are so low that they are forced to insist upon prompt payments. Being asked to pay, whether the student makes good grades or poor, has the effect of causing one to follow through with the course when he would otherwise drop it. The correspondence schools have not stressed this point sufficiently, for the truth is that their collection departments constitute the very finest sort of training on *decision, promptness,* and *the habit of finishing what one begins.*

I learned this from experience, more than forty-five years ago. I enrolled for a home study course in advertising. After completing eight or ten lessons I stopped studying, but the school did not stop sending me bills. Moreover it insisted upon payment, whether I kept up my studies or not. I decided that if I had to pay for the course (which I had legally obligated myself to do), I should complete the lessons and get my money's worth. I felt, at the time, that the collection system of the school was somewhat too well organized, but I learned later in life that it was a valuable part of my training for which no charge had been made. Being forced to pay, I went ahead and completed the course. Later in life I discovered that the efficient collection system of that school had been worth much in the form of money earned, because of the training in advertising I had so reluctantly taken.

Never Too Late to Learn

We have in this country what is said to be the greatest public school system in the world. One of the strange things about human beings is that they value only that which has a price. The free schools of America, and the free public libraries, do not impress people *because they are free*. This is the major reason why so many people find it necessary to acquire additional training after they quit school and go to work. It is also one of the major reasons why employers give greater consideration to employees who take home study courses. They have learned from experience that any person who has the ambition to give up a part of his spare time to studying at home has in him those qualities which make for leadership.

There is one weakness in people for which there is no remedy. It is the universal weakness of lack of ambition! People, especially salaried people who schedule their spare time to provide for home study seldom remain at the bottom very long. Their action opens the way for the upward climb, removes many obstacles from their path, and gains the friendly interest of those who have the power to put them in the way of opportunity.

The home study method of training is especially suited to the needs of employed people who find, after leaving school, that they must acquire additional specialized knowledge, but cannot spare the time to go back to school.

Stuart Austin Wier prepared himself as a construction engineer and followed this line of work until the depression limited his market to where it did not give him the income he required. He took inventory of himself, decided to change his profession to law, went back to school and took special courses by which he prepared himself as a corporation lawyer. He completed his training, passed the bar examination, and quickly built a lucrative law practice.

Just to keep the record straight, and to anticipate the alibis of those who will say, "I couldn't go to school because I have a family to support," or "I'm too old," I will add the information that Mr. Wier was past forty, and married when he went back to school. Moreover, by carefully selecting highly specialized courses in colleges best prepared to teach the subjects chosen, Mr. Wier completed in two years the work for which the majority of law students require four years. It pays to know how to purchase knowledge!

Bookkeeping on Wheels

Let us consider a specific instance. A salesman in a grocery store found himself suddenly unemployed. Having had some bookkeeping experience, he took a special course in accounting, familiarized himself with all the latest bookkeeping and office equipment, and went into business for himself. Starting with the grocer for whom he had formerly worked, he made contracts with more than one hundred small merchants to keep their books, at a very nominal monthly fee. His idea was so practical that he soon found it necessary to set up a portable office in a light delivery truck which he equipped with modern bookkeeping machinery. He now has a fleet of these bookkeeping offices "on wheels" and employs a large staff of assistants, thus providing small merchants with accounting service equal to the best that money can buy at very nominal cost.

Specialized knowledge plus imagination were the ingredients that went into this unique and successful business. Last year the owner of that business paid an income tax of almost ten times as much as was paid by the merchant for whom he worked when he lost his job.

The beginning of this successful business was an idea!

Inasmuch as I had the privilege of supplying the unemployed salesman with that idea, I now assume the further privilege of suggesting another idea which has within it the possibility of even greater income.

The idea was suggested by the salesman who gave up selling and went into the business of keeping books on a wholesale basis. When the plan was suggested as a solution of his unemployment problem, he quickly exclaimed, "I like the idea, but I would not know how to turn it into cash." In other words, he complained he would not know how to market his bookkeeping knowledge *after he acquired it*.

So, that brought up another problem which had to be solved. With the aid of a young woman typist who could put the story together, a very attractive book was prepared, describing the advantages of the new system of bookkeeping. The pages were neatly typed and pasted in an ordinary scrapbook which was used as a silent salesman with which the story of this new business was so effectively told that its owner soon had more accounts than he could handle.

A "Blueprint" that Built a Job

There are thousands of people all over the country who need the services of a merchandising specialist capable of preparing an attractive brief for use in marketing personal services.

The idea here described was born of necessity, to bridge an emergency which had to be covered, but it did not stop by serving merely one person. The woman who created the idea has a keen imagination. She saw in her newly born brain child the making of a new profession to serve thousands of people who need practical guidance in marketing personal services.

Spurred to action by the instantaneous success of her first "prepared plan to market personal services," this energetic woman turned next to the solution of a similar problem for her son who had just finished college, but had been totally unable to find a market for his services. The plan she originated for his use was the finest specimen of merchandising of personal services I have ever seen.

When the plan book had been completed, it contained nearly fifty pages of beautifully typed, properly organized information, telling the story of her son's native ability, schooling, personal experiences, and a great variety of other information too extensive for description. The plan book also contained a complete description of the position her son desired, together with a marvelous word picture of the exact plan he would use in filling the position.

The preparation of the plan book required several weeks' labor, during which time its creator sent her son to the public library almost daily, to procure data needed in selling his services to best advantage. She sent him also to all the competitors of his prospective employer, and gathered from them vital information concerning their business methods which was of great value in the formation of the plan he intended to use in filling the position he sought. When the plan had been finished, it contained more than half a dozen very fine suggestions for the use and benefit of the prospective employer.

He Saved Ten Years of "Beginning"

One may be inclined to ask, "Why go to all this trouble to secure a job?"

The answer is, "Doing a thing well never is trouble! The plan prepared by this woman for the benefit of her son helped him get the job for which he applied, at the first interview, at a salary fixed by himself."

Moreover—and this, too, is important—the position did not require the young man to start at the bottom. He began as a junior executive, at an executive's salary.

"Why go to all this trouble?"

Well, for one thing, the *planned presentation* of this young man's application for a position clipped off no less than ten years of time he would have required to get to where he began had he "started at the bottom and worked his way up."

This idea of starting at the bottom and working one's way up may appear to be sound, but the major objection to it is this—too many of those who begin at the bottom never manage to lift their heads high enough to be seen by opportunity, so they remain at the bottom. It should be remembered also that the outlook from the bottom is not so very bright or encouraging. It has a tendency to kill off ambition. We call it "getting into a rut," which means that we accept our fate because we form the habit of daily routine, a habit that finally becomes so strong we cease to try to throw it off. And that is another reason why it pays to start one or two steps above the bottom. By so doing one forms the habit of looking around, of observing how others get ahead, of seeing opportunity, and of embracing it without hesitation.

The World Loves a Winner

Dan Halpin is a splendid example of what I mean. During his college days, he was manager of the famous 1930 national championship Notre Dame football team when it was under the direction of the late Knute Rockne.

Halpin finished college at a mighty unfavorable time, when the depression had made jobs scarce, so after a fling at investment banking and motion pictures, he took the first opening with a potential future he could find—selling electrical hearing aids on a commission basis. Anyone could start in that sort of job, and Halpin knew it, but it was enough to open the door of opportunity to him.

For almost two years, he continued in a job not to his liking, and he would never have risen above that job if he had not done something about his dissatisfaction. He aimed first at the job of assistant sales manager of his company, and got the job. That one step upward placed him high enough above the crowd to enable him to see still greater opportunity. Also, it placed him where opportunity could see him.

He made such a fine record selling hearing aids that A. M. Andrews, chairman of the board of the Dictograph Products Company, a business competitor of the company for which Halpin worked, wanted to know something about that man Dan Halpin who was taking big sales away from the long established Dictograph Company. He sent for Halpin. When the interview was over, Halpin was the new sales manager

in charge of the Acousticon Division. Then, to test young
Halpin's mettle, Mr. Andrews went away to Florida for three
months leaving him to sink or swim in his new job. He did not
sink! Knute Rocke's spirit of "All the world loves a winner,
and has no time for a loser," inspired him to put so much
into his job that he was elected vice-president of the company,
a job which most men would be proud to earn through ten
years of loyal effort. Halpin turned the trick in little more than
six months.

One of the major points I am trying to emphasize through
this entire philosophy is that we rise to high positions or remain at the bottom because of conditions we can control if we
desire to control them.

Don't Linger at the Bottom

I am also trying to emphasize another point, namely, that
both success and failure are largely the results of *habit!* I have
not the slightest doubt that Dan Halpin's close association
with the greatest football coach America ever knew planted in
his mind the same brand of desire to excel which made the
Notre Dame football team world famous. Truly, there is
something to the idea that hero worship is helpful, provided
one worships a winner.

My belief in the theory that business associations are vital
factors, both in failure and in success, was clearly demonstrated when my son Blair was negotiating with Dan Halpin
for a position. Mr. Halpin offered him a beginning salary of
about one half what he could have gotten from a rival company. I brought parental pressure to bear, and induced him
to accept the place with Mr. Halpin, because I believe that
close association with one who refuses to compromise with

circumstances he does not like is an asset that can never be measured in terms of money.

The bottom is a monotonous, dreary, unprofitable place for any person. That is why I have taken the time to describe how lowly beginnings may be circumvented by proper planning.

You Can Market Yourself

The woman who prepared the "Personal Service Sales Plan" for her son now receives requests from all parts of the country for her cooperation in preparing similar plans for others who desire to market their personal services for more money.

It must not be supposed that her plan merely consists of clever salesmanship by which she helps men and women to demand and receive more money for the same services they formerly sold for less pay. She looks after the interests of the purchaser as well as the seller of personal services, and so prepares her plans that the employer receives full value for the additional money he pays.

If you have the imagination, and seek a more profitable outlet for your personal services, this suggestion may be the stimulus for which you have been searching. The idea is capable of yielding an income far greater than that of the "average" doctor, lawyer, or engineer whose education required several years in college.

There is no fixed price for sound ideas!

Back of all ideas is specialized knowledge. Unfortunately, for those who do not find riches in abundance, specialized knowledge is more abundant and more easily acquired than ideas. Because of this very truth, there is a universal demand and an ever-increasing opportunity for the person capable of helping men and women to sell their personal services advantageously. Capability means imagination, the one quality needed to combine specialized knowledge with ideas, in the form of organized plans designed to yield riches.

If you have imagination this chapter may present you with an idea sufficient to serve as the beginning of the riches you desire. Remember, the idea is the main thing. Specialized knowledge may be found just around the corner—any corner!

POINTS TO PIN DOWN:

Knowledge is only *potential* power. You can organize your knowledge to give you definite plans of action directed toward a definite end.

Open your mind to the education that comes from experience and from contact with other minds. Henry Ford was "ignorant" enough to make a fortune.

Use any or all of the five major sources of knowledge this chapter gives you. Knowledge is easy to acquire.

If you are not ready to sell a product, you can sell your services or your ideas at a very good price. Men past sixty have been highly successful in doing this. The plan has given a big upward boost to thousands of self-disciplined young men.

The blueprint given in this chapter can start you ten years ahead in any job.

Knowledge paves the road to riches—when you know which road to take.

Step 5 Toward Riches: Imagination

THE IMAGINATION IS LITERALLY THE WORKSHOP WHEREIN are fashioned all plans created by man. The impulse, the desire is given shape, form, and action through the aid of the imaginative faculty of the mind.

It is said that man can create anything he imagines.

Through the aid of his imaginative faculty, man has discovered and harnessed more of nature's forces during the past fifty years than during the entire history of the human race previous to that time. He has conquered the air so completely that the birds are a poor match for him in flying. He has analyzed and weighed the sun at a distance of millions of miles, and has determined, through the aid of *imagination,* the elements of which it consists. He has increased the speed of locomotion until he may now travel faster than sound.

All the "breaks" you need in life wait within your imagination. Imagination is the workshop of your mind, capable of turning mind-energy into accomplishment and wealth.

Man's only limitation, within reason, lies in his development and use of his imagination. He has not yet reached the apex of development in the use of his imaginative faculty. He has merely discovered that he has an imagination, and has commenced to use it in a very elementary way.

The Synthetic and the Creative

The imaginative faculty functions in two forms. One is known as "synthetic imagination" and the other as "creative imagination."

Synthetic Imagination: Through this faculty, one may arrange old concepts, ideas, or plans into new combinations. This faculty *creates* nothing. It merely works with the ma-

101

terial of experience, education, and observation with which
it is fed. It is the faculty used most by the inventor, with the
exception of the "genius" who draws upon the creative
imagination, when he cannot solve his problem through
synthetic imagination.

Creative Imagination: Through the faculty of creative
imagination, the finite mind of man has direct communication with Infinite Intelligence. It is the faculty through
which "hunches" and "inspirations" are received. It is by
this faculty that all basic or new ideas are handed over to
man. It is through this faculty that one individual may
"tune in" or communicate with the subconscious minds of
other men.

The creative imagination works automatically, in the manner described in subsequent pages. This faculty functions only
when the conscious mind is working at an exceedingly rapid
rate, as for example, when the conscious mind is stimulated
through the emotion of a *strong desire*.

The creative faculty becomes more alert in proportion to
its development through use.

The great leaders of business, industry, finance, and the
great artists, musicians, poets, and writers became great because they developed the faculty of creative imagination.

Both the synthetic and creative faculties of imagination
become more alert with use, just as any muscle or organ of the
body develops through use.

Desire is only a thought, an impulse. It is nebulous and
ephemeral. It is abstract, and of no value until it has been
transformed into its physical counterpart. While the synthetic
imagination is the one which will be used most frequently, in
the process of transforming the impulse of desire into money
you must keep in mind the fact that you may face circum-

stances and situations which demand use of the creative imagination as well.

Stimulate Your Imagination

Your imaginative faculty may have become weak through inaction. It can be revived and made alert through use. This faculty does not die, though it may become quiescent through lack of use.

Center your attention, for the time being, on the development of the synthetic imagination, because this is the faculty which you will use more often in the process of converting desire into money.

Transformation of the intangible impulse, of desire, into the tangible reality of money calls for the use of a plan, or plans. These plans must be formed with the aid of the imagination, and mainly with the synthetic faculty.

Read the entire book through, then come back to this chapter and begin at once to put your imagination to work on the building of a plan or plans for the transformation of your desire into money. Detailed instructions for the building of plans have been given in almost every chapter. Carry out the instructions best suited to your needs and reduce your plan to writing, if you have not already done so. The moment you complete this, you will have definitely given concrete form to the intangible desire. Read the preceding sentence once more. Read it aloud very slowly, and as you do so, remember that the moment you reduce the statement of your desire and a plan for its realization, to writing, you have actually taken the first of a series of steps which will enable you to convert the thought into its physical counterpart.

Nature Tells Us the Secret of Fortune

The earth on which you live, you, yourself, and every other material thing are the result of evolutionary change, through which microscopic bits of matter have been organized and arranged in an orderly fashion.

Moreover—and this statement is of stupendous importance —this earth, every one of the billions of individual cells of your body, and every atom of matter, *began as an intangible form of energy.*

Desire is thought impulse! Thought impulses are forms of energy. When you begin with the thought impulse, desire, to accumulate money, you are drafting into your service the same "stuff" that nature used in creating this earth and every material form in the universe, including the body and brain in which the thought impulses function.

You can build a fortune through the aid of laws which are immutable. But, first, you must become familiar with these laws and learn to use them. Through repetition, and by approaching the description of these principles from every conceivable angle, the author hopes to reveal to you the secret through which every great fortune has been accumulated. Strange and paradoxical as it may seem, the "secret" is not a secret. Nature herself advertises it in the earth on which we live, the stars, the planets suspended within our view, in the elements above and around us, in every blade of grass, and every form of life within our vision.

The principles which follow will open the way for understanding of imagination. Assimilate that which you understand, as you read this philosophy for the first time; then when you reread and study it, you will discover that something has happened to clarify it and give you a broader understanding of the whole. Above all, do not stop nor hesitate in your study of these principles until you have read the book at least *three* times, for then you will not want to stop.

Ideas Become Fortunes

Ideas are the beginning points of all fortunes. Ideas are products of the imagination. Let us examine a few well-known ideas which have yielded huge fortunes, with the hope that these illustrations will convey definite information concerning the method by which imagination may be used in accumulating riches.

One Ingredient Was Missing

Fifty years ago, an old country doctor drove to town, hitched his horse, quietly slipped into a drug store by the back door, and began "dickering" with the young drug clerk.

For more than an hour, behind the prescription counter, the old doctor and the clerk talked in low tones. Then the doctor left. He went out to the buggy and brought back a large, old-fashioned kettle and a big wooden paddle (used for stirring the contents of the kettle) and deposited them in the back of the store.

The clerk inspected the kettle, reached into his inside pocket, took out a roll of bills, and handed it over to the doctor. The roll contained exactly five hundred dollars—the clerk's entire savings!

The doctor handed over a small slip of paper on which was written a secret formula. The words on that small slip of paper were worth a king's ransom! *But not to the doctor!* Those magic words were needed to start the kettle to boiling, but neither the doctor nor the young clerk knew what fabulous fortunes were destined to flow from that kettle.

The old doctor was glad to sell the outfit for five hundred dollars. The clerk was taking a big chance by staking his entire life's savings on a mere scrap of paper and an old kettle! He never dreamed his investment would start a kettle to overflowing with gold that would one day surpass the miraculous performance of Aladdin's lamp.

What the clerk *really purchased* was an idea!

The old kettle and the wooden paddle and the secret message on a slip of paper were incidental. The strange performance of that kettle began to take place after the new owner mixed with the secret instructions an ingredient of which the doctor knew nothing.

See if you can discover what it was that the young man added to the secret message which caused the kettle to overflow with gold. Here you have a story of facts stranger than fiction, facts which began in the form of an idea.

Let us take a look at the vast fortunes of gold this idea has produced. It has paid and still pays huge fortunes to men and women all over the world who distribute the contents of the kettle to millions of people.

The old kettle is now one of the world's largest consumers of sugar, thus providing jobs for thousands of men and women engaged in growing sugar cane and in refining and marketing sugar.

The old kettle consumes, annually, millions of glass bottles, providing jobs to huge numbers of glass workers.

The old kettle gives employment to an army of clerks, stenographers, copywriters, and advertising experts throughout the nation. It has brought fame and fortune to scores of artists who have created magnificent pictures describing the product.

The old kettle has converted a small southern city into the

business capital of the South, where it now benefits, directly or indirectly, every business and practically every resident of the city.

The influence of this idea now benefits every civilized country in the world, pouring out a continuous stream of gold to all who touch it.

Gold from the kettle built and maintains one of the most prominent colleges of the South, where thousands of young people receive the training essential for success.

If the product of that old brass kettle could talk, it would tell thrilling tales of romance in every language. Romances of love, romances of business, romances of professional men and women who are daily being stimulated by it.

The author is sure of at least one such romance for he was a part of it, and it all began not far from the very spot on which the drug clerk purchased the old kettle. It was here that the author met his wife, and it was she who first told him of the enchanted kettle. It was the product of that kettle they were drinking when he asked her to accept him "for better or worse."

Whoever you are, wherever you may live, whatever occupation you may be engaged in, just remember in the future, every time you see the words *Coca-Cola,* that its vast empire of wealth and influence grew out of a single idea, and that the mysterious ingredient the drug clerk, Asa Candler, mixed with the secret formula was—*imagination!*

Stop and think of that for a moment.

Remember also that the steps to riches described in this book were the media through which the influence of Coca-Cola has been extended to every city, town, village, and crossroads of the world, and that any idea you may create, as *sound and meritorious* as Coca-Cola, has the possibility of duplicating the record of this world-wide thirst killer.

One Week to Get a Million Dollars

This story proves the truth of that old saying, "where there's a will, there's a way." It was told to me by that beloved educator and clergyman, the late Frank W. Gunsaulus, who began his preaching career in the stockyards region of Chicago.

While Dr. Gunsaulus was going through college, he observed many defects in our educational system, defects which he believed he could correct if he were the head of a college.

He made up his mind to organize a new college in which he could carry out his ideas, without being handicapped by orthodox methods of education.

He needed a million dollars to put the project across! Where was he to lay his hands on so large a sum of money? That was the question that absorbed most of this ambitious young preacher's thought.

But he couldn't seem to make any progress.

Every night he took that thought to bed with him. He got up with it in the morning. He took it with him everywhere he went. He turned it over and over in his mind until it became a consuming *obsession* with him.

Being a philosopher as well as a preacher, Dr. Gunsaulus recognized, as do all who succeed in life, that *definiteness of purpose* is the starting point from which one must begin. He recognized too that definiteness of purpose takes on animation, life, and power when backed by a burning desire to translate that purpose into its material equivalent.

He knew all these great truths, yet he did not know where, or how to lay his hands on a million dollars. The natural procedure would have been to give up and quit, by saying, "Ah well, my idea is a good one, but I cannot do anything with it, because I never can procure the necessary million dollars."

That is exactly what the majority of people would have said, but it is not what Dr. Gunsaulus said. What he said, and what he did are so important that I now introduce him, and let him speak for himself:

"One Saturday afternoon I sat in my room thinking of ways and means of raising the money to carry out my plans. For nearly two years, I had been thinking, but I *had done nothing but think!*

"I made up my mind, then and there, that I would get the necessary million dollars within a week. How? I was not concerned about that. The main thing of importance was the *decision* to get the money within a specified time, and I want to tell you that the moment I reached a definite decision to get the money within a specified time, a strange feeling of assurance came over me, such as I had never before experienced. Something inside me seemed to say, 'Why didn't you reach that decision a long time ago? The money was waiting for you all the time!'

"Things began to happen in a hurry. I called the newspapers and announced I would preach a sermon the following morning, entitled, 'What I Would Do If I Had a Million Dollars.'

"I went to work on the sermon immediately, but I must tell you, frankly, the task was not difficult, because I had been preparing that sermon for almost two years.

"Long before midnight I had finished writing the sermon. I went to bed and slept with a feeling of confidence, for *I could see myself already in possession of the million dollars.*

"Next morning I arose early, read the sermon, then knelt on my knees and asked that my sermon might come to the attention of someone who would supply the needed money.

"While I was praying I again had that feeling of assurance that the money would be forthcoming. In my excitement, I walked out without my sermon, and did not discover the oversight until I was in my pulpit and about ready to begin delivering it.

"It was too late to go back for my notes, and what a blessing that I couldn't go back! Instead, my own subconscious mind yielded the material I needed. When I arose to begin my sermon, I closed my eyes, and spoke with all my heart and soul of my dreams. I not only talked to my audience, but I fancy I talked also to God. I told what I would do with a million dollars if that amount were placed in my hands. I described the plan I had in mind for organizing a great educational institution, where young people would learn to do practical things, and at the same time develop their minds.

"When I had finished and sat down, a man slowly arose from his seat, about three rows from the rear, and made his way toward the pulpit. I wondered what he was going to do. He came into the pulpit, extended his hand, and said, 'Reverend, I liked your sermon. I believe you can do everything you said you would, if you had a million dollars. To prove that I believe in you and your sermon, if you will come to my office tomorrow morning, I will give you the million dollars. My name is Phillip D. Armour.' "

Young Gunsaulus went to Mr. Armour's office and the million dollars was presented to him. With the money he founded the Armour Institute of Technology, now known as Illinois Institute of Technology.

The necessary million dollars came as a result of an idea. Back of the idea was a desire which young Gunsaulus had been nursing in his mind for almost two years.

Observe this important fact—he got the money within thirty-six hours after he reached a definite decision in his own mind to get it, and decided upon a definite plan for getting it!

There was nothing new or unique about young Gunsaulus' vague thinking about a million dollars, and weakly hoping for it. Others before him and many since his time have had similar thoughts. But there was something very unique and different about the decision he reached on that memorable Saturday, when he put vagueness into the background and definitely said, "I *will* get that money within a week!"

Moreover, the principle through which Dr. Gunsaulus got his million dollars is still alive! It is available to you! This universal law is as workable today as it was when the young preacher made use of it so successfully.

Definite Purpose Plus Definite Plans

Observe that Asa Candler and Dr. Frank Gunsaulus had one characteristic in common. Both knew the astounding truth that ideas can be transmuted into cash through the power of definite purpose plus definite plans.

If you are one of those who believe that hard work and honesty alone will bring riches, perish the thought! It is not true! Riches, when they come in huge quantities, are never the result of hard work alone! Riches come, if they come at all, in response to definite demands based upon the application of definite principles, and not by chance or luck.

Generally speaking, an idea is an impulse of thought that impels action by an appeal to the imagination. All master salesmen know that ideas can be sold where merchandise cannot. Ordinary salesmen do not know this—that is why they are "ordinary."

A publisher of low-priced books made a discovery that should be worth much to publishers generally. He learned that many people buy titles, and not contents of books. By merely changing the name of one book that was not moving, his sales on that book jumped upward more than a million copies. The inside of the book was not changed in any way. He merely ripped off the cover bearing the title that did not sell and put on a new cover with a title that had "box-office" value.

That, as simple as it may seem, was an idea! It was imagination.

There is no standard price on ideas. The creator of ideas makes his own price and, if he is smart, gets it.

The story of practically every great fortune starts with the day when a creator of ideas and a seller of ideas got together and worked in harmony. Carnegie surrounded himself with men who could do all that he could not do, men who created ideas, and men who put ideas into operation, and made himself and the others fabulously rich.

Millions of people go through life hoping for favorable "breaks." Perhaps a favorable break can get one an opportunity, but the safest plan is not to depend upon luck. It was a favorable "break" that gave me the biggest opportunity of my life—*but*—twenty-five years of *determined effort* had to be devoted to that opportunity before it became an asset.

The "break" consisted of my good fortune in meeting and gaining the cooperation of Andrew Carnegie. On that occasion Carnegie planted in my mind the *idea* of organizing the principles of achievement into a philosophy of success. Thousands of people have profited by the discoveries made in the twenty-five years of research, and several fortunes have been accumulated through the application of the philosophy. The beginning was simple. It was an idea which anyone might have developed.

The favorable break came through Carnegie, but what about the determination, definiteness of purpose, the desire to attain the goal, and the persistent effort of twenty-five years? It was no ordinary desire that survived disappointment, discouragement, temporary defeat, criticism, and the constant reminding of "waste of time." It was a burning desire! An obsession!

When the idea was first planted in my mind by Mr. Carnegie, it was coaxed, nursed, and enticed to *remain alive*. Gradually, the idea became a giant under its own power, and it coaxed, nursed, and drove me. Ideas are like that. First you give life and action and guidance to ideas, then they take on power of their own and sweep aside all opposition.

Ideas are intangible forces, but they have more power than the physical brains that give birth to them. They have the power to live on, after the brain that creates them has returned to dust.

POINTS TO PIN DOWN:

You can use synthetic imagination and creative imagination, and with practice you make them work irresistibly together.

Imagination is the missing ingredient in many a failure, the catalyst of many a success. Asa Candler did not invent the formula for *Coca-Cola*; he supplied the imagination which turned a formula into a fortune.

Money without limit waits for you when you want it in definite amounts for a definite, imagination-backed purpose. This principle secured a million dollars for a clergyman who merely asked for it.

Many a fortune waits to be made with a simple idea. See how you may win thousands or millions even without an original plan—by coming up with a new *combination*.

The finest tool still needs a man who knows how to use it.

Step 6 Toward Riches: Organized Planning

You HAVE LEARNED THAT EVERYTHING MAN CREATES OR acquires begins in the form of desire, that desire is taken on the first lap of its journey from the abstract to the concrete into the workshop of the imagination, where plans for its transition are created and organized.

In the chapter on Desire, you were instructed to take six definite, practical steps as your first move in translating the desire for money into its monetary equivalent. One of these steps is the formation of a definite, practical plan, or plans, through which this transformation may be made.

You will now be instructed how to build practical plans.

1. Ally yourself with a group of as many people as you may need for the creation and carrying out of your

Your introduction to the electric secret of the Master Mind. You can find your own best field of work and become a leader and high money-maker in an amazingly short time.

plan or plans for the accumulation of money—making use of the "Master-Mind" principle described in a later chapter. (Compliance with this instruction is *absolutely essential*. Do not neglect it.)

2. Before forming your "Master-Mind" alliance, decide what advantages and benefits *you* may offer the individual members of your group in return for their cooperation. No one will work indefinitely without some form of compensation. No intelligent person will either request or expect another to work without adequate compensation, although this may not always be in the form of money.

3. Arrange to meet with the members of your "Master-Mind" group at least twice a week, and more often

if possible, until you have jointly perfected the necessary plan or plans for the accumulation of money.

4. Maintain perfect harmony between yourself and every member of your "Master-Mind" group. If you fail to carry out this instruction to the letter, you may expect to meet with failure. The "Master-Mind" principle *cannot* obtain where perfect harmony does not prevail.

Keep in mind these facts:

1. You are engaged in an undertaking of major importance to you. To be sure of success, you must have plans which are faultless.
2. You must have the advantage of the experience, education, native ability and imagination of other minds. This is in harmony with the methods followed by every person who has accumulated a great fortune.

No individual has sufficient experience, education, native ability, and knowledge to insure the accumulation of a great fortune without the cooperation of other people. Every plan you adopt, in your endeavor to accumulate wealth, should be the joint creation of yourself and every other member of your "Master-Mind" group. You may originate your own plans, either in whole or in part, but see that those plans are checked, and approved by the members of your "Master-Mind" alliance.

Defeat Makes You Stronger

If the first plan which you adopt does not work successfully, replace it with a new plan; if this new plan fails to work, replace it in turn with still another, and so on, until you find a plan which does work. Right here is the point at which the majority of men meet with failure because of their lack of persistence in creating new plans to take the place of those which fail.

The most intelligent man living cannot succeed in accumulating money—nor in any other undertaking—without plans which are practical and workable. Just keep this fact in mind, and remember, when your plans fail, that temporary defeat is not permanent failure. It may only mean that your plans have not been sound. Build other plans. Start all over again.

Temporary defeat should mean only one thing, the certain knowledge that there is something wrong with your plan. Millions of men go through life in misery and poverty because they lack a sound plan through which to accumulate a fortune.

Your achievement can be no greater than your plans are sound.

No man is ever whipped, until he quits—*in his own mind.*

James J. Hill met with temporary defeat when he first endeavored to raise the necessary capital to build a railroad from the East to the West, but he too turned defeat into victory *through new plans.*

Henry Ford met with temporary defeat, not only at the beginning of his automobile career, but after he had gone far toward the top. He created new plans, and went marching on to financial victory.

We see men who have accumulated great fortunes, but we often recognize only their triumph, overlooking the temporary defeats which they had to surmount before "arriving."

No follower of this philosophy can reasonably expect to accumulate a fortune without experiencing "temporary defeat." When defeat comes, accept it as a signal that your plans are not sound, rebuild those plans, and set sail once more toward your coveted goal. If you give up before your goal has been reached, you are a "quitter." *A quitter never wins —and a winner never quits.* Lift this sentence out, write it on a piece of paper in letters an inch high, and place it where you will see it every night before you go to sleep and every morning before you go to work.

When you begin to select members for your "Master-Mind" group, endeavor to select those who do not take defeat seriously.

Some people foolishly believe that only money can make money. This is not true! Desire, transmuted into its monetary equivalent through the principles laid down here, is the agency through which money is "made." Money, of itself, is nothing but inert matter. It cannot move, think, or talk, but it can "hear" when a man who desires it, calls it to come!

You Can Sell Services and Ideas

Intelligent planning is essential for success in any undertaking designed to accumulate riches. Here will be found detailed instructions to those who must begin the accumulation of riches by selling personal services.

It should be encouraging to know that practically all the great fortunes began in the form of compensation for personal services, or from the sale of ideas. What else, except ideas and personal services, would one not possessed of property have to give in return for riches?

Where Leadership Begins

Broadly speaking, there are two types of people in the world. One type is known as leaders, and the other as followers. Decide at the outset whether you intend to become a leader in your chosen calling, or remain a follower. The difference in compensation is vast. The follower cannot reasonably expect the compensation to which a leader is entitled, although many followers make the mistake of expecting such pay.

It is no disgrace to be a follower. On the other hand, it is no credit to remain a follower. Most great leaders began in the capacity of followers. They became great leaders because they were intelligent followers. With few exceptions, the man who cannot follow a leader intelligently, cannot become an efficient leader. The man who can follow a leader most efficiently, is usually the man who develops into leadership most rapidly. An intelligent follower has many advantages, among them the opportunity to acquire knowledge from his leader.

Eleven Secrets of Leadership

The following are important factors of leadership:

1. *Unwavering courage:* It is based upon knowledge of self, and of one's occupation. No follower wishes to be dominated by a leader who lacks self-confidence and courage. No intelligent follower will be dominated by such a leader very long.
2. *Self-control:* The man who cannot control himself can never control others. Self-control sets a mighty example for one's followers, which the more intelligent will emulate.
3. *A keen sense of justice:* Without a sense of fairness and justice, no leader can command and retain the respect of his followers.
4. *Definiteness of decision:* The man who wavers in

his decisions shows that he is not sure of himself, cannot lead others successfully.

5. *Definiteness of plans:* The successful leader must plan his work, and *work his plan.* A leader who moves by guesswork, without practical, definite plans is comparable to a ship without a rudder. Sooner or later he will land on the rocks.

6. *The habit of doing more than paid for:* One of the penalties of leadership is the necessity of willingness, upon the part of the leader, to do more than he requires of his followers.

7. *A pleasing personality:* No slovenly, careless person can become a successful leader. Leadership calls for respect. Followers will not respect a leader who does not grade high on all of the factors of a pleasing personality.

8. *Sympathy and understanding:* The successful leader must be in sympathy with his followers. Moreover, he must understand them and their problems.

9. *Mastery of detail:* Successful leadership calls for mastery of the details of the leader's position.

10. *Willingness to assume full responsibility:* The successful leader must be willing to assume responsibility for the mistakes and the shortcomings of his followers. If he tries to shift this responsibility, he will not remain the leader. If one of his followers makes a mistake, and shows himself incompetent, the leader must consider that it is *he* who failed.

11. *Cooperation:* The successful leader must understand and *apply* the principle of cooperative effort and be able to induce his followers to do the same.

> Leadership calls for power, and power calls for cooperation.

There are two forms of leadership. The first, and by far the most effective, is leadership by consent of, and with the sympathy of the followers. The second is leadership by force, without the consent and sympathy of the followers.

History is filled with evidences that leadership by force cannot endure. The downfall and disappearance of dictators and kings is significant. It means that people will not follow forced leadership indefinitely.

Napoleon, Mussolini, Hitler, were examples of leadership by force. Their leadership passed. *Leadership by consent* of the followers is the only brand which can endure!

Men may follow the forced leadership temporarily, but they will not do so willingly.

The new brand of leadership will embrace the eleven factors of leadership described in this chapter as well as some other factors. The man who makes these the basis of his leadership will find abundant opportunity to lead in any walk of life.

Why Leaders Fail

We come now to the major faults of leaders who fail, because it is just as essential to know *what not to do* as it is to know what to do:

1. *Inability to organize details:* Efficient leadership calls for ability to organize and to master details. No genuine leader is ever "too busy" to do anything which may be required of him in his capacity as leader. When a man, whether he is a leader or follower admits that he is "too busy" to change

his plans or to give attention to any emergency, he admits his inefficiency. The successful leader must be the master of all details connected with his position. That means, of course, that he must acquire the habit of relegating details to capable lieutenants.

2. *Unwillingness to render humble service:* Truly great leaders are willing, when occasion demands, to perform any sort of labor which they would ask another to perform. "The greatest among ye shall be the servant of all" is a truth which all able leaders observe and respect.

3. *Expectation of pay for what they "know" instead of what they do with that which they know:* The world does not pay men for that which they "know." It pays them for what they do, or induce others to do.

4. *Fear of competition from followers:* The leader who fears that one of his followers may take his position is practically sure to realize that fear sooner or later. The able leader trains understudies to whom he may delegate, at will, any of the details of his position. Only in this way may a leader multiply himself and prepare himself to be at many places, and give attention to many things at one time. It is an eternal truth that men receive more pay for their *ability to get others to perform,* than they could possibly earn by their own efforts. An efficient leader may, through his knowledge of his job and the magnetism of his personality, greatly increase the efficiency of others, and induce them to render more service and better service than they could render without his aid.

5. *Lack of imagination:* Without imagination, the leader is incapable of meeting emergencies, and of creating plans by which to guide his followers efficiently.

6. *Selfishness:* The leader who claims all the honor for the work of his followers is sure to be met by resentment. The really great leader claims none of the honors. He is contented to see the honors, when there are any, go to his followers because he knows that most men will work harder for commendation and recognition than they will for money alone.

7. *Intemperance:* Followers do not respect an intemperate leader. Moreover intemperance, in any of its various forms, destroys the endurance and the vitality of all who indulge in it.

8. *Disloyalty:* Perhaps this should have come at the head of the list. The leader who is not loyal to his trust, and to his associates, those above him, and those below him, cannot long maintain his leadership. Disloyalty marks one as being less than the dust of the earth, and brings down on one's head the contempt he deserves. Lack of loyalty is one of the major causes of failure in every walk of life.

9. *Emphasis of the "authority" of leadership:* The efficient leader leads by encouraging, and not by trying to instill fear in the hearts of his followers. The leader who tries to impress his followers with his "authority" comes within the category of leadership through force. If a leader is a real leader, he will have no need to advertise that fact except by his conduct—his sympathy, understanding, fairness, and a demonstration that he knows his job.

10. *Emphasis of title:* The competent leader requires no "title" to give him the respect of his followers. The man who makes too much over his title generally has little else to emphasize. The doors to the office of the real leader are open to all who wish to enter, and his working quarters are free from formality or ostentation.

These are among the more common of the causes of failure in leadership. Any one of these faults is sufficient to induce failure. Study the list carefully if you aspire to leadership and make sure that you are free of these faults.

Many Fields for Leadership

Before leaving this chapter, your attention is called to a few of the fertile fields in which there has been a decline of leadership, and in which the new type of leader may find an abundance of opportunity:

1. In the field of politics there is a most insistent demand for new leaders, a demand which indicates nothing less than an emergency.
2. The banking business is undergoing a reform.
3. Industry calls for new leaders. The future leader in industry, to endure, must regard himself as a quasi public official whose duty it is to manage his trust in such a way that it will work hardship on no individual or group of individuals.
4. The religious leader of the future will be forced to give more attention to the temporal needs of his followers, the solution of their economic and per-

sonal problems of the present, and less attention to
the dead past and the yet unborn future.

5. In the professions of law, medicine, and education,
    a new brand of leadership, and to some extent, new
    leaders will become a necessity. This is especially
    true in the field of education. The leader in that
    field must, in the future, find ways and means of
    teaching people how to apply the knowledge they
    receive in school. He must deal more with practice
    and less with theory.

6. New leaders will be required in the field of journal-
    ism.

These are but a few of the fields in which opportunities for
new leaders and a new brand of leadership are now available.
The world is undergoing a rapid change. This means that the
media through which the changes in human habits are promoted must be adapted to the changes. The media here
described are the ones which, more than any others, determine
the trend of civilization.

Five Ways to Get a Good Job

The information described here is the net result of many
years of experience, during which thousands of men and
women were helped to market their services effectively.

Experience has proved that the following media offer the
most direct and effective methods of bringing the buyer and
seller of personal services together:

1. *Employment bureaus:* Care must be taken to select
    only reputable bureaus, the management of which
    can show adequate records of achievement of sat-

isfactory results. There are comparatively few such bureaus.

2. *Advertising:* Try the newspapers, trade journals, magazines. Classified advertising may usually be relied upon to produce satisfactory results in the case of those who apply for clerical or ordinary salaried positions. Display advertising is more desirable in the case of those who seek executive connections, the copy to appear in the section of the paper which is most apt to come to the attention of the class of employer being sought. The copy should be prepared by an expert, who understands how to inject sufficient selling qualities to produce replies.

3. *Personal letters of application:* These are directed to particular firms or individuals most apt to need such services as are being offered. Letters should always be *neatly typed* and signed by hand. With the letter should be sent a complete "brief" or outline of the applicant's qualifications. Both the letter of application and the brief of experience or qualifications should be prepared by an expert. (See instructions as to information to be supplied.)

4. *Application through personal acquaintances:* When possible, the applicant should endeavor to approach prospective employers through some mutual acquaintance. This method of approach is particularly advantageous in the case of those who seek executive connections and do not wish to appear to be "peddling" themselves.

5. *Application in person:* In some instances, it may be more effective if the applicant personally offers his services to prospective employers, in which event a complete written statement of qualifications for the

position should be presented, for the reason that prospective employers often wish to discuss one's record with associates.

How to Prepare a "Brief" or Résumé

This brief should be prepared as carefully as a lawyer would prepare the brief of a case to be tried in court. Unless the applicant is experienced in the preparation of such briefs, an expert should be consulted and his services enlisted for this purpose. Successful merchants employ men and women who understand the art and the psychology of advertising to present the merits of their merchandise. One who has personal services for sale should do the same. The following information should appear in the brief:

1. *Education:* State briefly, but definitely, what schooling you have had and in what subjects you specialized in school, giving the reasons for that specialization.
2. *Experience:* If you have had experience in connection with positions similar to the one you seek, describe it fully, state names and addresses of former employers. Be sure to bring out clearly any *special* experience you may have had which would equip you to fill the position you seek.
3. *References:* Practically every business firm desires to know all about the previous records, antecedents, etc. of prospective employees who seek positions of responsibility. Attach to your brief photostatic copies of letters from:
    a. former employers

      b.   teachers under whom you studied

      c.   prominent people whose judgment may be relied upon.

4. *Photograph of self:* Attach to your brief a recent, unmounted photograph of yourself.

5. *Apply for a specific position:* Avoid application for a position without describing exactly what particular position you seek. Never apply for "just a position." That indicates you lack specialized qualifications.

6. *State your qualifications for the position:* Give full details as to the reason you believe you are qualified for the particular position you seek. This is the most important detail of your application. It will determine, more than anything else, what consideration you receive.

7. *Offer to go to work on probation:* This may appear to be a radical suggestion, but experience has proved that it seldom fails to win at least a trial. If you are sure of your qualifications, a trial is all you need. Incidentally, such an offer indicates that you have confidence in your ability to fill the position you seek; it is most convincing. Make clear the fact that your offer is based upon:

      a.   your confidence in your ability to fill the position

      b.   your confidence in your prospective employer's decision to employ you after trial

      c.   your determination to have the position.

8. *Knowledge of your prospective employer's business:* Before applying for a position, do sufficient research in connection with the business to familiarize yourself thoroughly with that business, and indicate in

your brief the knowledge you have acquired in this
field. This will be impressive, as it will indicate that
you have imagination and a real interest in the position you seek.

Remember that it is not the lawyer who knows the most
law, but the one who best prepares his case who wins. If your
"case" is properly prepared and presented, your victory will
have been more than half won at the outset.

Do not be afraid of making your brief too long. Employers
are just as much interested in purchasing the services of well-
qualified applicants as you are in securing employment. In
fact, the success of most successful employers is due, in the
main, to their ability to select well-qualified lieutenants. They
want all the information available.

Remember another thing: neatness in the preparation of
your brief will indicate that you are a painstaking person. I
have helped to prepare briefs for clients which were so strik-
ing and out of the ordinary that they resulted in the employment of the applicant without a personal interview.

When your brief has been completed, have it neatly bound
and lettered or typed similar to the following:

BRIEF OF THE QUALIFICATIONS OF
ROBERT K. SMITH
APPLYING FOR THE POSITION OF
PRIVATE SECRETARY TO
THE PRESIDENT OF
THE BLANK COMPANY, INC.

Change names each time brief is shown. This personal
touch is sure to command attention. Have your brief neatly
typed or mimeographed on the finest paper you can obtain,

and bound with a heavy paper of the book-cover variety, the binder to be changed and the proper firm name to be inserted if it is to be shown to more than one company. Your photograph should be pasted on one of the pages of your brief. Follow these instructions to the letter, improving upon them whenever your imagination suggests.

Successful salesmen groom themselves with care. They understand that first impressions are lasting. Your brief is your salesman. Give it a good suit of clothes, so it will stand out in bold contrast to anything your prospective employer ever saw in the way of an application for a position. If the position you seek is worth having, it is worth going after with care. Moreover, if you sell yourself to an employer in a manner that impresses him with your individuality, you will probably receive more money for your services from the very start than you would if you applied for employment in the usual conventional way.

If you seek employment through an advertising agency or an employment agency, have the agent use copies of your brief in marketing your services. This will help to gain preference for you, both with the agent and the prospective employers.

Find a Job You Like to Do

Everyone enjoys doing the kind of work for which he is best suited. An artist loves to work with paints, a craftsman with his hands, a writer loves to write. Those with less definite talents have their preferences for certain fields of business and industry. If America does anything well, it offers a full range of occupations, tilling the soil, manufacturing, marketing, and the professions.

1. Decide *exactly* what kind of a job you want. If the job doesn't already exist, perhaps you can create it.

2. Choose the company or individual for whom you wish to work.

3. Study your prospective employer, as to policies, personnel, and chances of advancement.

4. By analysis of yourself, your talents and capabilities, figure *what you can offer*, and plan ways and means of giving advantages, services, developments, ideas that *you believe* you can successfully deliver.

5. Forget about "a job." Forget whether or not there is an opening. Forget the usual routine of "have you got a job for me?" Concentrate on what *you can give*.

6. Once you have your plan in mind, arrange with an experienced writer to put it on paper in neat form, and in full detail.

7. Present it to the *proper person with authority* and he will do the rest. Every company is looking for men who can give something of value, whether it be ideas, services, or "connections." Every company has room for the man who has a definite plan of action which is to the advantage of that company.

This line of procedure may take a few days or weeks of extra time, but the difference in income, in advancement, and in gaining recognition will save years of hard work at small pay. It has many advantages, the main one being that it will often save from one to five years of time in reaching a chosen goal.

Every person who starts or "gets in" halfway up the ladder does so by deliberate and careful planning.

The Public Is Your Partner

Men and women who market their services to best advantage in the future must recognize the change which has taken place in connection with the relationship between employer and employee.

The future relationship between employers and their employees will be more in the nature of a partnership consisting of:

1. the employer
2. the employee
3. the public they serve.

This new way of marketing personal services is called new for many reasons. First, both the employer and the employee of the future will be considered as fellow employees whose business it will be to serve the public efficiently. In times past, employers and employees have bartered among themselves, driving the best bargains they could with one another, not considering that in the final analysis they were, in reality, bargaining at the expense of the third party, the public they served.

"Courtesy" and "service" are the watchwords of merchandising today, and apply to the person who is marketing personal services even more directly than to the employer whom he serves, because in the final analysis, both the employer and his employee are employed by the public they serve. If they fail to serve well, they pay by the loss of their privilege of serving.

We can all remember the time when the gas meter reader pounded on the door hard enough to break the panels. When the door was opened, he pushed his way in uninvited, with a scowl on his face which plainly said, "What the hell did you keep me waiting for?" All that has undergone a change. The meter man now conducts himself as a gentleman who is "delighted to be at your service, sir." Before the gas companies learned that their scowling meter men were accumulating liabilities never to be cleared away, the polite salesmen of oil burners came along and did a land-office business.

During the depression, I spent several months in the anthracite coal region of Pennsylvania, studying conditions which all but destroyed the coal industry. The coal operators and their employees drove sharp bargains with one another, adding the cost of the "bargaining" to the price of the coal, until finally they discovered they had built up a wonderful business for the manufacturers of oil-burning outfits and the producers of crude oil.

These illustrations are brought to the attention of those who have personal services to market, to show that we are where we are, and what we are, because of *our own conduct!* If there is a principle of cause and effect which controls business, finance, and transportation, this same principle controls individuals and determines their economic status.

Rate Yourself Three Ways

The causes of success in marketing services effectively and permanently have been clearly described. Unless those causes are studied, analyzed, understood, and applied no man can market his services effectively and permanently. Every person must be his own salesman of personal services. The quality and the quantity of service rendered and the spirit in which it is rendered determine to a large extent, the price and the duration of employment. To market personal services effectively (which means a permanent market, at a satisfactory price, under pleasant conditions), one must adopt and follow the "QQS" formula, which means that quality, plus quantity plus the proper spirit of cooperation equals perfect salesmanship of service. Remember the "QQS" formula, but do more —apply it as a habit!

Let us analyze the formula to make sure we understand exactly what it means:

1. *Quality* of service shall be construed to mean the performance of every detail, in connection with your position, in the most efficient manner possible, with the object of greater efficiency always in mind.
2. *Quantity* of service shall be understood to mean the habit of rendering all the service of which you are capable at all times with the purpose of increasing the amount of service rendered as greater skill is developed through practice and experience. Emphasis is again placed on the word *habit*.
3. *Spirit* of service shall be construed to mean the habit of agreeable, harmonious conduct which will induce cooperation from associates and fellow employees.

Adequacy of quality and quantity of service is not sufficient to maintain a permanent market for your services. The conduct, or the spirit in which you deliver service, is a strong determining factor in connection with both the price you receive and the duration of employment.

Andrew Carnegie stressed this point more than others in connection with his description of the factors which lead to success in the marketing of personal services. He emphasized again and again the necessity for harmonious conduct. He stressed the fact that he would not retain any man, no matter how great a quantity, or how efficient the quality of his work, *unless* he worked in a spirit of harmony. Mr. Carnegie insisted upon men being agreeable. To prove that he placed a high value upon this quality, he helped many men *who conformed to his standards* to become very wealthy. Those who did not conform had to make room for others.

The importance of a pleasing personality has been stressed because it is a factor which enables one to render service in the proper spirit. If one has a personality which pleases and renders service in a spirit of harmony, these assets often make up for deficiencies in both the quality and the quantity of service one renders. Nothing, however, can be successfully substituted for pleasing conduct.

Go-getter or Go-giver?

The person whose income is derived entirely from the sale of personal services is no less a merchant than the man who sells commodities, and it might well be added such a person is subject to exactly the same rules of conduct as the merchant who sells merchandise.

This has been emphasized because the majority of people who live by the sale of personal services make the mistake of considering themselves free from the rules of conduct, and the responsibilities attached to those who are engaged in marketing commodities.

The day of the "go-getter" has passed. He has been supplanted by the "go-giver."

The actual capital value of your brains may be determined by the amount of income you can produce (by marketing your services). A fair estimate of the capital value of your services may be made by multiplying your annual income by sixteen and two-thirds, as it is reasonable to estimate that your annual income represents 6% of your capital value. Money rents for 6% per annum. Money is worth no more than brains. It is often worth much less.

Competent "brains," if effectively marketed, represent a

much more desirable form of capital than that which is required to conduct a business dealing in commodities because "brains" are a form of capital which cannot be permanently depreciated through depressions, nor can this form of capital be stolen or spent. Moreover, the money which is essential for the conduct of business is as worthless as a sand dune until it has been mixed with efficient "brains."

Thirty-one Ways to Fail

Life's greatest tragedy consists of men and women who earnestly try, and fail! The tragedy lies in the overwhelmingly large majority of people who fail, as compared to the few who succeed.

I have had the privilege of analyzing several thousand men and women, 98% of whom were classed as "failures."

My analysis proved that there are thirty-one major reasons for failure and thirteen major principles through which people accumulate fortunes. In this chapter, a description of the thirty-one major causes of failure will be given. As you go over the list, check yourself by it point by point for the purpose of discovering how many of these causes of failure stand between you and success:

1. *Unfavorable hereditary background:* There is but little, if anything, which can be done for people who are born with a deficiency in brain power. This philosophy offers but one method of bridging this weakness—through the aid of the Master Mind. Observe with profit, however, that this is the only one of the thirty-one causes of failure which may not be *easily corrected* by any individual.

2. *Lack of a well-defined purpose in life:* There is no

hope of success for the person who does not have a central purpose or *definite goal* at which to aim. Ninety-eight out of every hundred of those whom I have analyzed had no such aim. Perhaps this was the major cause of their failure.

3. *Lack of ambition to aim above mediocrity:* We offer no hope for the person who is so indifferent as not to want to get ahead in life, and who is not willing to pay the price.

4. *Insufficient education:* This is a handicap which may be overcome with comparative ease. Experience has proven that the best-educated people are often those who are known as "self-made" or self-educated. It takes more than a college degree to make one a person of education. Any person who is educated is one who has learned to get whatever he wants in life without violating the rights of others. Education consists not so much of knowledge, but of knowledge effectively and persistently applied. Men are paid not merely for what they know, but more particularly for what they do with that which they know.

5. *Lack of self-discipline:* Discipline comes through self-control. This means that one must control all negative qualities. Before you can control conditions, you must first control yourself. Self-mastery is the hardest job you will ever tackle. If you do not conquer self, you will be conquered by self. You may see at one and the same time both your best friend and your greatest enemy by stepping in front of a mirror.

6. *Ill health:* No person may enjoy outstanding success without good health. Many of the causes of ill

health are subject to mastery and control. These
in the main are:

   a.   Overeating of foods not conducive to health
   b.   Wrong habits of thought; giving expression
        to negatives
   c.   Wrong use of, and over indulgence in sex
   d.   Lack of proper physical exercise
   e.   An inadequate supply of fresh air, due to
        improper breathing.

 7. *Unfavorable environmental influences during child-
    hood:* "Just as the twig is bent, the tree's inclined."
    Most people who have criminal tendencies acquire
    them as the result of bad environment and im-
    proper associates during childhood.

 8. *Procrastination:* This is one of the most common
    causes of failure. "Old Man Procrastination" stands
    within the shadow of every human being, waiting
    his opportunity to spoil one's chances of success.
    Most of us go through life as failures because we
    are waiting for the "time to be right" to start
    doing something worthwhile. Do not wait; the time
    will never be "just right." Start where you stand,
    and work with whatever tools you may have at
    your command, and better tools will be found as
    you go along.

 9. *Lack of persistence:* Most of us are good "starters"
    but poor "finishers" of everything we begin. More-
    over, people are prone to give up at the first signs
    of defeat. There is no substitute for persistence.
    The person who makes persistence his watchword
    discovers that "Old Man Failure" finally becomes
    tired and makes his departure. Failure cannot cope
    with persistence.

10. *Negative personality:* There is no hope of success

for the person who repels people through a negative personality. Success comes through the application of power, and power is attained through the co-operative efforts of other people. A negative personality will not induce cooperation.

11. *Lack of controlled sexual urge:* Sex energy is the most powerful of all the stimuli which move people into action. Because it is the most powerful of the emotions, it must be controlled through transmutation and converted into other channels.

12. *Uncontrolled desire for something for nothing:* The gambling instinct drives millions of people to failure. Evidence of this may be found in a study of the Wall Street crash of '29, during which millions of people tried to make money by gambling on stock margins.

13. *Lack of a well defined power of decision:* Men who succeed reach decisions promptly and change them, if at all, very slowly. Men who fail reach decisions, if at all, very slowly and change them frequently and quickly. Indecision and procrastination are twin brothers. Where one is found, the other may usually be found also. Kill off this pair before they completely hog-tie you to the treadmill of failure.

14. *One or more of the six basic fears:* These fears have been analyzed for you in a later chapter. They must be mastered before you can market your services effectively.

15. *Wrong selection of a mate in marriage:* This is a most common cause of failure. The relationship of marriage brings people intimately into contact. Unless this relationship is harmonious, failure is likely to follow. Moreover, it will be a form of

failure that is marked by misery and unhappiness, destroying all signs of ambition.

16. *Overcaution:* The person who takes no chances generally has to take whatever is left when others are through choosing. Overcaution is as bad as undercaution. Both are extremes to be guarded against. Life itself is filled with the element of chance.

17. *Wrong selection of associates in business:* This is one of the most common causes of failure in business. In marketing personal services, one should use great care to select an employer who will be an inspiration and who is himself intelligent and successful. We emulate those with whom we associate most closely. Pick an employer who is worth emulating.

18. *Superstition and prejudice:* Superstition is a form of fear. It is also a sign of ignorance. Men who succeed keep open minds and are afraid of nothing.

19. *Wrong selection of a vocation:* No man can succeed in a line of endeavor which he does not like. The most essential step in the marketing of personal services is that of selecting an occupation into which you can throw yourself wholeheartedly.

20. *Lack of concentration of effort:* The jack-of-all-trades seldom is good at any. Concentrate all of your efforts on one definite chief aim.

21. *The habit of indiscriminate spending:* The spendthrift cannot succeed, mainly because he stands eternally in fear of poverty. Form the habit of systematic saving by putting aside a definite percentage of your income. Money in the bank gives one a very safe foundation of courage when bar-

gaining for the sale of personal services. Without money, one must take what one is offered, and be glad to get it.

22. *Lack of enthusiasm:* Without enthusiasm one cannot be convincing. Moreover, enthusiasm is contagious and the person who has it, under control, is generally welcome in any group of people.

23. *Intolerance:* The person with a closed mind on any subject seldom gets ahead. Intolerance means that one has stopped acquiring knowledge. The most damaging forms of intolerance are those connected with religious, racial, and political differences of opinion.

24. *Intemperance:* The most damaging forms of intemperance are connected with eating, strong drink, and sexual activities. Overindulgence in any of these is fatal to success.

25. *Inability to cooperate with others:* More people lose their positions and their big opportunities in life because of this fault, than for all other reasons combined. It is a fault which no well-informed businessman or leader will tolerate.

26. *Possession of power that was not acquired through self-effort:* (Sons and daughters of wealthy men and others who inherit money which they did not earn.) Power in the hands of one who did not acquire it gradually is often fatal to success. Quick riches are more dangerous than poverty.

27. *Intentional dishonesty:* There is no substitute for honesty. One may be temporarily dishonest by force of circumstances over which one has no control without permanent damage. But there is no hope for the person who is dishonest by choice.

Sooner or later, his deeds will catch up with him, and he will pay by loss of reputation, and perhaps even loss of liberty.

28. *Egotism and vanity:* These qualities serve as red lights which warn others to keep away. They are fatal to success.

29. *Guessing instead of thinking:* Most people are too indifferent or lazy to acquire facts with which to think accurately. They prefer to act on "opinions" created by guesswork or snap judgments.

30. *Lack of capital:* This is a common cause of failure among those who start out in business for the first time without sufficient reserve of capital to absorb the shock of their mistakes, and to carry them over until they have established a reputation.

31. *Other:* Name any particular cause of failure from which you have suffered that has not been included in the foregoing list.

In these thirty-one major causes of failure is found a description of the tragedy of life, which obtains for practically every person who tries and fails. It will be helpful if you can induce someone who knows you well to go over this list with you, and help to analyze you by the thirty-one causes of failure. It may be beneficial if you try this alone. Most people cannot see themselves as others see them. You may be one who cannot.

How Do You Market Yourself?

The oldest of admonitions is "Man, know thyself!" If you market merchandise succesfully, you must know the merchandise. The same is true in marketing personal services.

You should know all of your weaknesses in order that you may either bridge them or eliminate them entirely. You should know your strength in order that you may call attention to it when selling your services. You can know yourself only through *accurate* analysis.

The folly of ignorance in connection with self was displayed by a young man who applied to the manager of a well-known business for a position. He made a very good impression until the manager asked him what salary he expected. He replied that he had no fixed sum in mind (*lack of a definite aim*). The manager then said, "We will pay you all you are worth, after we try you out for a week."

"I will not accept it," the applicant replied, "because I am getting more than that where I am now employed."

Before you even start to negotiate for a readjustment of your salary in your present position or to seek employment elsewhere be sure that you are worth more than you now receive.

It is one thing to want money—everyone wants more—but it is something entirely different to be worth more! Many people mistake their wants for their just dues. Your financial requirements or wants have nothing whatever to do with your worth. Your value is established entirely by your ability to render useful service or your capacity to induce others to render such service.

Did You Advance Last Year?

Annual self-analysis is an essential in the effective marketing of personal services, as is annual inventory in merchandising. Moreover, the yearly analysis should disclose a decrease in faults and an increase in virtues. One goes ahead, stands still, or goes backward in life. One's object should be, of course, to go ahead. Annual self-analysis will disclose whether advancement has been made, and if so, how much. It will also disclose any backward steps one may have made. The effective marketing of personal services requires one to move forward even if the progress is slow.

Your annual self-analysis should be made at the end of each year so you can include in your New Year's resolutions any improvements which the analysis indicates should be made. Take this inventory by asking yourself the following questions and by checking your answers with the aid of someone who will not permit you to deceive yourself as to their accuracy.

Twenty-eight Very Personal Questions

1. Have I attained the goal which I established as my objective for this year? (You should work with a definite yearly objective to be attained as a part of your major life objective.)
2. Have I delivered service of the best possible quality of which I was capable, or could I have improved any part of this service?
3. Have I delivered service in the greatest possible quantity of which I was capable?
4. Has the spirit of my conduct been harmonious and cooperative at all times?
5. Have I permitted the habit of procrastination to decrease my efficiency, and if so, to what extent?
6. Have I improved my personality, and if so, in what ways?
7. Have I been persistent in following my plans through to completion?

8.   Have I reached decisions promptly and definitely on all occasions?

9.   Have I permitted any one or more of the six basic fears to decrease my efficiency?

10. Have I been either overcautious, or undercautious?

11. Has my relationship with my associates in work been pleasant, or unpleasant? If it has been unpleasant, has the fault been partly or wholly mine?

12. Have I dissipated any of my energy through lack of concentration of effort?

13. Have I been open-minded and tolerant in connection with all subjects?

14. In what way have I improved my ability to render service?

15. Have I been intemperate in any of my habits?

16. Have I expressed, either openly or secretly, any form of egotism?

17. Has my conduct toward my associates been such that it has induced them to respect me?

18. Have my opinions and decisions been based upon guesswork or accuracy of analysis and thought?

19. Have I followed the habit of budgeting my time, my expenses, and my income, and have I been conservative in these budgets?

20. How much time have I devoted to unprofitable effort which I might have used to better advantage?

21. How may I rebudget my time, and change my habits so I will be more efficient during the coming year?

22. Have I been guilty of any conduct which was not approved by my conscience?

23. In what ways have I rendered more service and better service than I was paid to render?

24. Have I been unfair to anyone, and if so, in what way?
25. If I had been the purchaser of my own services for the year, would I be satisfied with my purchase?
26. Am I in the right vocation, and if not, why not?
27. Has the purchaser of my services been satisfied with the service I have rendered, and if not, why not?
28. What is my present rating on the fundamental principles of success? (Make this rating fairly and frankly, and have it checked by someone who is courageous enough to do it accurately.)

Having read and assimilated the information conveyed through this chapter, you are now ready to create a practical plan for marketing your personal services. In this chapter will be found an adequate description of every principle essential in planning the sale of personal services, including the major attributes of leadership, the most common causes of failure in leadership, a description of the fields of opportunity for leadership, the main causes of failure in all walks of life, and the important questions which should be used in self-analysis.

This extensive and detailed presentation of accurate information has been included because it will be needed by all who must begin the accumulation of riches by marketing personal services. Those who have lost their fortunes and those who are just beginning to earn money have nothing but personal services to offer in return for riches; therefore it is essential that they have available the practical information needed to market services to best advantage.

Complete assimilation and understanding of the information here conveyed will be helpful in marketing one's own services and it will also help one to become more analytical and capable of judging people. The information will be priceless to personnel directors, employment managers, and other executives charged with the selection of employees and the maintenance of efficient organizations. If you doubt this statement, test its soundness by answering in writing the twenty-eight self-analysis questions.

Your Vast Opportunities to Accumulate Riches

Now that we have analyzed the principles by which riches may be accumulated, we naturally ask, "Where may one find favorable opportunities to apply these principles?" Very well, let us take inventory and see what the United States of America offers the person seeking riches, great or small.

To begin with, let us remember, *all of us*, that we live in a country where *every law-abiding citizen enjoys freedom of thought and freedom of deed unequaled anywhere in the world*. Most of us have never taken inventory of the advantages of this freedom. We have never compared our unlimited freedom with the curtailed freedom in other countries.

Here we have freedom of thought, freedom in the choice and enjoyment of education, freedom in religion, freedom in politics, freedom in the choice of a business, profession, or occupation, freedom to accumulate and own without molestation *all the property we can accumulate*, freedom to choose our place of residence, freedom in marriage, freedom through equal opportunity to all races, freedom of travel from one state to another, freedom in our choice of foods, and freedom to *aim for any station in life for which we have prepared ourselves*, even for the Presidency of the United States.

We have other forms of freedom, but this list will give a bird's-eye view of the most important, which constitute opportunity of the highest order. This advantage of freedom is all the more conspicuous because the United States is the only country guaranteeing to every citizen, whether native born or naturalized, so broad and varied a list of freedoms.

Next, let us recount some of the blessings which our widespread freedom has placed within our hands. Take the average American family for example (meaning, the family of average income) and sum up the benefits available to every member of the family in this land of opportunity and plenty! Next to freedom of thought and deed comes food, clothing, and shelter, the three basic necessities of life.

Food: Because of our universal freedom the average American family has available at its very door the choicest selection of food to be found anywhere in the world, and at prices within its financial range.

Clothing: Anywhere in the United States, the woman of average clothing requirements can dress very comfortably and neatly for less than five hundred dollars a year, and the average man can dress for the same, or less.

Shelter: The average family lives in a comfortable apartment, heated by steam, lighted with electricity, with gas for cooking.

The toast they had for breakfast was toasted on an electric toaster which cost but a few dollars. The apartment is cleaned with a vacuum cleaner that is run by electricity. Hot and cold water is available at all times in the kitchen and the bathroom. The food is kept cool in a refrigerator that is run by electricity. The wife curls her hair, washes her clothes and irons them with electrical equipment, easily operated on power obtained by sticking a plug in the wall. The husband shaves with an electric shaver, and they receive entertainment from all over the world, twenty-four hours a day if they want it, without cost by merely turning the dial of their radio or television.

There are other conveniences in this apartment, but the foregoing list will give a fair idea of some of the concrete evidences of the freedom we, in America, enjoy.

Only the three basic necessities of food, clothing, and shelter have been mentioned. The average American citizen has other privileges and advantages available in return for modest effort, not exceeding eight hours per day of labor.

The average American has security of property rights not found in any other country in the world. He can place his surplus money in a bank with the assurance that his government will protect it and make good to him if the bank fails. If an American citizen wants to travel from one state to another he needs no passport, no one's permission. He may go when he pleases and return at will. Moreover, he may travel by train, private automobile, bus, airplane, or ship, as his pocketbook permits.

Give Credit to Capital

We often hear politicians proclaiming the freedom of America when they solicit votes, but seldom do they take the time or devote sufficient effort to the analysis of the source or nature of this "freedom." Having no axe to grind, no grudge to express, no ulterior motives to be carried out, I have the privilege of going into a frank analysis of that mysterious, abstract, greatly misunderstood "something" which gives to every citizen of the United States more blessings, more opportunities to accumulate wealth, more freedom of every nature than may be found in any other country.

I have the right to analyze the source and nature of this

unseen power because I know, and have known for more than half a century many of the men who organized that power and many who are now responsible for its maintenance.

The name of this mysterious benefactor of mankind is capital!

Capital consists not alone of money, but more particularly of highly organized, intelligent groups of men who plan ways and means of using money efficiently for the good of the public, and profitably to themselves.

These groups consist of scientists, educators, chemists, inventors, business analysts, publicity men, transportation experts, accountants, lawyers, doctors, and both men and women who have highly specialized knowledge in all fields of industry and business. They pioneer, experiment, and blaze trails in new fields of endeavor. They support colleges, hospitals, public schools, build good roads, publish newspapers, pay most of the cost of government, and take care of the multitudinous details essential to human progress. Stated briefly, the capitalists are the brains of civilization, because they supply the entire fabric of which all education, enlightenment and human progress consists.

Money without brains is always dangerous. Properly used, it is the most important essential of civilization.

Some slight idea of the importance of organized capital may be had by trying to imagine yourself burdened with the responsibility of collecting, without the aid of capital, and delivering to a family a simple breakfast.

To supply the tea, you would have to make a trip to China or India, both a very long way from America. Unless you are an excellent swimmer, you would become rather tired before making the round trip. Then too, another problem would confront you. What would you use for money, even if you had the physical endurance to swim the ocean?

To supply sugar, you would have to take another long swim

to the West Indies or a long walk to the sugar beet section of Utah. But even then you might come back without the sugar because organized effort and money are necessary to produce sugar, to say nothing of what is required to refine, transport, and deliver it to the breakfast table anywhere in the United States.

Eggs you could deliver easily enough from nearby farms, but you would have a very long walk to Florida and back before you could serve grapefruit juice.

You would have another long walk, to Kansas, or one of the other wheat-growing states, when you went after wheat bread.

Dry cereal would necessarily have to be omitted from the menu, because it would not be available except through the labor of a trained organization of men and suitable machinery, all of which call for capital.

While resting, you could take off for another little swim down to South America, where you would pick up a couple of bananas, and on your return, you could take a short walk to the nearest farm having a dairy and pick up some butter and cream. Then your family would be ready to sit down and enjoy breakfast.

Seems absurd, doesn't it? Well, the procedure described would be the only possible way these simple items of food could be delivered if we had no capitalistic system.

Civilization Is Built on Capital

The sum of money required for the building and maintenance of the railroads and steamships used in the delivery of that simple breakfast is so huge that it staggers one's imagination. It runs into hundreds of millions of dollars, not to mention the armies of trained employees required to man the ships and trains. But transportation is only a part of the requirements

of modern civilization in capitalistic America. Before there
can be anything to haul, something must be grown from the
ground or manufactured and prepared for market. This calls
for more millions of dollars for equipment, machinery, pack-
aging, boxing, marketing, and for the wages of millions of men
and women.

Steamships and railroads do not spring up from the earth
and function automatically. They come in response to the call
of civilization through the labor and ingenuity and organizing
ability of men who have imagination, faith, enthusiasm, decision, persistence! These men are known as capitalists. They
are motivated by the desire to build, construct, achieve, render
useful service, earn profits and accumulate riches. And because
they render service without which there would be no civilization, they put themselves in the way of great riches.

Just to keep the record simple and understandable, I will
add that these capitalists are the selfsame men of whom most
of us have heard soap-box orators speak. They are the same
men to whom radicals, racketeers, dishonest politicians and
grafting labor leaders refer as "the predatory interests" or
"Wall Street."

I am not attempting to present a brief for or against any
group of men or any system of economics.

The purpose of this book—*a purpose to which I have faith-
fully devoted more than half a century*—is to present to all
who want the knowledge, the most dependable philosophy
through which individuals may accumulate riches in whatever
amounts they desire.

I have here analyzed the economic advantages of the capitalistic system for the two-fold purpose of showing:

1. That all who seek riches must recognize and adapt
    themselves to the system that controls all approaches
    to fortunes, large or small.

2. To present the side of the picture opposite to that being shown by politicians and demagogues who deliberately becloud the issues they bring up by referring to organized capital as if it were something poisonous.

This is a capitalistic country. It was developed through the use of capital, and we who claim the right to partake of the blessings of freedom and opportunity, we who seek to accumulate riches here may as well know that neither riches nor opportunity would be available to us if organized capital had not provided these benefits.

There is but one dependable method of accumulating and legally holding riches, and that is by rendering useful service. No system has ever been created by which men can legally acquire riches through mere force of numbers, or without giving in return an equivalent value of one form or another.

Abundance Everywhere—Opportunity Everywhere

America provides all the freedom and all the opportunity to accumulate riches that any honest person may require. When one goes hunting for game, one selects hunting grounds where game is plentiful. When seeking riches, the same rule would naturally obtain.

If it is riches you are seeking, do not overlook the possibilities of a country whose citizens are so rich that women spend millions of dollars annually for lipstick, rouge and other cosmetics.

If it is money you are seeking, consider carefully a country that spends hundreds of millions of dollars annually for cigarettes.

Do not be in too big a hurry to get away from a country

whose people willingly, even eagerly, hand over millions of dollars annually for football, baseball, and prize fights.

Remember, also, that this is but the beginning of the available sources for the accumulation of wealth. Only a few of the luxuries and non-essentials have been mentioned. But, remember that the business of producing, transporting, and marketing these few items of merchandise gives regular employment to many millions of men and women, who receive for their services many millions of dollars monthly and spend it freely for both the luxuries and the necessities.

Especially remember that back of all this exchange of merchandise and personal services may be found an abundance of opportunity to accumulate riches. Here our American freedom comes to one's aid. There is nothing to stop you or anyone from engaging in any portion of the effort necessary to carry on these businesses. If one has superior talent, training, experience, one may accumulate riches in large amounts. Those not so fortunate may accumulate small amounts. Anyone may earn a living in return for a very nominal amount of labor.

So—there you are!

Opportunity has spread its wares before you. Step up to the front, select what you want, create your plan, put the plan into action, and follow through with persistence. Capitalistic America will do the rest. You can depend upon this much—capitalistic America insures every person the opportunity to render useful service and to collect riches in proportion to the value of the service.

The "system" denies no one this right, but it does not and cannot promise something for nothing because the system itself is irrevocably controlled by the law of economics, which neither recognizes nor tolerates for long getting without giving.

POINTS TO PIN DOWN:

Four dynamic principles guide you in forming a "Master-Mind" group which vastly expands your money-making power.

You can choose people who inspire you, share mind power with you, reflect and magnify your own great faith.

Exploit eleven secrets of successful leadership; ten reasons why would-be leaders fail; rise far above any negative influences you see; six fields for new leadership, and five ways to get a good job in any field you wish.

Write a brief, or résumé according to the plan given here and doors open for you, employers invite you to take important, well-paid jobs.

American prosperity is built on capital, not too different, in principle, from the illimitable capital you carry within yourself.

Success requires no explanations. Failure permits no alibis.

Step 7 Toward Riches: Decision

ANALYSIS OF OVER TWENTY-FIVE THOUSAND MEN AND women who had experienced failure disclosed the fact that lack of decision was near the head of the list of the thirty-one major causes of failure.

Procrastination, the opposite of decision, is a common enemy which practically every man must conquer.

You will have an opportunity to test your capacity to reach *quick* and *definite* decisions when you finish reading this book, and are ready to begin putting into action the principles which it describes.

Analysis of several hundred people who had accumulated fortunes well beyond the million-dollar mark disclosed the fact that *every one of them* had the habit of reaching decisions promptly, and of changing these decisions slowly, if and

You see how to crystallize opinion into decision and proceed on that decision. You understand how and when to change a decision for greater benefit and profit.

---

when they were changed. People who fail to accumulate money, *without exception*, have the habit of reaching decisions very *slowly*, if at all, and of *changing these decisions quickly and often.*

One of Henry Ford's most outstanding qualities was his *habit* of reaching decisions quickly and definitely, and changing them slowly. This quality was so pronounced in Mr. Ford, that it gave him the reputation of being obstinate. It was this quality which promoted Mr. Ford to continue to manufacture his famous Model T (the world's ugliest car), when all of his advisors and many of the purchasers of the car were urging him to change it.

Perhaps Mr. Ford delayed too long in making the change, but the other side of the story is that Mr. Ford's firmness of decision yielded a huge fortune before the change in model became *necessary*. There is but little doubt that Mr. Ford's habit of definiteness of decision assumed the proportion of obstinacy, but this quality is preferable to slowness in reaching decisions and quickness in changing them.

Opinion—A Cheap Commodity

The majority of people who fail to accumulate money sufficient for their needs are generally easily influenced by the opinions of others. They permit the newspapers and the gossiping neighbors to do their thinking for them. Opinions are the cheapest commodities on earth. Everyone has a flock of opinions ready to be wished upon anyone who will accept them. If you are influenced by opinions when you reach decisions you will not succeed in any undertaking, much less in that of transmuting your own desire into money.

If you are influenced by the opinions of others, you will have no desire of your own.

Keep your own counsel, when you begin to put into practice the principles described here, by *reaching your own decisions* and following them. Take no one into your confidence, except the members of your "Master-Mind" group, and be very sure, in your selection of this group, that you choose only those who will be in complete sympathy and harmony with your purpose.

Close friends and relatives, while not meaning to do so, often handicap one through "opinions" and sometimes through ridicule, which is meant to be humorous. Thousands of men and women carry inferiority complexes with them all through life, because some well-meaning but ignorant person destroyed their confidence through "opinions" or ridicule.

You have a brain and mind of your own. Use it and reach your own decisions. If you need facts or information from other people to enable you to reach decisions, as you probably will in many instances, acquire these facts or secure the information you need quietly, without disclosing your purpose.

It is characteristic of people who have but a smattering or a veneer of knowledge to try to give the impression that they have much knowledge. Such people generally do too much talking, and too little listening. Keep your eyes and ears wide open—and your mouth closed, if you wish to acquire the habit of prompt decision. Those who talk too much do little else. If you talk more than you listen, you not only deprive yourself of many opportunities to accumulate useful knowledge, but you also disclose your plans and purposes to people who will take great delight in defeating you because they envy you.

Remember also that every time you open your mouth in the presence of a person who has an abundance of knowledge, you display to that person your exact stock of knowledge or your lack of it! Genuine wisdom is usually conspicuous through *modesty and silence.*

Keep in mind the fact that every person with whom you associate is, like yourself, seeking the opportunity to accumulate money. If you talk about your plans too freely, you may be surprised when you learn that some other person has beaten you to your goal by putting into action ahead of you the plans of which you talked unwisely.

Let one of your first decisions be to keep a closed mouth and open ears and eyes.

As a reminder to yourself to follow this advice, it will be helpful if you copy the following epigram in large letters and place it where you will see it daily: "Tell the world what you intend to do, but first show it."

This is the equivalent of saying that "Deeds, and not words, are what count most."

History Made by Decisions

The value of decisions depends upon the courage required to render them. The great decisions which served as the foundation of civilization were reached by assuming great risks which often meant the chance of death.

Lincoln's decision to issue his famous Emancipation Proclamation, which gave freedom to the colored people of America, was rendered with full understanding that his act would turn thousands of friends and political supporters against him.

Socrates' decision to drink the cup of poison rather than compromise in his personal belief was a decision of courage. It turned time ahead a thousand years, and gave to people then unborn the right to freedom of thought and of speech.

The decision of Gen. Robert E. Lee when he came to the parting of the ways with the Union and took up the cause of the South was a decision of courage, for he well knew that it might cost him his own life, that it would surely cost the lives of others.

An Incident in Boston

But the greatest decision of all time, as far as any American citizen is concerned, was reached in Philadelphia, July 4, 1776, when fifty-six men signed their names to a document which they well knew would bring freedom to all Americans, or *leave every one of the fifty-six hanging from a gallows!*

You have heard of this famous document, but you may not have drawn from it the great lesson in personal achievement it so plainly taught.

We all remember the date of this momentous decision, but few of us realize what courage that decision required. We remember our history as it was taught; we remember dates and the names of the men who fought; we remember Valley Forge and Yorktown; we remember George Washington, and Lord Cornwallis. But we know little of the real forces back of these names, dates, and places. We know still less of that intangible power which insured us freedom *long before Washington's armies reached Yorktown.*

It is nothing short of tragedy that the writers of history have missed entirely even the slightest reference to the irresistible power which gave birth and freedom to the nation destined to set up new standards of independence for all the peoples of the earth. I say it is a tragedy because it is the self-same power which must be used by every individual who surmounts the difficulties of life and forces life to pay the price asked.

Let us briefly review the events which gave birth to this power. The story begins with an incident in Boston, March 5, 1770. British soldiers were patrolling the streets, openly threatening the citizens by their presence. The colonists resented armed men marching in their midst. They began to express their resentment openly, hurling stones as well as epithets at the marching soldiers, until the commanding officer gave orders, "Fix bayonets . . . Charge!"

The battle was on. It resulted in the death and injury of many. The incident aroused such resentment that the Provincial Assembly (made up of prominent colonists) called a meeting for the purpose of taking definite action. Two of the members of that Assembly were John Hancock and Samuel Adams. They spoke up courageously and declared that a move must be made to eject all British soldiers from Boston.

Remember this—a decision, in the minds of two men, might properly be called the beginning of the freedom which we of the United States now enjoy. Remember too that the decision of these two men called for faith and courage because it was dangerous.

Before the Assembly adjourned, Samuel Adams was appointed to call on the governor of the province, Hutchinson, and demand the withdrawal of the British troops.

The request was granted, the troops were removed from Boston, but the incident was not closed. It had caused a situation which was destined to change the entire trend of civilization.

Minds Begin to Work Together

Richard Henry Lee became an important factor in this story because he and Samuel Adams corresponded frequently, sharing freely their fears and their hopes concerning the welfare of the people of their provinces. From this practice, Adams conceived the idea that a mutual exchange of letters between the thirteen colonies might help to bring about the coordination of effort so badly needed in connection with the solution of their problems. Two years after the clash with the soldiers in Boston (March '72), Adams presented this idea to the Assembly in the form of a motion that a Correspondence Committee be established among the colonies, with definitely appointed correspondents in each colony, "for the purpose of friendly cooperation for the betterment of the colonies of British America."

It was the beginning of the organization of the farflung power destined to give freedom to you and to me. The "Master-Mind" group had already been organized. It consisted of Adams, Lee, and Hancock.

The Committee of Correspondence was organized. The citizens of the colonies had been waging disorganized warfare against the British soldiers through incidents similar to the Boston riot, but nothing of benefit had been accomplished. Their individual grievances had not been consolidated under one "Master-Mind" group. No group of individuals had put their hearts, minds, souls, and bodies together in one definite decision to settle their difficulty with the British once and for all until Adams, Hancock, and Lee got together.

Meanwhile, the British were not idle. They, too, were doing some planning and "Master-Minding" on their own account, with the advantage of having back of them money and organized soldiery.

An Instant Decision Changes History

The Crown appointed Gage to supplant Hutchinson as the governor of Massachusetts. One of the new governor's first acts was to send a messenger to call on Samuel Adams, for the purpose of endeavoring to stop his opposition—by fear.

We can best understand the spirit of what happened by quoting the conversation between Colonel Fenton (the messenger sent by Gage) and Adams:

Colonel Fenton: "I have been authorized by Governor Gage, to assure you, Mr. Adams, that the governor has been empowered to confer upon you such benefits as would be satisfactory [endeavor to win Adams by promise of bribes] upon the condition that you engage to cease in your opposition to the measures of the government. It is the governor's advice to you, Sir, not to incur the further displeasure of His Majesty. Your conduct has been such as makes you liable to penalties of an Act of Henry VIII, by which persons can be sent to England for trial for treason, or misprison of treason, at the discretion of a governor of a province. But, by changing your political course, you will not only receive great personal advantages, but you will make your peace with the King."

Samuel Adams had the choice of two decisions. He could cease his opposition and receive personal bribes, or he could continue and run the risk of being hanged!

Clearly, the time had come when Adams was *forced* to reach *instantly* a decision which could have cost his life.

Adams insisted upon Colonel Fenton's word of honor that the colonel would deliver to the governor the answer exactly as Adams would give it to him.

Adams' answer: "Then you may tell Governor Gage that I trust I have long since made my peace with the King of Kings. No personal consideration shall induce me to abandon the righteous cause of my country. And, tell Governor Gage it is the advice of Samuel Adams to him, no longer to insult the feelings of an exasperated people."

When Governor Gage received Adams' caustic reply, he flew into a rage and issued a proclamation which read, "I do, hereby, in His Majesty's name, offer and promise his most gracious pardon to all persons who shall forthwith lay down their arms, and return to the duties of peaceable subjects, excepting only from the benefit of such pardon, Samuel Adams and John Hancock, whose offences are of too flagitious a nature to admit of any other consideration but that of condign punishment."

As one might say in modern slang, Adams and Hancock were "on the spot!" The threat of the irate governor forced the two men to reach another decision, equally as dangerous. They hurriedly called a secret meeting of their staunchest followers. After the meeting had been called to order, Adams locked the door, placed the key in his pocket, and informed all present that it was imperative that a congress of the colonists be organized, and that no man should leave the room until the decision for such a congress had been reached.

Great excitement followed. Some weighed the possible consequences of such radicalism. Some expressed grave doubt as to the wisdom of so *definite a decision* in defiance of the Crown. Locked in that room were two men immune to fear, blind to the possibility of failure, Hancock and Adams. Through the influence of their minds, the others were induced to agree that, through the Correspondence Committee, arrangements should be made for a meeting of the First Continental Congress, to be held in Philadelphia, September 5, 1774.

Remember this date. It is more important than July 4, 1776. If there had been no *decision* to hold a Continental Congress, there could have been no signing of the Declaration of Independence.

Before the first meeting of the new Congress, another leader, in a different section of the country, was deep in the throes of publishing a "Summary View of the Rights of British America." He was Thomas Jefferson, of the Province of Virginia, whose relationship to Lord Dunmore (representative of the Crown in Virginia) was as strained as that of Hancock and Adams with their governor.

Shortly after his famous Summary of Rights was published, Jefferson was informed that he was subject to prosecution for high treason against His Majesty's government. Inspired by the threat, one of Jefferson's colleagues, Patrick Henry, boldly spoke his mind, concluding his remarks with a sentence which shall· remain forever a classic, "*If this be treason, make the most of it.*"

It was such men as these who, without power, without authority, without military strength, without money sat in solemn consideration of the destiny of the colonies, beginning at the opening of the First Continental Congress, and continuing at intervals for two years—until on June 7, 1776, Richard Henry Lee arose, addressed the Chair, and to the startled Assembly made this motion:

"Gentlemen, I make the motion that these United Colonies are, and of right ought to be free and independent States, that they be absolved from all allegiance to the British Crown, and that all political connection between them and the state of Great Britain is, and ought to be totally dissolved."

Thomas Jefferson Reads Aloud

Lee's astounding motion was discussed fervently, and at such length that he began to lose patience. Finally, after days of argument, he again took the floor, and declared in a clear, firm voice, "Mr. President, we have discussed this issue for days. It is the only course for us to follow. Why then, sir, do we longer delay? Why still deliberate? Let this happy day give birth to an American Republic. Let her arise, not to devastate and to conquer, but to re-establish the reign of peace, and of law."

Before his motion was finally voted upon, Lee was called back to Virginia because of serious family illness, but before leaving, he placed his cause in the hands of his friend, Thomas Jefferson, who promised to fight until favorable action was taken. Shortly thereafter the President of the Congress (Hancock) appointed Jefferson as chairman of a committee to draw up a Declaration of Independence.

Long and hard the committee labored on a document which would mean, when accepted by the Congress, that every man who signed it would be signing his own death warrant should the colonies lose in the fight with Great Britain, which was sure to follow.

The document was drawn, and on June 28, the original draft was read before the Congress. For several days it was discussed, altered, and made ready. On July 4, 1776, Thomas Jefferson stood before the Assembly and fearlessly read the most momentous decision ever placed upon paper:

"When, in the course of human events, it becomes necessary for one people to dissolve the political bands which have connected them with another, and to assume among the powers of the earth the separate and equal station to which the laws of nature and of nature's God entitle them, a decent respect to the opinions of mankind requires that they should declare the causes which impel them to the separation. . . ."

When Jefferson finished, the document was voted upon, accepted, and signed by the fifty-six men, every one staking his own life upon his decision to write his name. By that decision came into existence a nation destined to bring to mankind forever the privilege of making decisions.

Analyze the events which led to the Declaration of Independence, and be convinced that this nation, which now holds a position of commanding respect and power among all nations of the world, was born of a decision created by a "Master-Mind" group consisting of fifty-six men. Note well the fact that it was their decision which insured the success of Washington's armies, because the *spirit* of that decision was in the heart of every soldier who fought with him, and served as a spiritual power which recognizes no such thing as failure.

Note also (with great personal benefit) that the power which gave this nation its freedom is the selfsame power that must be used by every individual who becomes self-determining. This power is made up of the principles described in this book. It will not be difficult to detect in the story of the Declaration of Independence at least six of these principles: *desire, decision, faith, persistence, the "Master-Mind" group, and organized planning.*

The Power of a Made-up Mind

Throughout this philosophy will be found the suggestion that thought, backed by strong desire, has a tendency to transmute itself into its physical equivalent. One may find in this story and in the story of the organization of the United States Steel Corporation a perfect description of the method by which thought makes this astounding transformation.

In your search for the secret of the method do not look for a miracle, because you will not find it. You will find only the eternal laws of nature. These laws are available to every person who has the faith and the courage to use them. They may be used to bring freedom to a nation or to accumulate riches.

Those who reach decisions promptly and definitely know what they want, and generally get it. The leaders in every walk of life decide quickly and firmly. That is the major reason why they are leaders. The world has the habit of making room for the man whose words and actions show that he knows where he is going.

Indecision is a habit which usually begins in youth. The habit takes on permanency as the youth goes through grade school, high school, and even through college without definiteness of purpose.

The habit of indecision goes with the student into the occupation he chooses—if, in fact, he does choose his occupation. Generally, the youth just out of school seeks any job that can be found. He takes the first place he finds, because he has fallen into the habit of indecision. Ninety-eight out of every hundred people working for wages today are in the positions they hold because they lacked the definiteness of decision to plan a definite position, and the knowledge of how to choose an employer.

Definiteness of decision always requires courage, sometimes very great courage. The fifty-six men who signed the Declaration of Independence staked their lives on the decision to affix their signatures to that document. The person who reaches a definite decision to procure the particular job and make life pay the price he asks does not stake his life on that decision; he stakes his economic freedom. Financial independence, riches, desirable business and professional positions are not within reach of the person who neglects or refuses to expect, plan, and demand these things. The person who desires riches in the same spirit that Samuel Adams desired freedom for the colonies is sure to accumulate wealth.

POINTS TO PIN DOWN:

Lack of decision is a major cause of failure. Everyone has an opinion, but in the end it is *your* opinion that swings *your* world. How a decision made in Philadelphia in 1776 works for your strength and confidence today.

A made-up mind attunes itself to tremendous extra power. Indecision often begins in youth; how to avoid it and help others avoid it.

Analyze the events which have led to great decisions, and you give yourself a lifelong guide to decided and effective action in every part of your life.

A great desire for freedom brings freedom; a great desire for wealth brings wealth.

Every powerful man has himself within his own power.

Step 8 Toward Riches:
Persistence

PERSISTENCE IS AN ESSENTIAL FACTOR IN THE PROCEDURE of transmuting desire into its monetary equivalent. The basis of persistence is the power of will.

Will power and desire when properly combined make an irresistible pair. Men who accumulate great fortunes are generally known as cold-blooded, and sometimes ruthless. Often they are misunderstood. What they have is will-power, which they mix with persistence and place back of their desires to *insure* the attainment of their objectives.

The majority of people are ready to throw their aims and purposes overboard and give up at the first sign of opposition or misfortune. A few carry on despite all opposition until they attain their goal.

There may be no heroic connotation to the word "per-

170

You recognize and sweep aside certain weaknesses which stand between you and your goals. Your persistence develops into a respected, proved, progressive power.

---

sistence," but the quality is to the character of man what carbon is to steel.

The building of a fortune generally involves the application of the entire thirteen factors of this philosophy. These principles must be understood, they must be applied with persistence by all who accumulate money.

Weak Desires Bring Weak Results

If you are following this book with the intention of applying the knowledge it conveys, your first test as to your persistence will come when you begin to follow the six steps described in the second chapter. Unless you are one of the two out of every hundred who already have a definite goal at which you

are aiming and a definite plan for its attainment, you may
read the instructions and then pass on with your daily routine
and never comply with those instructions.

Lack of persistence is one of the major causes of failure.
Moreover, experience with thousands of people has proved
that lack of persistence is a weakness common to the majority
of men. It is a weakness which may be overcome by effort.
The ease with which lack of persistence may be conquered
will depend *entirely* upon the intensity of one's desire.

The starting point of all achievement is desire. Keep this
constantly in mind. Weak desires bring weak results, just as
a small amount of fire makes a small amount of heat. If you
find yourself lacking in persistence, this weakness may be
remedied by building a stronger fire under your desires.

Continue to read through to the end, then go back to
the chapter on Desire and start *immediately* to carry out the
instructions given with regard to the six steps. The eagerness
with which you follow these instructions will indicate clearly
how much or how little you really desire to accumulate money.
If you find that you are indifferent, you may be sure that you
have not yet acquired the "money consciousness" which you
must possess before you can be sure of accumulating a fortune.

Fortunes gravitate to men whose minds have been prepared to attract them just as surely as water gravitates to the
ocean.

If you find you are weak in persistence, center your attention upon the instructions contained in the chapter on
"Power"; surround yourself with a "Master-Mind" group, and
through the cooperative efforts of the members of this group
you can develop persistence. You will find additional instructions for the development of persistence in the chapters on
autosuggestion and the subconscious mind. Follow the in-

structions outlined in these chapters until your habit nature hands over to your subconscious mind a clear picture of the object of your desire. From that point on, you will not be handicapped by lack of persistence.

Your subconscious mind works continuously, while you are awake and while you are asleep.

The Magic of "Money Consciousness"

Spasmodic or occasional effort to apply the rules will be of no value to you. To get results, you must apply all of the rules until their application becomes a fixed habit with you. In no other way can you develop the necessary "money consciousness."

Poverty is attracted to the one whose mind is favorable to it, as money is attracted to him whose mind has been deliberately prepared to attract it, and through the same laws. Poverty consciousness will voluntarily seize the mind which is not occupied with the money consciousness. A poverty consciousness develops without *conscious* application of habits favorable to it. The money consciousness must be created to order unless one is born with such a consciousness.

Catch the full significance of the statements in the preceding paragraph and you will understand the importance of persistence in the accumulation of a fortune. Without persistence, you will be defeated even before you start. With persistence you will win.

If you have ever experienced a nightmare, you will realize the value of persistence. You are lying in bed, half awake, with a feeling that you are about to smother. You are unable to turn over or to move a muscle. You realize that you must begin to regain control over your muscles. Through persistent effort of will power, you finally manage to move the fingers of one hand. By continuing to move your fingers, you extend your control to the muscles of one arm, until you can lift it. Then you gain control of the other arm in the same manner. You finally gain control over the muscles of one leg, and then extend it to the other leg. Then—with one supreme effort of will —you regain complete control over your muscular system and "snap out of" your nightmare. The trick has been turned step by step.

You Have a Hidden Guide

You may find it necessary to "snap out of" your mental inertia through a similar procedure, moving slowly at first, then increasing your speed until you gain complete control over your will. Be persistent no matter how slowly you may, at first, have to move. With persistence will come success.

If you select your "Master-Mind" group with care, you will have in it at least one person who will aid you in the development of persistence. Some men who have accumulated great fortunes did so because of necessity. They developed the habit of persistence because they were so closely driven by circumstances that they *had to become persistent*.

Those who have cultivated the habit of persistence seem to enjoy insurance against failure. No matter how many times they are defeated, they finally arrive up toward the top of the ladder. Sometimes it appears that there is a hidden guide whose duty is to test men through all sorts of discouraging experiences. Those who pick themselves up after defeat and keep on trying arrive; and the world cries, "Bravo! I knew you could do it!" The hidden guide lets no one enjoy great achievement without passing the persistence test. Those who can't take it simply do not make the grade.

Those who can take it are bountifully rewarded for their

persistence. They receive, as their compensation, whatever goal they are pursuing. That is not all! They receive something infinitely more important than material compensation— the knowledge that "every failure brings with it the seed of an equivalent advantage."

Defeat: A Temporary Condition

There are exceptions to this rule; a few people know from experience the soundness of persistence. They are the ones who have not accepted defeat as being anything more than temporary. They are the ones whose desires are so persistently applied that defeat is finally changed into victory. We who stand on the sidelines of life see the overwhelmingly large number who go down in defeat, never to rise again. We see the few who take the punishment of defeat *as an urge to greater effort*. These, fortunately, never learn to accept life's reverse gear. But what we do not see, what most of us never suspect of existing, is the silent but irresistible power which comes to the rescue of those who fight on in the face of discouragement. If we speak of this power at all we call it persistence and let it go at that. One thing we all know, if one does not possess persistence, one does not achieve noteworthy success in any calling.

As these lines are being written, I look up from my work and see before me, less than a block away, the great mysterious Broadway, the "Graveyard of Dead Hopes," and the "Front Porch of Opportunity." From all over the world people have come to Broadway seeking fame, fortune, power, love, or whatever it is that human beings call success. Once in a great while someone steps out from the long procession of seekers, and the world hears that another person has mastered Broadway. But Broadway is not easily nor quickly conquered.

She acknowledges talent, recognizes genius, pays off in money, only *after* one has refused to quit.

Then we know he has discovered the secret of how to conquer Broadway. The secret is always inseparably attached to one word, *persistence!*

The secret is told in the struggle of Fannie Hurst, whose persistence conquered the Great White Way. She came to New York in 1915, to convert writing into riches. The conversion did not come quickly, but it came. For four years Miss Hurst learned about "The Sidewalks of New York" from first-hand experience. She spent her days laboring, and her nights hoping. When hope grew dim she did not say, "All right Broadway, you win!" She said, "Very well, Broadway, you may whip some, but not me. I'm going to force you to give up."

One publisher (*The Saturday Evening Post*) sent her *thirty-six* rejection slips, before she broke the ice and got a story across. The average writer, like the average in other walks of life, would have given up the job when the first rejection slip came. She pounded the pavements for four years, because she was determined to win.

Then came the payoff. The spell had been broken, the unseen Guide had tested Fannie Hurst, and she could take it. From that time on publishers made a beaten path to her door. Money came so fast she hardly had time to count it. Then the moving-picture men discovered her, and money came not in small change, but in floods.

Briefly, you have a description of what persistence is capable of achieving. Fannie Hurst is no exception. Wherever men and women accumulate great riches, you may be sure they first acquired persistence. Broadway will give any beggar a cup of coffee and a sandwich, but it demands persistence of those who go after the big stakes.

Kate Smith will say "amen" when she reads this. For years she sang, without money and without price, before any microphone she could reach. Broadway said to her, "Come and get it, if you can take it." She did take it until one happy day Broadway got tired and said, "Aw, what's the use? You don't know when you're whipped, so name your price, and go to work in earnest." Miss Smith named her price. It was plenty.

Anyone Can Learn Persistence

Persistence is a state of mind, therefore it can be cultivated. Like all states of mind, persistence is based upon definite causes, among them:

1. *Definiteness of purpose:* Knowing what one wants is the first and, perhaps, the most important step toward the development of persistence. A strong motive forces one to surmount many difficulties.

2. *Desire:* It is comparatively easy to acquire and to maintain persistence in pursuing the object of intense desire.

3. *Self-reliance:* Belief in one's ability to carry out a plan encourages one to follow the plan through with persistence. (Self-reliance can be developed through the principle described in the chapter on autosuggestion.)

4. *Definiteness of plans:* Organized plans, even though they may be weak and entirely impractical, encourage persistence.

5. *Accurate knowledge:* Knowing that one's plans are sound, based upon experience or observation, encourages persistence; guessing instead of knowing destroys persistence.

6. *Cooperation:* Sympathy, understanding, and harmonious cooperation with others tend to develop persistence.

7. *Will-power:* The habit of concentrating one's thoughts upon the building of plans for the attainment of a definite purpose leads to persistence.

8. *Habit:* Persistence is the direct result of habit. The mind absorbs and becomes a part of the daily experiences upon which it feeds. Fear, the worst of all enemies, can be effectively cured by *forced repetition of acts of courage.* Everyone who has seen active service in war knows this.

An Eight-Point "Persistence Inventory"

Before leaving the subject of persistence, take inventory of yourself, and determine in what particular, if any, you are lacking in this essential quality. Measure yourself courageously, point by point, and see how many of the eight factors of persistence you lack. The analysis may lead to discoveries that will give you a new grip on yourself.

Here you will find the real enemies which stand between you and noteworthy achievement. Here you will find not only the "symptoms" indicating weakness of persistence, but also the deeply seated subconscious causes of this weakness. Study the list carefully and face yourself squarely if you really wish to know who you are and what you are capable of doing. These are the weaknesses which must be mastered by all who accumulate riches:

1. Failure to recognize and to define clearly exactly what one wants.

2. Procrastination, with or without cause (usually

backed up with a formidable array of alibis and excuses).

3. Lack of interest in acquiring specialized knowledge.

4. Indecision, the habit of "passing the buck" on all occasions, instead of facing issues squarely (also backed by alibis).

5. The habit of relying upon alibis instead of creating definite plans for the solution of problems.

6. Self-satisfaction. There is but little remedy for this affliction, and no hope for those who suffer from it.

7. Indifference, usually reflected in one's readiness to compromise on all occasions rather than meet opposition and fight it.

8. The habit of blaming others for one's mistakes and accepting unfavorable circumstances as being unavoidable.

9. Weakness of desire, due to neglect in the choice of motives that impel action.

10. Willingness, even eagerness to quit at the first sign of defeat (based upon one or more of the six basic fears).

11. Lack of organized plans placed in writing where they may be analyzed.

12. The habit of neglecting to move on ideas, or to grasp opportunity when it presents itself.

13. Wishing instead of willing.

14. The habit of compromising with poverty instead of aiming at riches, general absence of ambition to *be*, to *do*, to *own*.

15. Searching for all the short-cuts to riches, trying to get without giving a fair equivalent (usually

reflected in the habit of gambling, endeavoring to
drive "sharp" bargains.

16. Fear of criticism, failure to create plans and to
put them into action because of what other people
will think, do, or say. This enemy belongs at the
head of the list because it generally exists in one's
subconscious mind, where its presence is not recognized. (See the Six Basic Fears in a later chapter.)

Anyone Can Criticize

Let us examine some of the symptoms of the fear of criticism. The majority of people permit relatives, friends, and the
public at large to so influence them that they cannot live their
own lives because they fear criticism.

Huge numbers of people make mistakes in marriage, stand
by the bargain, and go through life miserable and unhappy,
because they fear criticism which may follow if they correct
the mistake. (Anyone who has submitted to this form of
fear knows the irreparable damage it does by destroying one's
ambition and the desire to achieve.)

Millions of people neglect to acquire belated educations
after having left school because they fear criticism.

Countless numbers of men and women, both young and
old, permit relatives to wreck their lives in the name of duty
because they fear criticism. (Duty does not require any person
to submit to the destruction of his personal ambitions and
the right to live his own life in his own way.)

People refuse to take chances in business because they fear
the criticism which may follow if they fail. *The fear of criticism in such cases is stronger than the desire for success.*

Too many people refuse to set high goals for themselves

or even neglect selecting a career because they fear the criticism of relatives and "friends" who may say, "Don't aim so high, people will think you are crazy."

When Andrew Carnegie suggested that I devote twenty years to the organization of a philosophy of individual achievement, my first impulse of thought was fear of what people might say. The suggestion set up a goal for me far out of proportion to any I had ever conceived. As quick as a flash, my mind began to create alibis and excuses, all of them traceable to the inherent fear of criticism. Something inside of me said, "You can't do it—the job is too big and requires too much time—what will your relatives think of you? How will you earn a living? No one has ever organized a philosophy of success, what right have you to believe you can do it? Who are you, anyway, to aim so high? Remember your humble birth—what do you know about philosophy? People will think you are crazy (and they did). Why hasn't some other person done this before now?"

These, and many other questions flashed into my mind, and demanded attention. It seemed as if the whole world had suddenly turned its attention to me with the purpose of ridiculing me into giving up all desire to carry out Mr. Carnegie's suggestion.

I had a fine opportunity then and there to kill off ambition before it gained control of me. Later in life, after having analyzed thousands of people, I discovered that most ideas are stillborn and need the breath of life injected into them through definite plans of immediate action. The time to nurse an idea is at the time of its birth. Every minute it lives gives it a better chance of surviving. The fear of criticism is at the bottom of the destruction of most ideas which never reach the planning and action stage.

They Made Their Own "Breaks"

Many people believe that material success is the result of favorable "breaks." There is an element of ground for the belief, but those depending entirely upon luck are nearly always disappointed because they overlook another important factor which must be present before one can be sure of success. It is the knowledge with which favorable "breaks" can be made to order.

During the depression, W. C. Fields, the comedian, lost all his money and found himself without income, without a job, and his means of earning a living (vaudeville) no longer existed. Moreover, he was past sixty, when many men consider themselves "old." He was so eager to stage a comeback that he offered to work without pay in a new field (movies). In addition to his other troubles, he fell and injured his neck. To many that would have been the place to give up and quit. But Fields was persistent. He knew that if he carried on he would get the "breaks" sooner or later, and he did get them, but not by chance.

Marie Dressler found herself down and out, with her money gone, with no job when she was about sixty. She too went after the "breaks," and got them. Her persistence brought an astonishing triumph late in life, long beyond the age when most men and women are done with ambition to achieve.

Eddie Cantor lost his money in the 1929 stock market crash, but he still had his persistence and his courage. With these, plus two prominent eyes, he exploited himself back into an income of $10,000 a week! Truly, if one has persistence one can get along very well without many other qualities.

The only "break" anyone can afford to rely upon is a self-made "break." These come through the application of persistence. The starting point is definiteness of purpose.

All They Wanted Was Each Other

Once there was a man who was king of a great empire. Yet in his heart he was not a king, but a lonely man. As the Prince of Wales, for more than forty years he had been sought in marriage; princesses throughout Europe languished at his feet. He lived without privacy, and when he became Edward VIII he faced only a personal emptiness, hardly understood by his cheering subjects—an emptiness that could be filled only by love.

And what of Wallis Simpson? Twice, when she had failed to find love, she had had the courage to continue her search. Her first duty was to love. What is the greatest thing on earth? The Master called it love—not man-made rules, criticism, bitterness or slander, not political marriage, but love.

When you think of Wallis Simpson, think of one who knew what she wanted, and shook a great empire to get it. Women who complain that this is a man's world, that women do not have an equal chance to win, owe it to themselves to study carefully the life of this unusual woman who, at an age most women consider "old," won the world's most sought after bachelor.

And what of King Edward? Did he pay too high a price for the love of the only woman he wanted?

We only can conjecture. But we can see the *decision,* we can see that the decision had a price, and that the price was paid, and paid openly.

The British Empire has given way to a new order in the world. The Duke of Windsor and his wife were finally reconciled with the Royal Family. Their story of love, of *persist-*

ence, of a price paid and love made triumphant seems to belong to a long-ago time. But we still should remember how these two people sought the world's greatest treasure and claimed it.

Examine the first hundred people you meet, ask them what they want most in life, and ninety-eight of them will not be able to tell you. If you press them for an answer, some will say "security"; many will say "money"; a few will say "happiness"; others will say "fame and power"; and still others will say "social recognition," "ease in living," "ability to sing, dance, or write"; but none of them will be able to define these terms or give the slightest indication of a plan by which they hope to attain these vaguely expressed wishes. Riches do not respond to wishes. They respond only to definite plans, backed by definite desires, through constant persistence.

Four Steps to Persistence

There are four simple steps which lead to the habit of persistence. They call for no great amount of intelligence, no particular amount of education, and but little time or effort. The necessary steps are:

1. A definite purpose backed by burning desire for its fulfillment.
2. A definite plan, expressed in continuous action.
3. A mind closed tightly against all negative and discouraging influences, including negative suggestions of relatives, friends and acquaintances.
4. A friendly alliance with one or more persons who will encourage one to follow through with both plan and purpose.

The preceding four steps are essential for success in all walks of life. The entire purpose of the thirteen principles of this philosophy is to enable one to take these steps as a matter of *habit*.

They are the steps by which one may control one's economic destiny.

They are the steps that lead to freedom and independence of thought.

They are the steps that lead to riches, in small or great quantities.

They are the steps that lead the way to power, fame, and worldly recognition.

They are the four steps that guarantee favorable "breaks."

They are the steps that convert dreams into physical realities.

They are the steps that lead to the mastery of fear, discouragement, indifference.

There is a magnificent reward for all who learn to take these four steps. It is the privilege of writing one's own ticket, and of making life yield whatever price is asked.

Can You Get Help from Infinite Intelligence?

What mystical power gives to men of persistence the capacity to master difficulties? Does the quality of persistence set up in one's mind some form of spiritual, mental or chemical activity which gives one access to supernatural forces? Does Infinite Intelligence throw itself on the side of the person who still fights on after the battle has been lost, with the whole world on the opposing side?

These and many other similar questions have arisen in

my mind as I have observed men like Henry Ford, who started from scratch, and built an industrial empire of huge proportions with little else in the way of a beginning but persistence. Or Thomas A. Edison who with less than three months of schooling became the world's leading inventor, and converted persistence into the talking machine, the moving picture machine, and the incandescent light, to say nothing of half a hundred other useful inventions.

I had the happy privilege of analyzing both Mr. Edison and Mr. Ford, year by year over a long period of years, and therefore the opportunity to study them at close range, so I speak from actual knowledge when I say that I found no quality save persistence, in either of them, that even remotely suggested the major source of their stupendous achievements.

As one makes an impartial study of the prophets, philosophers, miracle men, and religious leaders of the past, one is drawn to the inevitable conclusion that persistence, concentration of effort, and definiteness of purpose were the major sources of their achievements.

Consider, for example, the strange and fascinating story of Mohammed; analyze his life, compare him with men of achievement in this modern age of industry and finance, and observe how they have one outstanding trait in common, persistence!

If you are keenly interested in studying the strange power which gives potency to persistence, read a biography of Mohammed, especially the one by Essad Bey. This brief review of that book, by Thomas Sugrue, in the *Herald Tribune*, will provide a preview of the rare treat in store for those who take the time to read the entire story of one of the most astounding examples of the power of persistence known to civilization:

THE LAST GREAT PROPHET
Reviewed by Thomas Sugrue

Mohammed was a prophet, but he never performed a miracle. He was not a mystic; he had no formal schooling; he did not begin his mission until he was forty. When he announced that he was the Messenger of God, bringing word of the true religion, he was ridiculed and labeled a lunatic. Children tripped him and women threw filth upon him. He was banished from his native city, Mecca, and his followers were stripped of their worldly goods and sent into the desert after him. When he had been preaching ten years he had nothing to show for it but banishment, poverty and ridicule. Yet before another ten years had passed, he was dictator of all Arabia, ruler of Mecca, and the head of a new world religion which was to sweep to the Danube and the Pyrenees before exhausting the impetus he gave it. That impetus was threefold: the power of words, the efficacy of prayer and man's kinship with God.

His career never made sense. Mohammed was born to impoverished members of a leading family of Mecca. Because Mecca, the crossroads of the world, home of the magic stone called the Caaba, great city of trade and the center of trade routes, was unsanitary, its children were sent to be raised in the desert by Bedouins. Mohammed was thus nurtured, drawing strength and health from the milk of nomad, vicarious mothers. He tended sheep and soon hired out to a rich widow as leader of her caravans. He traveled to all parts of the Eastern World, talked with many men of diverse beliefs and observed the decline of Christianity into warring sects. When he was twenty-eight, Khadija, the widow, looked upon him with favor, and married him. Her father would have objected to such a marriage, so she got him drunk and held him up while he gave the paternal blessing. For the next twelve years Mohammed lived as a rich and respected and very shrewd trader. Then he took to wandering in the desert, and one day he returned with the first verse of the Koran and told Khadija that the archangel Gabriel had appeared to him and said that he was to be the Messenger of God.

The Koran, the revealed word of God, was the closest thing to a miracle in Mohammed's life. He had not been a poet; he had no gift of words. Yet the verses of the Koran, as he received them and recited them to the faithful, were better than any verses which the professional poets of the tribes could produce. This, to the Arabs, was a miracle. To them the gift of words was the greatest gift, the poet was all-powerful. In addition the Koran said that all men were equal before God, that the world should be a democratic state—Islam. It was this political heresy, plus Mohammed's desire to destroy all the 360 idols in the courtyard of the Caaba, which brought about his banishment. The idols brought the desert tribes to Mecca, and that meant trade. So the businessmen of Mecca, the capitalists, of which he had been one, set upon Mohammed. Then he retreated to the desert and demanded sovereignty over the world.

The rise of Islam began. Out of the desert came a flame which would not be extinguished—a democratic army fighting as a unit and prepared to die without wincing. Mohammed had invited the Jews and Christians to join him; for he was not building a new religion. He was calling all who believed in one God to join in a single faith. If the Jews and Christians had accepted his invitation Islam would have conquered the world. They didn't. They would not even accept Mohammed's innovation of humane warfare. When the armies of the prophet entered Jerusalem not a single person was killed because of his faith. When the crusaders entered the city, centuries later, not a Moslem man, woman, or child was spared. But the Christians did accept one Moslem idea—the place of learning, the university.

POINTS TO PIN DOWN:

Persistence changes a man's character as carbon changes brittle iron into invincible steel. With persistence you develop a magical quotient of money consciousness, and your subconscious mind is at work continuously to get you the money you require.

An eight-point persistence inventory shows you where to build persistence within yourself. Eight areas for special training provide pin-pointed targets for your persistence.

People such as Fannie Hurst, Kate Smith, W. C. Fields teach us lessons in the value of persistence. Mohammed and others show us how persistence changes the course of history.

Four simple steps lead to the *habit* of persistence, also fend off any negative or discouraging influences which may have affected you until now.

Watch where the going gets tough; you'll see how the tough get going.

Step 9 Toward Riches: Power of the Master Mind

POWER IS ESSENTIAL FOR SUCCESS IN THE ACCUMULATION of money.

Plans are inert and useless without sufficient power to translate them into action. This chapter will describe the method by which an individual may attain and apply power.

Power may be defined as "organized and intelligently directed knowledge." Power, as the term is here used, refers to organized effort sufficient to enable an individual to transmute desire into its monetary equivalent. Organized effort is produced through the co-ordination of effort of two or more people who work toward a definite end in a spirit of harmony.

Power is required for the accumulation of money! Power is necessary for the retention of money after it has been accumulated!

Let us ascertain how power may be acquired. If power

An economic principle and a psychic principle give you a remarkable cooperative alliance. Master-mind power helps you accumulate money and keep your money growing.

is "organized knowledge," let us examine the sources of knowledge:

1. *Infinite Intelligence:* This source of knowledge may be contacted through the procedure described in another chapter, with the aid of creative imagination.
2. *Accumulated experience:* The accumulated experience of man (or that portion of it which has been organized and recorded) may be found in any well-equipped public library. An important part of this accumulated experience is taught in public schools and colleges, where it has been classified and organized.
3. *Experiment and research:* In the field of science

and in practically every other walk of life men are gathering, classifying, and organizing new facts daily. This is the source to which one must turn when knowledge is not available through "accumulated experience." Here, too, the creative imagination must often be used.

Knowledge may be acquired from any of the foregoing sources. It may be converted into power by organizing it into definite plans and by expressing those plans in terms of action.

Examination of the three major sources of knowledge will readily disclose the difficulty an individual would have, if he depended upon his efforts alone, in assembling knowledge and expressing it through definite plans in terms of action. If his plans are comprehensive, and if they encompass extensive activity, he must, generally, induce others to cooperate with him before he can inject into them the necessary element of power.

Andrew Carnegie's Secret of Success

The "Master Mind" may be defined as: "coordination of knowledge and effort, in a spirit of harmony, between two or more people for the attainment of a definite purpose."

No individual may have great power without availing himself of the "Master Mind." In a preceding chapter, instructions were given for the creation of plans for the purpose of translating desire into its monetary equivalent. If you carry out these instructions with persistence and intelligence, and use discrimination in the selection of your "Master-Mind" group, your objective will have been halfway reached even before you begin to recognize it.

So you may better understand the intangible potentialities of power available to you through a properly chosen "Master-Mind" group, we will here explain the two characteristics of the Master-Mind principle, one of which is economic in nature, and the other psychic. The economic feature is obvious. Economic advantages may be created by any person who surrounds himself with the advice, counsel, and personal co-operation of a group of men who are willing to lend him wholehearted aid in a spirit of perfect harmony. This form of cooperative alliance has been the basis of nearly every great fortune. Your understanding of this great truth may definitely determine your financial status.

The psychic phase of the Master-Mind principle is much more difficult to comprehend. You may catch a significant suggestion from this statement: "No two minds ever come together without, thereby, creating a third invisible, intangible force which may be likened to a third mind."

The human mind is a form of energy, a part of it being spiritual in nature. When the minds of two people are co-ordinated in a spirit of harmony, the spiritual units of energy of each mind form an affinity, which constitutes the "psychic" phase of the Master Mind.

The Master-Mind principle, or rather the economic feature of it, was first called to my attention by Andrew Carnegie more than fifty years ago. Discovery of this principle was responsible for the choice of my life's work.

Mr. Carnegie's Master-Mind group consisted of a staff of approximately fifty men, with whom he surrounded himself for the definite purpose of manufacturing and marketing steel. He attributed his entire fortune to the power he accumulated through this "Master Mind."

Analyze the record of any man who has accumulated a

great fortune, and many of those who have accumulated modest fortunes, and you will find that they have either consciously or unconsciously employed the "Master Mind" principle.

Great power can be accumulated through no other principle!

You Can Use More Brains Than Your Own

Man's brain may be compared to an electric battery. It is a well-known fact that a group of electric batteries will provide more energy than a single battery. It is also a well-known fact that an individual battery will provide energy in proportion to the number and capacity of the cells it contains.

The brain functions in a similar fashion. This accounts for the fact that some brains are more efficient than others, and leads to this significant statement—a group of brains coordinated (or connected) in a spirit of harmony will provide more thought energy than a single brain, just as a group of electric batteries will provide more energy than a single battery.

Through this metaphor it becomes immediately obvious that the Master-Mind principle holds the secret of the power wielded by men who surround themselves with other men of brains.

There follows now another statement which will lead still nearer to an understanding of the psychic phase of the Master-Mind principle: when a group of individual brains are coordinated and function in harmony, the increased energy created through that alliance becomes available to every individual brain in the group.

It is a well-known fact that Henry Ford began his business

career under the handicaps of poverty, illiteracy, and ignorance. It is an equally well-known fact that, within the inconceivably short period of ten years, Mr. Ford mastered these three handicaps, and that within twenty-five years he made himself one of the richest men in America. Connect with this fact the additional knowledge that Mr. Ford's most rapid strides became noticeable from the time he became a personal friend of Thomas A. Edison, and you will begin to understand what the influence of one mind upon another can accomplish. Go a step farther, and consider the fact that Mr. Ford's most outstanding achievements began from the time that he formed the acquaintances of Harvey Firestone, John Burroughs, and Luther Burbank (each a man of great brain capacity) and you will have further evidence that power may be produced through friendly alliance of minds.

Men take on the nature and the habits and the power of thought of those with whom they associate in a spirit of sympathy and harmony. Through his association with Edison, Burbank, Burroughs, and Firestone, Mr. Ford added to his own brain power the sum and substance of the intelligence, experience, knowledge, and spiritual forces of these four men. Moreover, he appropriated and made use of the Master-Mind principle through the methods of procedure described in this book.

This principle is available to you!

We have already mentioned Mahatma Gandhi.

Let us study the method by which he attained his stupendous power. It may be explained in a few words. He came by power through inducing over two hundred million people to coordinate, with mind and body, in a spirit of harmony, for a definite purpose.

In brief, Gandhi accomplished a miracle, for it is a miracle

when two hundred million people can be induced—not forced
—to cooperate in a spirit of harmony. If you doubt that this
is a miracle, try to induce any two people to cooperate in a
spirit of harmony for *any length of time.*

Every man who manages a business knows what a difficult
matter it is to get employees to work together in a spirit even
remotely resembling harmony.

The list of the chief sources from which power may be
attained is, as you have seen, headed by Infinite Intelligence.
When two or more people coordinate in a spirit of harmony
and work toward a definite objective, they place themselves
in position, through that alliance, to absorb power directly
from the great universal storehouse of Infinite Intelligence.
This is the greatest of all sources of power. It is the source to
which the genius and the great leader turn (whether they are
conscious of the fact or not).

The other two major sources from which the knowledge
necessary for the accumulation of power may be obtained
are no more reliable than the five senses of man. The senses
are not always reliable.

In subsequent chapters, the methods by which Infinite
Intelligence may be most readily contacted will be adequately
described.

This is not a course on religion. No fundamental principle
described in this book should be interpreted as being intended to interfere either directly or indirectly with any
man's religious habits. This book has been confined ex-
clusively to instructing the reader how to transmute the definite purpose of desire for money into its monetary equivalent.

Read, *think,* and meditate as you read. Soon, the entire
subject will unfold, and you will see it in perspective. You
are now seeing the detail of the individual chapters.

Poverty Needs No Plan

Money is shy and elusive. It must be wooed and won by methods not unlike those used by a determined lover in pursuit of the girl of his choice. And, coincidental as it is, the power used in the "wooing" of money is not greatly different from that used in wooing a maiden. That power, when successfully used in the pursuit of money, must be mixed with faith. It must be mixed with desire. It must be mixed with persistence. It must be applied through a plan, and that plan must be set into action.

When money comes in quantities known as "the big money," it flows to the one who accumulates it as easily as water flows down hill. There exists a great unseen stream of power, which may be compared to a river, except that one side flows in one direction, carrying all who get into that side of the stream, onward and upward to wealth—and the other side flows in the opposite direction, carrying all who are unfortunate enough to get into it (and not able to extricate themselves from it) downward to misery and poverty.

Every man who has accumulated a great fortune has recognized the existence of this stream of life. It consists of one's thinking process. The positive emotions of thought form the side of the stream which carries one to fortune. The negative emotions form the side which carries one down to poverty.

This carries a thought of stupendous importance to the person who is following this book with the object of accumulating a fortune.

If you are in the side of the stream of power which leads to poverty, this may serve as an oar by which you may propel yourself over into the other side of the stream. It can serve you only through application and use. Merely reading and passing judgment on it, either one way or another, will in no way benefit you.

Poverty and riches often change places. When riches take the place of poverty, the change is usually brought about through well-conceived and carefully executed plans. Poverty needs no plan. It needs no one to aid it, because it is bold and ruthless. Riches are shy and timid. They have to be "attracted."

POINTS TO PIN DOWN:

Andrew Carnegie's greatest contribution to personal and business success—the Master Mind—is yours to use as you desire. It is the master way to use organized and directed knowledge as a road to lifelong power.

The human mind is a form of energy. When two or more minds cooperate in harmony, they form a great "bank" of energy, plus a third, invisible force which can be likened to a Master Mind.

It is necessary to plan and to organize in order to get rich. Staying poor is very easy; poverty needs no plan.

Three major sources of accumulated mind power stand ready to aid you. They can be used at will by those who know how to use them—as you do now.

Happiness is found in doing, not merely in possessing.

Step 10 Toward Riches: The Mystery of Sex Transmutation

T HE MEANING OF THE WORD "TRANSMUTE" IS, IN SIMPLE language, "the changing, or transferring of one element, or form of energy, into another."

The emotion of sex brings into being a state of mind.

Because of ignorance on the subject, this state of mind is generally associated with the physical, and because of improper influences to which most people have been subjected in acquiring knowledge of sex, things essentially physical have highly biased the mind.

The emotion of sex has back of it the possibility of three constructive potentialities. They are:

1. The perpetuation of mankind.
2. The maintenance of health (as a therapeutic agency, it has no equal).

You see how any man can direct his great reservoir of sex energy in helping his prosperity drive. You understand how women help men become successful, and how to take full advantage of this ancient truth.

---

3. The transformation of mediocrity into genius through transmutation.

Sex transmutation is simple and easily explained. It means the switching of the mind from thoughts of physical expression to thoughts of some other nature.

Sex desire is the most powerful of human desires. When driven by this desire, men develop keenness of imagination, courage, will power, persistence, and creative ability unknown to them at other times. So strong and impelling is the desire for sexual contact that men freely run the risk of life and reputation to indulge it. When harnessed and redirected along other lines, this motivating force maintains all of its attributes of keenness of imagination, courage, etc. which may be used as powerful creative forces in literature, art, or in any other profession or calling, including, of course, the accumulation of riches.

The transmutation of sex energy calls for the exercise of will power, to be sure, but the reward is worth the effort. The desire for sexual expression is inborn and natural. The desire cannot and should not be submerged or eliminated. But it should be given an outlet through forms of expression which enrich the body, mind, and spirit of man. If not given this form of outlet, through transmutation, it will seek outlets through purely physical channels.

A river may be dammed and its water controlled for a time, but eventually it will force an outlet. The same is true of the emotion of sex. It may be submerged and controlled for a time, but its very nature causes it to be ever seeking means of expression. If it is not transmuted into some creative effort it will find a less worthy outlet.

The Driving Power of Sex

Fortunate indeed is the person who has discovered how to give sex emotion an outlet through some form of creative effort. Scientific research has disclosed these significant facts:

1. The men of greatest achievement are men with highly developed sex natures, men who have learned the art of sex transmutation.
2. The men who have accumulated great fortunes and achieved outstanding recognition in literature, art, industry, architecture, and the professions were motivated by the influence of a woman.

The research from which these discoveries were made went back through the pages of biography and history for more than two thousand years. Wherever there was evidence available in connection with the lives of men and women of great achievement, it indicated most convincingly that they possessed highly developed sex natures.

The emotion of sex is an "irresistible force" against which there can be no such opposition as an "immovable body." When driven by this emotion, men become gifted with a super power for action. Understand this truth, and you will catch the significance of the statement that sex transmutation contains the secret of creative ability.

Destroy the sex glands, whether in man or beast, and you have removed the major source of action. For proof of this observe what happens to any animal after it has been castrated. A bull becomes as docile as a cow after it has been altered sexually. Sex alteration takes out of the male, whether man or beast, all the fight that was in him.

Mind Stimuli—Good and Bad

The human mind responds to stimuli, through which it may be "keyed up" to high rates of vibration, known as enthusiasm, creative imagination, intense desire, etc. The stimuli to which the mind responds most freely are:

1. The desire for sex expression.
2. Love.
3. A burning desire for fame, power, financial gain, or money.
4. Music.
5. Friendship between either those of the same sex or those of the opposite sex.
6. A Master Mind alliance based upon the harmony

of two or more people who ally themselves for spiritual or temporal advancement.

7. Mutual suffering, such as that experienced by people who are persecuted.

8. Autosuggestion.

9. Fear.

10. Narcotics and alcohol.

The desire for sex expression comes at the head of the list of stimuli which most effectively "step up" the mind and start the "wheels" of physical action. Eight of these stimuli are natural and constructive. Two are destructive. The list is here presented for the purpose of enabling you to make a comparative study of the major sources of mind stimulation. From this study, it will be readily seen that the emotion of sex is, by great odds, the most intense and powerful of all mind stimuli.

Some wiseacre has said that a genius is a man who "wears long hair, eats queer food, lives alone, and serves as a target for the joke makers." A better definition of a genius is, "a man who has discovered how to increase the intensity of thought to the point where he can freely communicate with sources of knowledge not available through the ordinary rate of thought."

The person who thinks will want to ask some questions concerning this definition of genius. The first question will be, "How may one communicate with sources of knowledge which are not available through ordinary thought?"

The next question will be, "Are there known sources of knowledge which are available only to geniuses, and if so, what are these sources, and exactly how may they be reached?"

We shall offer evidence, through which you may secure your own proof through experimentation, and in doing so we shall answer both of these questions.

Your Sixth Sense—Creative Imagination

The reality of a sixth sense has been fairly well established. This sixth sense is creative imagination. The faculty of creative imagination is one which the majority of people never use during an entire lifetime, and if used at all, it usually happens by mere accident. A relatively small number of people use, with deliberation and purpose aforethought, the faculty of creative imagination. Those who use this faculty voluntarily, and with understanding of its functions, are geniuses.

The faculty of creative imagination is the direct link between the finite mind of man and Infinite Intelligence. All so-called revelations referred to in the realm of religion, and all discoveries of basic or new principles in the field of invention take place through the faculty of creative imagination.

An Exalted Plane of Thought

When ideas or concepts flash into one's mind through what is popularly called a "hunch" they come from one or more of the following sources:

1. Infinite Intelligence.

2. One's subconscious mind, wherein is stored every sense impression and thought impulse which ever reached the brain through any of the five senses.

3. From the mind of some other person who has just

released the thought or picture of the idea or concept through conscious thought.

4. From the other person's subconscious storehouse.

There are no other known sources from which "inspired"
ideas or "hunches" may be received.

When brain action has been stimulated through one or
more of the ten mind stimulants, it has the effect of lifting
the individual far above the horizon of ordinary thought, and
permits him to envision distance, scope, and quality of
thoughts not available on the lower plane, such as that occupied while one is engaged in the solution of the problems
of business and professional routine.

When lifted to this higher level of thought through any
form of mind stimulation, an individual occupies, relatively,
the same position as one who has ascended in an airplane
to a height from which he may see over and beyond the
horizon line which limits his vision while on the ground.
Moreover, while on this higher level of thought the individual is not hampered or bound by any of the stimuli which
circumscribe and limit his vision while wrestling with the
problems of gaining the three basic necessities of food, clothing, and shelter. He is in a world of thought in which the ordinary, workaday thoughts have been as effectively removed
as are the hills and valleys and other limitations of physical
vision when he rises in an airplane.

While on this exalted plane of thought, the creative faculty
of the mind is given freedom for action. The way has been
cleared for the sixth sense to function. It becomes receptive
to ideas which could not reach the individual under any other
circumstances. The "sixth sense" is the faculty which marks
the difference between a genius and an ordinary individual.

The Voice Within

The creative faculty becomes more alert and receptive to factors originating outside the individual's subconscious mind the more this faculty is used, and the more the individual relies upon it and makes demands upon it for thought impulses. This faculty can be cultivated and developed only through use.

That which is known as one's "conscience" operates entirely through the faculty of the sixth sense.

The great artists, writers, musicians, and poets become great because they acquire the habit of relying upon the "still small voice" which speaks from within, through the faculty of creative imagination. It is a fact well known to people who have "keen" imaginations that their best ideas come through so-called "hunches."

There is a great orator who does not attain to greatness until he closes his eyes and begins to rely entirely upon the faculty of creative imagination. When asked why he closed his eyes just before the climaxes of his oratory, he replied, "I do it because then I speak through ideas which come to me from within."

One of America's most successful and best known financiers followed the habit of closing his eyes for two or three minutes before making a decision. When asked why he did this, he replied, "With my eyes closed, I am able to draw upon a source of superior intelligence."

"Sitting for Ideas"

The late Dr. Elmer R. Gates of Chevy Chase, Maryland, created more than two hundred useful patents, many of them basic, through the process of cultivating and using the creative faculty. His method is both significant and interesting to one interested in attaining to the status of genius, in which category Dr. Gates unquestionably belonged. Dr. Gates was one of the really great, though less publicized, scientists of the world.

In his laboratory, he had what he called his "personal communication room." It was practically sound proof, and so arranged that all light could be shut out. It was equipped with a small table, on which he kept a pad of writing paper. In front of the table, on the wall, was an electric pushbutton which controlled the lights. When Dr. Gates desired to draw upon the forces available to him through his creative imagination, he would go into this room, seat himself at the table, shut off the lights, and *concentrate* upon the *known* factors of the invention on which he was working, remaining in that position until ideas began to "flash" into his mind in connection with the unknown factors of the invention.

On one occasion, ideas came through so fast that he was forced to write for almost three hours. When the thoughts stopped flowing and he examined his notes, he found they contained a minute description of principles which had not a parallel among the known data of the scientific world. Moreover, the answer to his problem was intelligently presented in those notes.

Dr. Gates earned his living by "sitting for ideas" for individuals and corporations. Some of the largest corporations in America paid him substantial fees, by the hour, for "sitting for ideas."

The reasoning faculty is often faulty because it is largely guided by one's accumulated experience. Not all knowledge which one accumulates through experience is accurate. Ideas received through the creative faculty are much more reliable, for the reason that they come from sources more reliable than any which are available to the reasoning faculty of the mind.

The Source of Genius Is Available to You

The major difference between the genius and the ordinary crank inventor may be found in the fact that the genius works through his faculty of creative imagination, while the "crank" knows nothing of this faculty. The scientific inventor makes use of both the synthetic and the creative faculties of imagination.

For example, the scientific inventor begins an invention by organizing and combining the known ideas or principles accumulated through experience, through the synthetic faculty (the reasoning faculty). If he find this accumulated knowledge to be insufficient for the completion of his invention, he then draws upon the sources of knowledge available to him through his *creative* faculty. The method by which he does this varies with the individual, but this is the essence of his procedure:

1. He stimulates his mind so that it functions on a higher-than-average plane, using one or more of the ten mind stimulants or some other stimulant of his choice.

2. He concentrates upon the known factors (the finished part) of his invention, and creates in his mind a perfect picture of unknown factors (the unfinished part) of his invention. He holds this picture in mind until it has been taken over by the subconscious mind, then relaxes by clearing his mind of all thought, and waits for his answer to "flash" into his mind.

Sometimes the results are both definite and immediate. At other times the results are negative, depending upon the state of development of the sixth sense, or creative faculty.

Mr. Edison tried out more than ten thousand different combinations of ideas through the synthetic faculty of his imagination before he "tuned in" through the creative faculty and got the answer which perfected the incandescent light. His experience was similar when he produced the phonograph.

There is plenty of reliable evidence that the faculty of creative imagination exists. This evidence is available through accurate analysis of men who have become leaders in their respective callings, without having had extensive educations. Lincoln was a notable example of a great leader who achieved greatness through the discovery and use of his faculty of creative imagination. He discovered, and began to use this faculty as the result of the stimulation of love which he experienced after he met Ann Rutledge, a statement of the highest significance in connection with the study of the source of genius.

Sex Energy Is Transmuted

The pages of history are filled with the records of great leaders whose achievements may be traced directly to the influence of women who aroused the creative faculties of their minds through the stimulation of sex desire. Napoleon Bonaparte was one of these. When inspired by his first wife, Josephine, he was irresistible and invincible. When his "better judgment" or reasoning faculty prompted him to put Josephine aside, he began to decline. His defeat and St. Helena were not far distant.

If good taste would permit, we might easily mention scores of men, well known to the American people, who climbed to great heights of achievement under the stimulating influence of their wives, only to drop back to destruction after money and power went to their heads, and they put aside the old wife for a new one. Napoleon was not the only man to discover that sex influence *from the right source* is more powerful than any substitute of expediency which may be created by mere reason.

The human mind responds to stimulation!

Among the greatest, and most powerful of these stimuli is the urge of sex. When harnessed and transmuted, this driving force is capable of lifting men into that higher sphere of thought which enables them to master the sources of worry and petty annoyance which beset their pathway on the lower plane.

For the purpose of refreshing the memory, in connection with the facts available from the biographies of certain men, we here present the names of a few men of outstanding achievement, each of whom was known to have been of a highly sexed nature. The genius which was theirs undoubtedly found its source of power in transmuted sex energy:

GEORGE WASHINGTON	THOMAS JEFFERSON
NAPOLEON BONAPARTE	ELBERT HUBBARD
WILLIAM SHAKESPEARE	ELBERT H. GARY
ABRAHAM LINCOLN	WOODROW WILSON
RALPH WALDO EMERSON	JOHN H. PATTERSON
ROBERT BURNS	ANDREW JACKSON

ENRICO CARUSO

Your own knowledge of biography will enable you to add to this list. Find, if you can, a single man, in all history of civilization, who achieved outstanding success in any calling, who was not driven by a well-developed sex nature.

If you do not wish to rely upon biographies of men not now

living, take inventory of those whom you know to be men of great achievement, and see if you can find one among them who is not highly sexed.

Sex energy is the creative energy of all geniuses. *There never has been, and never will be a great leader, builder, or artist lacking in this driving force of sex.*

Surely no one will misunderstand these statements to mean that all who are highly sexed are geniuses. Man attains to the status of a genius only when, and if, he stimulates his mind so that it draws upon the forces available, through the creative faculty of the imagination. Chief among the stimuli with which this "stepping up" may be produced is sex energy. The mere *possession* of this energy is not sufficient to produce a genius. The energy must be *transmuted* from desire for physical contact into some *other* form of desire and action before it will lift one to the status of a genius.

Far from becoming geniuses because of great sex desires, the majority of men *lower* themselves, through misunderstanding and misuse of this great force, to the status of the lower animals.

Much Sex Energy Is Wasted

I discovered, from the analysis of over twenty-five thousand people, that men who succeed in an outstanding way, seldom do so before the age of forty, and more often they do not strike their real pace until they are well beyond the age of fifty. This fact was so astounding that it prompted me to go into the study of its cause most carefully.

This study disclosed the fact that the major reason why the majority of men who succeed do not begin to do so before the age of forty to fifty, is their tendency to dissipate their energies through overindulgence in physical expression of the emotion of sex. The majority of men *never* learn that the urge of sex has other possibilities, which far transcend in importance that of mere physical expression. The majority of those who make this discovery, do so *after having wasted many years* at a period when the sex energy is at its height, prior to the age of forty-five to fifty. This usually is followed by noteworthy achievement.

The lives of many men up to, and sometimes well past the age of forty, reflect a continued dissipation of energies which could have been more profitably turned into better channels. Their finer and more powerful emotions are sown wildly to the four winds. Out of this habit of the male grew the term, "sowing his wild oats."

The desire for sexual expression is by far the strongest and most impelling of all the human emotions, and for this very reason this desire, when *harnessed and transmuted* into action other than that of physical expression, may raise one to great accomplishment.

Nature Gives Great Stimulants

History is not lacking in examples of men who attained to the status of genius as the result of the use of artificial mind stimulants in the form of alcohol and narcotics. Edgar Allan Poe wrote "The Raven" while under the influence of liquor, "dreaming dreams that mortal never dared to dream before." James Whitcomb Riley did his best writing while under the influence of alcohol. Perhaps it was thus he saw "the ordered intermingling of the real and the dream, the mill above the river, and the mist above the stream." Robert Burns wrote best when intoxicated. "For Auld Lang Syne, my dear, we'll take a cup of kindness yet, for Auld Lang Syne."

But let it be remembered that many such men have destroyed themselves in the end. Nature has prepared her own potions with which men may safely stimulate their minds to tune in to fine and rare thoughts which come from—no man knows where! No satisfactory substitute for nature's stimulants has ever been found.

It is a fact well known to psychologists that there is a very close relationship between sex desires and spiritual urges—a fact which accounts for the peculiar behavior of people who participate in the orgies known as religious "revivals," common among the primitive types.

The world is ruled and the destiny of civilization is established by the human emotions. People are influenced in their actions, not by reason so much as by "feelings." The creative faculty of the mind is set into action entirely by emotions, and *not by cold reason*. The most powerful of all human emotions is that of sex. There are other mind stimulants, some of which have been listed, but no one of them, nor all of them combined, can equal the driving power of sex.

A mind stimulant is any influence which will either temporarily or permanently increase the intensity of thought. The ten major stimulants described are those most commonly resorted to. Through these sources one may commune with Infinite Intelligence, or enter at will the storehouse of the subconscious mind, either one's own or that of another person, a procedure *which is all there is of genius*.

Sex and Salesmanship

A teacher, who has trained and directed the efforts of more than 30,000 salespeople, made the astounding discovery that highly sexed men are most efficient salesmen. The explanation is, that the factor of personality known as "personal magnetism" is nothing more nor less than sex energy. Highly sexed people always have a plentiful supply of magnetism. Through cultivation and understanding, this vital force may be drawn upon and used to great advantage in the relationships between people. This energy may be communicated to others through the following media:

1. *The handshake:* The touch of the hand indicates instantly the presence of magnetism, or the lack of it.
2. *The tone of voice:* Magnetism, or sex energy is the factor with which the voice may be colored, or made musical and charming.
3. *Posture and carriage of the body:* Highly sexed people move briskly, and with grace and ease.
4. *The vibrations of thought:* Highly sexed people mix the emotion of sex with their thoughts, or may do so at will, and in that way may influence those around them.
5. *Body adornment:* People who are highly sexed are usually very careful about their personal appearance. They usually select clothing of a style becoming to their personality, physique, complexion, etc.

When employing salesmen, the more capable sales manager looks for the quality of personal magnetism as the *first requirement* of a salesman. People who lack sex energy will never become enthusiastic nor inspire others with enthusiasm, and enthusiasm is one of the most important requisites in salesmanship, no matter what one is selling.

The public speaker, orator, preacher, lawyer, or salesman who is lacking in sex energy is a "flop" as far as being able to influence others is concerned. Couple with this the fact that most people can be influenced only through an appeal to their emotions, and you will understand the importance of sex

energy as a part of the salesman's native ability. Master salesmen attain the status of mastery in selling because they either
consciously or unconsciously *transmute* the energy of sex into
sales enthusiasm! In this statement may be found a very practical suggestion as to the actual meaning of sex transmutation.

The salesman who knows how to take his mind off the subject of sex and direct it in sales effort with as much enthusiasm
and determination as he would apply to its original purpose
has acquired the art of sex transmutation, whether he knows
it or not. The majority of salesmen who transmute their sex
energy do so without being in the least aware of what they are
doing, or how they are doing it.

Transmutation of sex energy calls for more will power than
the average person cares to use for this purpose. Those who
find it difficult to summon will power sufficient for transmutation may gradually acquire this ability. Though this requires
will power, the reward for the practice is more than worth the
effort.

Too Many False Beliefs About Sex

The entire subject of sex is one about which the majority of
people appear to be unpardonably ignorant. The urge of sex
has been grossly misunderstood, slandered, and burlesqued by
the ignorant and the evil minded.

Men and women who are known to be blessed—yes, blessed
—with highly sexed natures, are usually looked upon as being
people who will bear watching. Instead of being called blessed,
they are usually called cursed.

Millions of people, even in this age of enlightenment, have
inferiority complexes which they developed because of this
false belief that a highly sexed nature is a curse. These statements of the virtue of sex energy should not be construed as

justification for the libertine. The emotion of sex is a virtue only when used intelligently and with discrimination. It may be misused, and often is, to such an extent that it debases, instead of enriches, both body and mind.

It seemed quite significant to the author, when he made the discovery that practically every great leader whom he had the privilege of analyzing was a man whose achievements were largely inspired by a woman. In many instances, the "woman in the case" was a modest, self-denying wife, of whom the public had heard but little or nothing. In a few instances, the source of inspiration has been traced to the "other woman."

Every intelligent person knows that stimulation in excess through alcoholic drink and narcotics is a destructive form of intemperance. Not every person knows, however, that overindulgence in sex expression may become a habit as destructive and as detrimental to creative effort as narcotics or liquor.

A sex-mad man is not essentially different from a dope-mad man! Both have lost control over their faculties of reason and will power. Many cases of hypochondria (imaginary illness) grow out of habits developed in ignorance of the true function of sex.

It may be readily seen that ignorance on the subject of sex transmutation forces stupendous penalties upon the ignorant on the one hand, and withholds from them equally stupendous benefits on the other.

Widespread ignorance on the subject of sex is due to the fact that the subject has been surrounded with mystery and dark silence. The conspiracy of mystery and silence has had the same effect upon the minds of young people that the psychology of prohibition had. The result has been increased curiosity, and desire to acquire more knowledge on this *"verboten"* subject; and to the shame of all lawmakers, and most physicians—by training best qualified to educate youth on that subject—information has not been easily available.

The Lesson of the Fruitful Years

Seldom does an individual enter upon highly creative effort in any field of endeavor before the age of forty. The average man reaches the period of his greatest capacity to create between forty and sixty. These statements are based upon analysis of thousands of men and women who have been carefully observed. They should be encouraging to those who fail to arrive before the age of forty, and to those who become frightened at the approach of "old age" around the forty-year mark. The years between forty and fifty are, as a rule, the most fruitful. Man should approach this age, not with fear and trembling, but with hope and eager anticipation.

If you want evidence that most men do not begin to do their best work before the age of forty, study the records of the most successful men known to the American people and you will find it. Henry Ford had not hit his pace of achievement until he had passed the age of forty. Andrew Carnegie was well past forty before he began to reap the reward of his efforts. James J. Hill was still running a telegraph key at the age of forty. His stupendous achievements took place after that age. Biographies of American industrialists and financiers are filled with evidence that the period from forty to sixty is the most productive age of man.

Between the ages of thirty and forty, man begins to learn (if he ever learns) the art of sex transmutation. This discovery is generally accidental, and more often than otherwise, the man who makes it is totally unconscious of his discovery. He may observe that his powers of achievement have increased around the age of thirty-five to forty, but in most cases, he is not familiar with the cause of this change, that nature begins to harmonize the emotions of love and sex in the individual between the ages of thirty and forty, so that he may draw upon these great forces and apply them jointly as stimuli to action.

Only You Can Lead Yourself to Genius

Sex, alone, is a mighty urge to action, but its forces are like a cyclone—they are often uncontrollable. When the emotion of love begins to mix itself with the emotion of sex, the result is calmness of purpose, poise, accuracy of judgment, and balance. What person, who has attained to the age of forty, is so unfortunate as to be unable to analyze these statements, and to corroborate them by his own experience?

When driven by his desire to please a woman, based solely upon the emotion of sex, a man may be, and usually is, capable of great achievement, but his actions may be disorganized, distorted, and totally destructive. When driven by his desire to please a woman, based upon the motive of sex alone, a man may steal, cheat, and even commit murder. But when the emotion of love is mixed with the emotion of sex that same man will guide his actions with more sanity, balance, and reason.

Love, romance, and sex are all emotions capable of driving men to heights of superachievement. Love is the emotion which serves as a safety valve and insures balance, poise, and constructive effort. When combined, these three emotions may lift one to an altitude of a genius.

The emotions are states of mind. Nature has provided man with a "chemistry of the mind" which operates in a manner similar to the principles of chemistry of matter. It is a well-known fact that, through the aid of chemistry of matter, a chemist may create a deadly poison by mixing certain elements, none of which is—in itself—harmful in the right proportions. The emotions may, likewise, be combined so as to create a deadly poison. The emotions of sex and jealousy, when mixed, may turn a person into an insane beast.

The presence of any one or more of the destructive emotions in the human mind through the chemistry of the mind sets up a poison which may destroy one's sense of justice and fairness.

The road to genius consists of the development, control, and use of sex, love, and romance. Briefly, the process may be stated as follows:

Encourage the presence of these emotions as the dominating thoughts in one's mind and discourage the presence of all the destructive emotions. The mind is a creature of habit. It thrives upon the *dominating* thoughts fed it. Through the faculty of will power, one may discourage the presence of any emotion and encourage the presence of any other. Control of the mind through the power of will is not difficult. Control comes from persistence and habit. The secret of control lies in understanding the process of transmutation. When any negative emotion presents itself in one's mind, it can be transmuted into a positive or constructive emotion by the simple procedure of changing one's thoughts.

There is no other road to genius than through voluntary self effort! A man may attain to great heights of financial or business achievement solely by the driving force of sex energy, but history is filled with evidence that he may, and usually does, carry with him certain traits of character which rob him of the ability to either hold or enjoy his fortune. This is worthy of analysis, thought, and meditation, for it states a truth, the knowledge of which may be helpful to women as well as men. Ignorance of this has cost thousands of people their privilege of happiness, even though they possessed riches.

The Mighty Experience of Love

Memories of love never pass. They linger, guide, and influence long after the source of stimulation has faded. There is nothing new in this. Every person who has been moved by genuine love knows that it leaves enduring traces upon the human heart. The effect of love endures because love is spiritual in nature. The man who cannot be stimulated to great heights of achievement by love is hopeless—he is dead, though he may seem to live.

Go back into your yesteryears, at times, and bathe your mind in the beautiful memories of past love. It will soften the influence of the present worries and annoyances. It will give you a source of escape from the unpleasant realities of life, and maybe—who knows?—your mind will yield to you, during this temporary retreat into the world of fantasy, ideas or plans which may change the entire financial or spiritual status of your life.

If you believe yourself unfortunate because you have loved and lost, perish the thought. One who has loved truly can never lose entirely. Love is whimsical and temperamental. It comes when it pleases and goes away without warning. Accept and enjoy it while it remains, but spend no time worrying about its departure. Worry will never bring it back.

Dismiss also the thought that love never comes but once. Love may come and go times without number, but there are no two love experiences which affect one in just the same way. There may be, and there usually is, one love experience which leaves a deeper imprint on the heart than all the others, but all love experiences are beneficial, except to the person who becomes resentful and cynical when love makes its departure.

There should be no disappointment over love, and there

would be none if people understood the difference between the emotions of love and sex. The major difference is that love is spiritual, while sex is biological. No experience which touches the human heart with a spiritual force can possibly be harmful, except through ignorance or jealousy.

Love is, without question, life's greatest experience. It brings one into communion with Infinite Intelligence. When mixed with the emotions of romance and sex, it may lead one far up the ladder of creative effort. The emotions of love, sex and romance are sides of the eternal triangle of achievement building genius.

Love is an emotion with many sides, shades, and colors. But the most intense and burning of all kinds of love is that experienced in the blending of the emotions of love and sex. Marriages not blessed with the eternal affinity of love properly balanced and proportioned with sex cannot be happy ones— and seldom endure. Love alone will not bring happiness in marriage, nor will sex alone. When these two beautiful emotions are blended, marriage may bring about a state of mind closest to the spiritual that one may ever know on this earthly plane.

When the emotion of romance is added to those of love and sex, the obstructions between the finite mind of man and Infinite Intelligence are removed. Then a genius has been born!

Trivialities Can Wreck a Marriage

Here is an interpretation which would, when properly understood, bring harmony out of the chaos which exists in too many marriages. The disharmonies often expressed in the form of nagging may usually be traced to *lack of knowledge* on the subject of sex. Where love, romance and the proper understanding of the emotion and function of sex abide, there is no disharmony between married people.

Fortunate is the husband whose wife understands the true relationship between the emotions of love, sex, and romance. When motivated by this holy triumvirate, no form of labor is burdensome, because even the most lowly form of effort takes on the nature of a labor of love.

It is a very old saying that " a man's wife may either make him or break him," but the reason is not always clear. The "making" and "breaking" are the results of the wife's understanding or lack of understanding of the emotions of love, sex, and romance.

If a woman permits her husband to lose interest in her and became more interested in other women, it is usually because of her ignorance or indifference toward the subjects of sex, love, and romance. This statement presupposes, of course, that genuine love once existed between a man and his wife. The facts are equally applicable to a man who permits his wife's interest in him to die.

Married people often bicker over a multitude of trivialities. If these are analyzed accurately, the real cause of the trouble will often be found to be indifference or ignorance on these subjects.

How Women Get Their Power

Man's greatest motivating force is his desire to please woman! The hunter who excelled during prehistoric days, before the dawn of civilization, did so because of his desire to appear great in the eyes of woman. Man's nature has not changed in this respect. The "hunter" of today brings home no skins of wild animals, but he indicates his desire for her favor by supplying fine clothes, automobiles, and wealth. Man has the same desire to please woman that he had before the dawn of civilization. The only thing that has changed is his method of pleasing. Men who accumulate large fortunes and attain to great heights of power and fame do so, mainly, to satisfy their *desire to please women*. Take women out of their lives, and great wealth would be useless to most men. *It is this inherent desire of man to please woman which gives woman the power to make or break a man.*

The woman who understands man's nature and tactfully caters to it need have no fear of competition from other women. Men may be "giants" with indomitable will power when dealing with other men, but they are easily managed by the women of their choice.

Most men will not admit that they are easily influenced by the women they prefer because it is in the nature of the male to want to be recognized as the stronger of the species. Moreover, the intelligent woman recognizes this manly trait and very wisely makes no issue of it.

Some men know that they are being influenced by the women of their choice—their wives, sweethearts, mothers, or sisters—but they tactfully refrain from rebelling against the influence because they are intelligent enough to know that no man is happy or complete without the modifying influence of the right woman. The man who does not recognize this important truth deprives himself of the power which has done more to help men achieve success than all other forces combined.

POINTS TO PIN DOWN:

Two amazing facts about sex energy give you new insight into this vast source of personal power. Sex energy can be a source of genius just as potent as Thomas Edison's or Andrew Jackson's.

Sex energy stands behind your enthusiasm, creative imagination, intense desire, persistence, and all other qualities which can make you rich and happy.

You help yourself find the exalted plane of thought which can give you priceless "hunches." You can tune-in on other peoples' subconscious storehouse of ideas.

The great secret of every gifted inventor now goes to work for you in two simple but startling stages. You see too that even "reason" may not help you so much as you are helped and guided by sex energy—never denied its natural expression—but also used in a way that many men discover too late.

In the sources of every vital power lie the sources of endless wealth.

Step 11 Toward Riches: The Subconscious Mind

THE SUBCONSCIOUS MIND CONSISTS OF A FIELD OF CONSCIOUSNESS in which every impulse of thought that reaches the conscious mind through any of the five senses is classified and recorded, and from which thoughts may be recalled or withdrawn as letters may be taken from a filing cabinet.

It receives and files sense impressions or thoughts, regardless of their nature. You may voluntarily plant in your subconscious mind any plan, thought, or purpose which you desire to translate into its physical or monetary equivalent. The subconscious acts first on the dominating desires which have been mixed with emotional feeling, such as faith.

Consider this in connection with the instructions given in the chapter on Desire, for taking the six steps there outlined and the instructions given in the chapter on the building and

You see how your subconscious mind waits like a sleeping giant to back up every plan and purpose. At last you can fill your subconscious with positively-directed thoughts that bring anything you want in life.

---

execution of plans, and you will understand the importance of the thought conveyed.

The subconscious mind works day and night. Through a method of procedure unknown to man the subconscious mind draws upon the forces of Infinite Intelligence for the power with which it voluntarily transmutes one's desires into their physical equivalent, making use always of the most practical media by which this end may be accomplished.

You cannot *entirely* control your subconscious mind, but you can voluntarily hand over to it any plan, desire, or purpose which you wish transformed into concrete form. Read again instructions for using the subconscious mind in the chapter on Autosuggestion.

There is plenty of evidence to support the belief that the

subconscious mind is the connecting link between the finite mind of man and Infinite Intelligence. It is the intermediary through which one may draw upon the forces of Infinite Intelligence at will. It alone contains the secret process by which mental impulses are modified and changed into their spiritual equivalent. It alone is the medium through which prayer may be transmitted to the source capable of answering prayer.

The First Creation Must Be Thought

The possibilities of creative effort connected with the subconscious mind are stupendous and imponderable. They inspire one with awe.

I never approach the discussion of the subconscious mind without a feeling of littleness and inferiority due, perhaps, to the fact that man's entire stock of knowledge on this subject is so pitifully limited.

After you have accepted as a reality the existence of the subconscious mind, and understand its possibilities as a medium for transmuting your desires into their physical or monetary equivalent, you will comprehend the full significance of the instructions given in the chapter on Desire. You will also understand why you have been repeatedly admonished to make your desires clear, and to reduce them to writing. You will also understand the necessity of persistence in carrying out instructions.

The thirteen principles are the stimuli with which you acquire the ability to reach and to influence your subconscious mind. Do not become discouraged if you cannot do this upon the first attempt. Remember that the subconscious mind may be voluntarily directed *only through habit*, under the directions given in the chapter on Faith. You have not yet had time to master faith. Be patient. Be persistent.

A good many statements in the chapters on Faith and Auto-suggestion will be repeated here for the benefit of your subconscious mind. Remember, your subconscious mind functions voluntarily, *whether you make any effort to influence it or not.* This, naturally, suggests to you that thoughts of fear and poverty and all negative thoughts serve as stimuli to your subconscious mind *unless* you master these impulses and give it more desirable food upon which it may feed.

The subconscious mind will not remain idle! If you fail to plant desires in your subconscious mind, it will feed upon the thoughts which reach it as the *result of your neglect.* We have already explained that thought impulses, both negative and positive, are reaching the subconscious mind continuously from the four sources which were mentioned in the chapter on Sex Transmutation.

For the present, it is sufficient if you remember that you are living *daily* in the midst of all manner of thought impulses which are reaching your subconscious mind without your knowledge. Some of these impulses are negative, some are positive. You are now engaged in trying to help shut off the flow of negative impulses, and to aid in voluntarily influencing your subconscious mind through positive impulses of desire.

When you achieve this, you will possess the key which unlocks the door to your subconscious mind. Moreover you will control that door so completely that no undesirable thought may influence your subconscious mind.

Everything which man creates begins in the form of a thought impulse. Man can create nothing which he does not first conceive in thought. Through the aid of the imagination thought impulses may be assembled into plans. The imagination, when under control, may be used for the creation of plans or purposes that lead to success in one's chosen occupation.

All thought impulses intended for transmutation into their physical equivalent, voluntarily planted in the subconscious mind, must pass through the imagination and be mixed with faith. The "mixing" of faith with a plan or purpose intended for submission to the subconscious mind may be done only through the imagination.

From these statements, you will readily observe that voluntary use of the subconscious mind calls for coordination and application of all the principles.

How to Harness Your Positive Emotions

The subconscious mind is more susceptible to influence by impulses of thought mixed with "feeling" or emotion than by those originating solely in the reasoning portion of the mind. In fact, there is much evidence to support the theory that only emotionalized thoughts have any action influence upon the subconscious mind. It is a well-known fact that emotion or feeling rules the majority of people. If it is true that the subconscious mind responds more quickly to, and is influenced more readily by thought impulses which are well mixed with emotion, it is essential to become familiar with the more important of the emotions. There are seven major positive emotions and seven major negative emotions. The negatives *voluntarily* inject themselves into the thought impulses, which insure passage into the subconscious mind. The positives must be injected, through the principle of autosuggestion, into the thought impulses which an individual wishes to pass on to his subconscious mind. (Instructions have been given in the chapter on Autosuggestion.)

These emotions, or feeling impulses, may be likened to yeast in a loaf of bread, because they constitute the action element which transforms thought impulses from the passive to the active state. Thus may one understand why thought impulses which have been well mixed with emotion are acted upon more readily than thought impulses originating in "cold reason."

You are preparing yourself to influence and control the "inner audience" of your subconscious mind in order to hand over to it the desire for money, which you wish transmuted into its monetary equivalent. It is essential, therefore, that you understand the method of approach to this "inner audience." You must speak its language, or it will not heed your call. It understands best the language of emotion or feeling. Let us therefore describe here the seven major positive emotions and the seven major negative emotions, so that you may draw upon the positives and avoid the negatives when giving instructions to your subconscious mind.

THE SEVEN MAJOR POSITIVE EMOTIONS

> Desire
> Faith
> Love
> Sex
> Enthusiasm
> Romance
> Hope

There are other positive emotions, but these are the seven most powerful, and the ones most commonly used in creative effort. Master these seven emotions (they can be mastered only by use) and the other positive emotions will be at your command when you need them. Remember, in this connection, that you are studying a book which is intended to help you develop a "money consciousness" by *filling your mind with positive emotions.*

THE SEVEN MAJOR NEGATIVE EMOTIONS
(*To Be Avoided*)

Fear
Jealousy
Hatred
Revenge
Greed
Superstition
Anger

Positive and negative emotions cannot occupy the mind at the same time. One or the other must dominate. It is your responsibility to make sure that positive emotions constitute the dominating influence of your mind. Here the law of habit will come to your aid. *Form the habit* of applying and using the positive emotions! Eventually they will dominate your mind so completely that the negatives *cannot enter it.*

Only by following these instructions literally and continuously can you gain control over your subconscious mind. The presence of a single negative in your conscious mind is sufficient to *destroy* all changes of constructive aid from your subconscious mind.

Prayer and the Subconscious Mind

If you are an observing person, you must have noticed that most people resort to prayer only after everything else has failed! Or else they pray by a ritual of meaningless words. And, because it is a fact that most people who pray do so only after everything else has failed, they go to prayer with their minds filled with fear and doubt, *which are the emotions the subconscious mind acts upon* and passes on to Infinite Intelligence. Likewise, that is the emotion which Infinite Intelligence receives and acts upon.

If you pray for a thing but have fear as you pray that you may not receive it, or that your prayer will not be acted upon by Infinite Intelligence, your prayer *will have been in vain.*

Prayer does, sometimes, result in the realization of that for which one prays. If you have ever had the experience of receiving that for which you prayed, go back in your memory and recall your actual state of mind while you were praying, and you will know for sure that the theory here described is more than a theory.

The method by which you may communicate with Infinite Intelligence is very similar to that through which the vibration of sound is communicated by radio. If you understand the working principle of radio, you of course know that sound cannot be communicated until it has been changed into a rate of vibration which the human ear cannot detect. The radio sending station picks up the sound of the human voice, and modifies it by stepping up the vibration millions of times. Only in this way can the energy of sound be communicated through space. After this transformation has taken place, the energy (which originally was in the form of vibrations of sound) is carried to radio receivers, and these receiving sets reconvert that energy to its original rate of vibration so it is recognized as sound.

The subconscious mind is the intermediary which translates one's prayers into terms which Infinite Intelligence can recognize, presents the message, and brings back the answer in the form of a definite plan or idea for procuring the object of the prayer. Understand this principle and you will know why mere words read from a prayer book cannot and will never serve as an agency of communication between the mind of man and Infinite Intelligence.

POINTS TO PIN DOWN:

Your subconscious mind can feed upon random thoughts—upon thoughts of defeat—or upon thoughts of success and riches. The choice is yours; the results can make you or break you.

You recognize seven major negative emotions and make sure they cannot possibly take root in your mind. At the same time, you recognize and firmly harness your all-important positive emotions.

Beyond your own mind lies an Infinite Intelligence to which your mind can be tuned like a radio set, both sending and receiving. The energy of the entire universe can help your prayers be answered.

Day by day you build your power to use your mighty subconscious. Soon you control the primal impulses which stand behind every plan and every piece of work.

A man is as big as the measure of his thinking.

Step 12 Toward Riches: The Brain

MORE THAN FORTY YEARS AGO, THE AUTHOR, WORKING in conjunction with the late Dr. Alexander Graham Bell and Dr. Elmer R. Gates, observed that every human brain is both a broadcasting and receiving station for the vibration of thought.

In a fashion similar to that employed by the radio broadcasting principle, every human brain is capable of picking up vibrations of thought which are being released by other brains.

In connection with the statement in the preceding paragraph, compare and consider the description of the creative imagination, as outlined in the chapter on Imagination. The creative imagination is the "receiving set" of the brain, which receives thoughts released by the brains of others. It is the

You find amazing new powers in every part of your mind. You see how to step up these powers of quick, clear, effective thinking.

agency of communication between one's conscious or reasoning mind and the four sources from which one may receive thought stimuli.

When stimulated, or stepped up to a high rate of vibration, the mind becomes more receptive to thought which reaches it through outside sources. This stepping-up process takes place through the positive emotions or the negative emotions. Through the emotions, the vibrations of thought may be increased.

The emotion of sex stands at the head of the list of human emotions as far as intensity and driving force are concerned. The brain which has been stimulated by the emotion of sex functions at a much more rapid rate than it does when that emotion is quiescent or absent.

The result of sex transmutation is the increase of thoughts to such a pitch that the creative imagination becomes highly receptive to ideas. On the other hand, when the brain is functioning at a rapid rate, it not only attracts thoughts and ideas released by other brains, but it gives to one's own thoughts that feeling which is essential before those thoughts will be picked up and acted upon by one's subconscious mind.

The subconscious mind is the "sending station" of the brain, through which vibrations of thought are broadcast. The creative imagination is the "receiving set," through which the energies of thought are picked up.

Along with the important factors of the subconscious mind and the faculty of the creative imagination, which constitute the sending and receiving sets of your mental broadcasting machinery, consider now the principle of autosuggestion, which is the medium by which you may put into operation your "broadcasting" station.

Through the instructions described in the chapter on Autosuggestion, you were definitely informed of the method by which desire may be transmuted into its monetary equivalent.

Operation of your mental "broadcasting" station is a comparatively simple procedure. You have but three principles to bear in mind and to apply when you wish to use your broadcasting station—the subconscious mind, creative imagination, and autosuggestion. The stimuli through which you put these three principles into action have been described— and the procedure begins with desire.

We Are Ruled by Intangible Forces

Through the ages which have passed, man has depended too much upon his physical senses and has limited his knowledge to physical things, which he could see, touch, weigh, and measure.

We are now entering the most marvelous of all ages—an age which will teach us something of the intangible forces of the world about us. Perhaps we shall learn, as we pass through this age, that the "other self" is more powerful than the physical self we see when we look into a mirror.

Sometimes men speak lightly of the intangibles—the things which they cannot perceive through any of their five senses, and when we hear them, it should remind us that *all of us are controlled by forces which are unseen and intangible.*

The whole of mankind has not the power to cope with nor to control the intangible force wrapped up in the rolling waves of the oceans. Man has not the capacity to understand the intangible force of gravity, which keeps this little earth suspended in space and keeps man from falling from it, much less the power to control that force. Man is entirely subservient to the intangible force which comes with a thunder storm and he is just as helpless in the presence of the intangible force of electricity.

Nor is this by any means the end of man's ignorance in connection with things unseen and intangible. He does not understand the intangible force (and intelligence) wrapped up in the soil of the earth—*the force which provides him with every morsel of food he eats, every article of clothing he wears, every dollar he carries in his pockets.*

Brain-to-Brain Communication

Last, but not least, man, with all of his boasted culture and education, understands little or nothing of the intangible force (the greatest of all the intangibles) of *thought*. He knows but little concerning the physical brain and its vast network of intricate machinery through which the power of thought is translated into its material equivalent, but he is now entering an age which will yield enlightenment on the subject. Men of science have begun to turn their attention to the study of this stupendous thing called a brain, and while they are still in the kindergarten stage of their studies, they have uncovered enough knowledge to know that the central switchboard of the human brain, the number of lines which connect the brain cells with one another, equals the figure one, followed by fifteen million ciphers.

"The figure is so stupendous," said Dr. C. Judson Herrick, of the University of Chicago, "that astronomical figures dealing with hundreds of millions of light years, become insignificant by comparison. . . . It has been determined that there are from ten billion to fourteen billion nerve cells in the human cerebral cortex, and we know that these are arranged in definite patterns. These arrangements are not haphazard. They are orderly. Recently developed methods of electrophysiology draw off action currents from very precisely located cells, or fibers with micro-electrodes, amplify them with radio tubes, and record potential differences to a millionth of a volt."

It is inconceivable that such a network of intricate machinery should be in existence for the sole purpose of carrying on the physical functions incidental to growth and maintenance of the physical body. Is it not likely that the same system which gives billions of brain cells the media for communication one with another provides also the means of communication with other intangible forces?

The New York Times published an editorial showing that

at least one great university and one intelligent investigator in the field of mental phenomena are carrying on an organized research through which conclusions have been reached that parallel many of those described in this and the following chapter. The following editorial briefly analyzed the work carried on by Dr. Rhine and his associates at Duke University:

WHAT IS "TELEPATHY"?

A month ago we cited on this page some of the remarkable results achieved by Professor Rhine and his associates at Duke University from more than a hundred thousand tests to determine the existence of "telepathy" and "clairvoyance." These results were summarized in the first two articles in *Harper's Magazine*. In the second which has now appeared, the author, E. H. Wright, attempts to summarize what has been learned, or what it seems reasonable to infer, regarding the exact nature of these "extrasensory" modes of perception.

The actual existence of telepathy and clairvoyance now seems to some scientists enormously probable as the result of Rhine's experiments. Various percipients were asked to name as many cards in a special pack as they could without looking at them and without other sensory access to them. About a score of men and women were discovered who could regularly name so many of the cards correctly that "there was not one chance in many a million million of their having done their feats by luck or accident."

But how did they do them? These powers, assuming that they exist, do not seem to be sensory. There is no

known organ for them. The experiments worked just as
well at distances of several hundred miles as they did in
the same room. These facts also dispose, in Mr. Wright's
opinion, of the attempt to explain telepathy or clairvoyance
through any physical theory of radiation. All known forms
of radiant energy decline inversely as the square of the
distance traversed. Telepathy and clairvoyance do not. But
they do vary through physical cause as our other mental
powers do. Contrary to widespread opinion, they do not
improve when the percipient is asleep or half-asleep, but,
on the contrary, when he is most wide-awake and alert.
Rhine discovered that a narcotic will invariably lower a
percipient's score, while a stimulant will always send it
higher. The most reliable performer apparently cannot
make a good score unless he tries to do his best.

One conclusion that Wright draws with some confidence
is that telepathy and clairvoyance are really one and the
same gift. That is, the faculty that "sees" a card face down
on a table seems to be exactly the same one that "reads" a
thought residing only in another mind. There are several
grounds for believing this. So far, for example, the two
gifts have been found in every person who enjoys either of
them. In every one so far the two have been of equal vigor,
almost exactly. Screens, walls, distances, have no effect at
all on either. Wright advances from this conclusion to
express what he puts forward as no more than the mere
"hunch" that other extrasensory experiences, prophetic
dreams, premonitions of disaster, and the like, may also
prove to be part of the same faculty. The reader is not asked
to accept any of these conclusions unless he finds it necessary, but the evidence that Rhine has piled up must remain
impressive.

Minds "Tuned" to Each Other

In view of Dr. Rhine's announcement in connection with the conditions under which the mind responds to what he terms "extrasensory" modes of perception, I now feel privileged to add to his testimony by stating that my associates and I have discovered what we believe to be the ideal conditions under which the mind can be stimulated so that the sixth sense described in the next chapter can be made to function in a practical way.

The conditions to which I refer consist of a close working alliance between myself and two members of my staff. Through experimentation and practice, we have discovered how to stimulate our minds (by applying the principle used in connection with the "invisible counselors" described in the next chapter) so that we can, by a process of blending our three minds into one, find the solution to a great variety of personal problems which are submitted by my clients.

The procedure is very simple. We sit down at a conference table, clearly state the nature of the problem we have under consideration, then begin discussing it. Each contributes whatever thoughts may occur. The strange thing about this method of mind stimulation is that it places each participant in communication with unknown sources of knowledge definitely outside his own experience.

If you understand the principle described in the chapter on the Master Mind, you of course recognize the round-table procedure here described as being a practical application of the Master Mind.

This method of mind stimulation, through harmonious discussion of definite subjects between three people, illustrates the simplest and most practical use of the Master Mind.

By adopting and following a similar plan any student of this philosophy may come into possession of the famous Carnegie formula briefly described in the introduction. If it means nothing to you at this time, mark this page and read it again after you have finished the last chapter.

POINTS TO PIN DOWN:

Three simple principles now coordinate your powers of thought and accomplishment. Your new grip on the all-important *intangibles* can exert an influence denied to many men.

"Far out" discoveries of mind science now become practical tools of your own self-improvement. You now command the key secret of the conference table.

Ten trillion tiny servants—every cell in your brain—form patterns of *thought, imagination* and *will*. Your mind can gather in any amount of money-making knowledge.

Most people wish for riches, but few provide the definite plan and the burning desire which pave the road to wealth.

Step 13 Toward Riches:

The Sixth Sense

THE THIRTEENTH PRINCIPLE IS KNOWN AS THE SIXTH SENSE, through which Infinite Intelligence may and will communicate voluntarily, without any effort from, or demands by, the individual.

This principle is the apex of the philosophy. It can be assimilated, understood, and applied only by first mastering the other twelve principles.

The sixth sense is that portion of the subconscious mind which has been referred to as the creative imagination. It has also been referred to as the "receiving set" through which ideas, plans, and thoughts flash into the mind. The flashes are sometimes called hunches or inspirations.

The sixth sense defies description! It cannot be described to a person who has not mastered the other principles of this

You open the door to the Temple of Wisdom. Glorious paths of creative adventure beckon on the road to wealth.

---

philosophy, because such a person has no knowledge and no experience with which the sixth sense may be compared. Understanding of the sixth sense comes only by meditation through mind development *from within*.

After you have mastered the principles described in this book, you will be prepared to accept as truth a statement which may, otherwise, be incredible to you, namely:

Through the aid of the sixth sense, you will be warned of impending dangers in time to avoid them and notified of opportunities in time to embrace them.

There comes to your aid and to do your bidding, with the development of the sixth sense, a "guardian angel" who will open to you at all times the door to the temple of wisdom.

The Great First Cause

The author is not a believer in, nor an advocate of "miracles," for the reason that he has enough knowledge of nature to understand that Nature *never deviates from her established laws.* Some of her laws are so incomprehensible that they produce what appear to be "miracles." The sixth sense comes as near to being a miracle as anything I have ever experienced.

This much the author does know—that there is a power, or a First Cause, or an Intelligence, which permeates every atom of matter, and embraces every unit of energy perceptible to man—that this Infinite Intelligence converts acorns into oak trees, causes water to flow down hill in response to the law of gravity, follows night with day and winter with summer, each maintaining its proper place and relationship to the other. This Intelligence may, through the principles of this philosophy, be induced to aid in transmuting desires into concrete or material form. The author has this knowledge, because he has experimented with it—and has experienced it.

Step by step, through the preceding chapters, you have been led to this, the last principle. If you have mastered each of the preceding principles, you are now prepared to accept, *without being skeptical,* the stupendous claims made here. If you have not mastered the other principles, you must do so before you may determine definitely whether or not the claims made in this chapter are fact or fiction.

While I was passing through the age of "hero worship," I found myself trying to imitate those whom I most admired. Moreover, I discovered that the element of faith, with which I endeavored to imitate my idols, gave me great capacity *to do so quite successfully.*

You Can Employ "Invisible Counselors"

I have never entirely divested myself of this habit of hero worship. My experience has taught me that the next best thing to being truly great is to emulate the great, by feeling and action, as nearly as possible.

Long before I had ever written a line for publication or endeavored to deliver a speech in public, I followed the habit of reshaping my own character by trying to imitate the nine men whose lives and lifeworks had been most impressive to me. These nine men were Emerson, Paine, Edison, Darwin, Lincoln, Burbank, Napoleon, Ford, and Carnegie. Every night, over a long period of years, I held an imaginary council meeting with this group whom I called my "invisible counselors."

The procedure was this. Just before going to sleep at night, I would shut my eyes and see, in my imagination, this group of men seated with me around my council table. Here I had not only an opportunity to sit among those whom I considered to be great, but I actually dominated the group, by serving as the chairman.

I had a very definite purpose in indulging my imagination through these nightly meetings. My purpose was to rebuild my own character so it would represent a composite of the characters of my imaginary counselors. Realizing, as I did early in life, that I had to overcome the handicap of birth in an environment of ignorance and superstition, I deliberately assigned myself the task of voluntary rebirth through the method I have described above.

A Time for Self-suggestion

I knew, of course, that all men have become what they are because of their dominating thoughts and desires. I knew that every deeply seated desire has the effect of causing one to seek outward expression through which that desire may be transmuted into reality. I knew that self-suggestion is a powerful factor in building character, that it is, in fact, the sole principle through which character is built.

With this knowledge of the principles of mind operation, I was fairly well armed with the equipment needed in rebuilding my character. In these imaginary council meetings I called on my cabinet members for the knowledge I wished each to contribute, addressing myself to each member in audible words, as follows:

"Mr. Emerson, I desire to acquire from you the marvelous understanding of nature which distinguished your life. I ask that you make an impress upon my subconscious mind of whatever qualities you possessed which enabled you to understand and adapt yourself to the laws of nature.

"Mr. Burbank, I request that you pass on to me the knowledge which enabled you to so harmonize the laws of nature that you caused the cactus to shed its thorns and become an edible food. Give me access to the knowledge which enabled you to make two blades of grass grow where but one grew before.

"Napoleon, I desire to acquire from you, by emulation, the marvelous ability you possessed to inspire men, and to arouse them to greater and more determined spirit of action. Also to acquire the spirit of enduring faith, which enabled you to turn defeat into victory and to surmount staggering obstacles.

"Mr. Paine, I desire to acquire from you the freedom of thought and the courage and clarity with which to express convictions which so distinguished you!

"Mr. Darwin, I wish to acquire from you the marvelous patience and ability to study cause and effect without bias or prejudice, so exemplified by you in the field of natural science.

"Mr. Lincoln, I desire to build into my own character the keen sense of justice, the untiring spirit of patience, the sense of humor, the human understanding, and the tolerance which were your distinguishing characteristics.

"Mr. Carnegie, I wish to acquire a thorough understanding of the principles of *organized effort*, which you used so effectively in the building of a great industrial enterprise.

"Mr. Ford, I wish to acquire your spirit of persistence, the determination, poise, and self-confidence which have enabled you to master poverty, and to organize, unify, and simplify human effort, so I may help others to follow in your footsteps.

"Mr. Edison, I wish to acquire from you the marvelous spirit of faith, with which you have uncovered so many of nature's secrets, the spirit of unremitting toil with which you have so often wrested victory from defeat."

The Imaginary "Cabinet"

My method of addressing the members of the imaginary cabinet would vary, according to the traits of character which I was, for the moment, most interested in acquiring. I studied the records of their lives with painstaking care. After some months of this nightly procedure, I was astounded by the discovery that these imaginary figures became apparently *real*.

Each of these nine men developed individual characteristics, which surprised me. For example, Lincoln developed the habit of always being late, then walking around in solemn parade. He always wore an expression of seriousness upon his face. Rarely did I see him smile.

That was not true of the others. Burbank and Paine often indulged in witty repartee which seemed, at times, to shock the other members of the cabinet. On one occasion Burbank was late. When he came, he was excited and enthusiastic and explained that he had been late because of an experiment he was making, through which he hoped to be able to grow apples on any sort of tree. Paine chided him by reminding him that it was an apple which started all the trouble between man and woman. Darwin chuckled heartily as he suggested that Paine should watch out for little serpents when he went into the forest to gather apples, as they had the habit of growing into big snakes. Emerson observed—"No serpents, no apples," and Napoleon remarked, "No apples, no state!"

These meetings became so realistic that I became fearful of their consequences, and discontinued them for several months. The experiences were so uncanny, I was afraid if I continued them I would lose sight of the fact that the meetings were purely *experiences of my imagination.*

This is the first time that I have had the courage to mention this. Heretofore I have remained quiet on the subject, because I knew, from my own attitude in connection with such matters, that I would be misunderstood if I described my unusual experience. I have been emboldened now to reduce my experience to the printed page because I am now less concerned about what "they say" than I was in the years that have passed.

Lest I be misunderstood, I wish here to state most emphatically that I still regard my cabinet meetings as being purely imaginary, but I feel entitled to suggest that, while the members of my cabinet may be purely fictional and the meetings existent only in my own imagination, they have led me into glorious paths of adventure, rekindled an appreciation of true greatness, encouraged creative endeavor, and emboldened the expression of honest thought.

How to Inspire the Sixth Sense

Somewhere in the cell structure of the brain is located an organ which receives vibrations of thought ordinarily called "hunches." So far, science has not discovered where this organ of the sixth sense is located, but this is not important. The fact remains that human beings do receive accurate knowledge through sources other than the physical senses. Such knowledge, generally, is received when the mind is under the influence of extraordinary stimulation. Any emergency which arouses the emotions and causes the heart to beat more rapidly than normal may, and generally does, bring the sixth sense into action. Anyone who has experienced a near accident while driving, knows that on such occasions the sixth sense often comes to one's rescue and aids, by split seconds, in avoiding the accident.

These facts are mentioned preliminary to a statement of fact which I shall now make, namely, that during my meetings with the "Invisible Counselors" I find my mind most receptive to ideas, thoughts, and knowledge which reach me through the sixth sense.

On scores of occasions when I have faced emergencies, some of them so grave that my life was in jeopardy, I have been miraculously guided past these difficulties through the influence of my "Invisible Counselors."

My original purpose in conducting council meetings with imaginary beings was solely that of impressing my own subconscious mind, through the principle of autosuggestion, with certain characteristics which I desired to acquire. In more recent years, my experimentation has taken on an entirely different trend. I now go to my imaginary counselors with every difficult problem which confronts me and my clients.

The results are often astonishing, although I do not depend
entirely on this form of counsel.

You Will Own a Great New Power

The sixth sense is not something that one can take off and
put on at will. Ability to use this great power comes slowly,
through application of the other principles outlined in this
book.

No matter who you are or what may have been your purpose in reading this book, you cannot profit by it without
understanding the principle described in this chapter. This
is especially true if your major purpose is that of accumulation
of money or other material things.

The chapter on the sixth sense was included, because the
book is designed for the purpose of presenting a complete
philosophy by which individuals may unerringly guide themselves in attaining whatever they ask of life. The starting point
of all achievement is desire. The finishing point is that brand
of knowledge which leads to understanding—understanding
of self, understanding of others, understanding of the laws of
nature, recognition and understanding of happiness.

This sort of understanding comes in its fullness only
through familiarity with, and use of the principle of the sixth
sense.

Having read the chapter, you must have observed that
while reading it you were lifted to a high level of mental
stimulation. Splendid! Come back to this again a month from
now, read it once more, and observe that your mind will soar
to a still higher level of stimulation. Repeat this experience
from time to time, giving no concern as to how much or how
little you learn at the time, and eventually you will find yourself in possession of a power that will enable you to throw off

discouragement, master fear, overcome procrastination, and draw freely upon your imagination. Then you will have felt the touch of that unknown "something" which has been the moving spirit of every truly great thinker, leader, artist, musician, writer, statesman. Then you will be in position to transmute your desires into their physical or financial counterpart as easily as you may lie down and quit at the first sign of opposition.

POINTS TO PIN DOWN:

Inspirations and "hunches" no longer pass you by, now they flood you with dynamism through your Creative Imagination —your Sixth Sense.

The author chose Henry Ford and either other successful men to become his "invisible counselors." You can win your goals, just as he did, with the same startling method.

Now you are in touch with the unknown "something" which has stood steadfast for all great men of all time. It still works seeming miracles in the arts and sciences and in business of every kind.

If your major purpose is the accumulation of money or any other material thing, this chapter is especially important in guiding you.

The ladder of success is never crowded at the top.

The Six Ghosts of Fear

BEFORE YOU CAN PUT ANY PORTION OF THIS PHILOSOPHY into successful use, your mind must be prepared to receive it. The preparation is not difficult. It begins with study, analysis, and understanding of three enemies which you will have to clear out—indecision, doubt, and fear.

The Sixth Sense will never function while these three negatives, or any one of them, remain in your mind. The members of this unholy trio are closely related; where one is found, the other two are close at hand.

Indecision is the seedling of fear! Remember this as you read. Indecision crystallizes into doubt, the two blend and become fear! The blending process often is slow. This is one reason why these three enemies are so dangerous. They germinate and grow *without their presence being observed.*

You take inventory of yourself, see if any remnants of fear are standing in your way. You Think and Grow Rich— because nothing, absolutely nothing, can stand in your way.

The remainder of this chapter describes an end which must be attained before the philosophy as a whole can be put into practical use. It also analyzes a condition which has reduced huge numbers of people to poverty, and it states a truth which must be understood by all who accumulate riches, whether measured in terms of money or a state of mind of far greater value than money.

The purpose of this chapter is to turn the spotlight of attention upon the cause and the cure of the six basic fears. Before we can master an enemy, we must know its name, its habits, and its place of abode. As you read, analyze yourself carefully and determine which, if any, of the six common fears have attached themselves to you.

Do not be deceived by the habits of these subtle enemies.

Sometimes they remain hidden in the subconscious mind, where they are difficult to locate and still more difficult to eliminate.

Fear Is Only a State of Mind

There are six basic fears, with some combination of which every human suffers at one time or another. Most people are fortunate if they do not suffer from the entire six. Named in the order of their most common appearance, they are:

> Poverty
> Criticism
> Ill health
> Lost love
> Old age
> Death.

The first three are at the bottom of most of one's worries.

All other fears are of minor importance; they can be grouped under these six headings.

Fears are nothing more than states of mind. One's state of mind is subject to control and direction.

Man can create nothing which he does not first conceive in the form of an impulse of thought. Following this statement comes another of still greater importance, namely, man's thought impulses begin immediately to translate themselves into their physical equivalent, whether those thoughts are voluntary or involuntary. Thought impulses which are picked up by mere chance (thoughts which have been released by other minds) may determine one's financial, business, professional, or social destiny just as surely as do the thought impulses which one creates by intent and design.

We are here laying the foundation for the presentation of

a fact of great importance to the person who does not understand why some people appear to be "lucky" while others of equal or greater ability, training, experience, and brain capacity seem destined to ride with misfortune. This fact may be explained by the statement that *every human being has the ability to completely control his own mind,* and with this control, obviously, every person may open his mind to the tramp thought impulses which are being released by other brains, or close the doors tightly and admit only thought impulses of his own choice.

Nature has endowed man with absolute control over but one thing, and that is thought. This fact, coupled with the additional fact that everything which man creates begins in the form of a thought, leads one very near to the principle by which fear may be mastered.

If it is true that all thought has a tendency to clothe itself in its physical equivalent (and this is true, beyond any reasonable room for doubt), it is equally true that thought impulses of fear and poverty cannot be translated into terms of courage and financial gain.

Roads that Lead in Opposite Directions

There can be no compromise between poverty and riches! The two roads that lead to poverty and riches travel in opposite directions. If you want riches, you must refuse to accept any circumstance that leads toward poverty. (The word "riches" is here used in its broadest sense, meaning financial, spiritual, mental and material estates.) The starting point of the path that leads to riches is desire. In the chapter on Desire, you received full instructions for its proper use. In this chapter on fear, you have complete instructions for preparing your mind to make practical use of desire.

Here, then, is the place to give yourself a challenge which will definitely determine how much of this philosophy you have absorbed. Here is the point at which you can turn prophet and foretell accurately what the future holds in store for you. If, after reading this chapter you are willing to accept poverty, you may as well make up your mind to receive poverty. This is one decision you cannot avoid.

If you demand riches, determine what form, and how much will be required to satisfy you. You know the road that leads to riches. You have been given a road map which, if followed, will keep you on that road. If you neglect to make the start or stop before you arrive, no one will be to blame, but you. This responsibility is yours. No alibi will save you from accepting the responsibility if you now fail or refuse to demand riches of life, because the acceptance calls for but one thing —incidentally, the only thing you can control—and that is a state of mind. A state of mind is something that one assumes. It cannot be purchased, it must be created.

Analyze Your Fears

Fear of poverty is a state of mind, nothing else! But it is sufficient to destroy one's chances of achievement in any undertaking.

This fear paralyzes the faculty of reason, destroys the faculty of imagination, kills off self-reliance, undermines enthusiasm, discourages initiative, leads to uncertainty of purpose, encourages procrastination, wipes out enthusiasm and makes self-control an impossibility. It takes the charm from one's personality, destroys the possibility of accurate thinking, diverts concentration of effort; it masters persistence, turns the will power into nothingness, destroys ambition, beclouds the memory and invites failure in every conceivable form; it kills love and assassinates the finer emotions of the heart, discourages friendship and invites disaster in a hundred forms, leads to sleeplessness, misery and unhappiness—and all this despite the obvious truth that we live in a world of overabundance of everything the heart could desire, with nothing standing between us and our desires, excepting lack of a definite purpose.

The fear of poverty is, without doubt, the most destructive of the six basic fears. It has been placed at the head of the list because it is the most difficult to master. The fear of poverty grew out of man's inherited tendency to prey upon his fellow man economically. Nearly all animals lower than man are motivated by instinct, but their capacity to think is limited, therefore, they prey upon one another physically. Man, with his superior sense of intuition, with the capacity to think and to reason, does not eat his fellow man bodily; he gets more satisfaction out of "eating" him financially. Man is so avaricious that every conceivable law has been passed to safeguard him from his fellow man.

Nothing brings man so much suffering and humility as poverty! Only those who have experienced poverty understand the full meaning of this.

It is no wonder that man *fears* poverty. Through a long line of inherited experiences man has learned, for sure, that some men cannot be trusted where matters of money and earthly possessions are concerned.

So eager is man to possess wealth that he will acquire it in whatever manner he can—through legal methods if possible —through other methods if necessary or expedient.

Self-analysis may disclose weaknesses which one does not like to acknowledge. This form of examination is essential to all who demand of life more than mediocrity and poverty. Remember, as you check yourself point by point, that you are both the court and the jury, the prosecuting attorney and the attorney for the defense, and that you are the plaintiff and the defendant; also, that you are on trial. Face the facts squarely. Ask yourself definite questions and demand direct replies. When the examination is over, you will know more about yourself. If you do not feel that you can be an impartial judge in this self-examination, call upon someone who knows you well to serve as judge while you cross-examine yourself. You are after the truth. *Get it, no matter at what cost even though it may temporarily embarrass you!*

The majority of people, if asked what they fear most, would reply, "I fear nothing." The reply would be inaccurate because few people realize that they are bound, handicapped, whipped spiritually and physically through some form of fear. So subtle and deeply seated is the emotion of fear that one may go through life burdened with it, never recognizing its presence. Only a courageous analysis will disclose the presence of this universal enemy. When you begin such an analysis, search deeply into your character. Here is a list of the symptoms for which you should look:

Six Symptoms that Show Fear of Poverty

1. *Indifference:* Commonly expressed through lack of ambition, willingness to tolerate poverty, acceptance of whatever compensation life may offer without protest, mental and physical laziness, lack of initiative, imagination, enthusiasm and self-control.
2. *Indecision:* The habit of permitting others to do one's thinking. Staying "on the fence."
3. *Doubt:* Generally expressed through alibis and excuses designed to cover up, explain away, or apologize for one's failures, sometimes expressed in

the form of envy for those who are successful, or by criticizing them.

4. *Worry:* Usually expressed by finding fault with others, a tendency to spend beyond one's income, neglect of personal appearance, scowling and frowning: intemperance in the use of alcoholic drink, sometimes through the use of narcotics: nervousness, lack of poise and self-consciousness.

5. *Overcaution:* The habit of looking for the negative side of every circumstance, thinking and talking of possible failure instead of concentrating upon the means of succeeding: knowing all the roads to disaster, but never searching for the plans to avoid failure: waiting for "the right time" to begin putting ideas and plans into action until the waiting becomes a permanent habit: remembering those who have failed and forgetting those who have succeeded: seeing the hole in the doughnut, but overlooking the doughnut: pessimism, leading to indigestion, poor elimination, autointoxication, bad breath and bad disposition.

6. *Procrastination:* The habit of putting off until tomorrow that which should have been done last year. Spending enough time in creating alibis and excuses to have done the job. This symptom is closely related to overcaution, doubt and worry: refusal to accept responsibility when it can be avoided: willingness to compromise rather than put up a stiff fight: compromising with difficulties instead of harnessing them and using them as stepping stones to advancement: bargaining with life for a penny, instead of demanding prosperity, opulence, riches, contentment and happiness: planning what to do if and

when overtaken by failure, instead of burning all bridges and making retreat impossible: weakness, and often total lack of self-confidence, definiteness of purpose, self-control, initiative, enthusiasm, ambition, thrift and sound reasoning ability: expecting poverty instead of demanding riches: association with those who accept poverty instead of seeking the company of those who demand and receive riches.

"Just Money"

Some will ask, "Why did you write a book about money? Why measure riches in dollars, alone?" Some will believe, and rightly so, that there are other forms of riches more desirable than money. Yes, there are riches which cannot be measured in terms of dollars, but there are millions of people who will say, "Give me all the money I need, and I will find everything else I want."

The major reason I wrote this book on how to get money is the fact that millions of men and women are paralyzed with the fear of poverty. What this sort of fear does to one was well described by Westbrook Pegler:

Money is only clam shells or metal discs or scraps of paper, and there are treasures of the heart and soul which money cannot buy, but most people, being broke, are unable to keep this in mind and sustain their spirits. When a man is down and out and on the street, unable to get any job at all, something happens to his spirit which can be observed in the droop of his shoulders, the set of his hat, his walk and his gaze. He cannot escape a feeling of inferiority among people with regular employment, even though he knows they are definitely not his equals in character, intelligence or ability.

These people—even his friends—feel, on the other hand, a sense of superiority and regard him, perhaps unconsciously, as a casualty. He may borrow for a time, but not enough to carry on in his accustomed way, and he cannot continue to borrow very long. But borrowing in itself, when a man is borrowing merely to live, is a depressing experience, and the money lacks the power of earned money to revive his spirits. Of course, none of this applies to bums or habitual ne'er-do-wells, but only to men of normal ambitions and self-respect.

Women in the same predicament must be different. We somehow do not think of women at all in considering the down-and-outers. They are scarce in the breadlines, they rarely are seen begging on the streets, and they are not recognizable in crowds by the same plain signs which identify busted men. Of course, I do not mean the shuffling hags of the city streets who are the opposite number of the confirmed male bums. I mean reasonably young, decent and intelligent women. There must be many of them, but their despair is not apparent. Maybe they kill themselves.

When a man is down and out he has time on his hands for brooding. He may travel miles to see a man about a job and discover that the job is filled or that it is one of those jobs with no base pay but only a commission on the sale of some useless knick-knack which nobody would buy, except out of pity. Turning that down, he finds himself back on the street with nowhere to go but just anywhere. So he walks and walks. He gazes into store windows at luxuries which are not for him, and feels inferior and gives way to people who stop to look with an active interest. He wanders into the railroad station or puts himself down in the library to ease his legs and soak up a little heat, but that isn't looking for a job, so he gets going again. He may not know it, but his aimlessness would give him away even if the very lines of his figure did not. He may be well dressed in the clothes left over from the days when he had a steady job, but the clothes cannot disguise the droop.

He sees thousands of other people, bookkeepers or clerks or chemists or wagon hands, busy at their work and envies them from the bottom of his soul. They have their independence, their self-respect and manhood, and he simply cannot convince himself that he is a good man, too, though he argue it out and arrive at a favorable verdict hour after hour.

It is just money which makes this difference in him. With a little money he would be himself again.

Do You Fear Criticism?

Just how man originally came by this fear, no one can state definitely, but one thing is certain—he has it in a highly developed form.

This author is inclined to attribute the basic fear of criticism to that part of man's inherited nature which prompts him not only to take away his fellow man's goods and wares, but to justify his action by criticism of his fellow man's character. It is a well-known fact that a thief will criticize the man from whom he steals—that politicians seek office, not by displaying their own virtues and qualifications, but by attempting to besmirch their opponents.

The astute manufacturers of clothing have not been slow to capitalize this basic fear of criticism, with which all mankind has been cursed. Every season the styles in many articles of wearing apparel change. Who establishes the styles? Certainly not the purchaser of clothing, but the manufacturer. Why does he change the styles so often? The answer is obvious. He changes the styles so he can sell more clothes.

For the same reason the manufacturers of automobiles change styles of models every season. No man wants to drive an automobile which is not of the latest style.

We have been describing the manner in which people behave under the influence of fear of criticism as applied to the small and petty things of life. Let us now examine human behavior when this fear affects people in connection with the more important events of human relationship. Take for example practically any person who has reached the age of mental maturity (from 35 to 40 years of age, as a general average), and if you could read the secret thoughts of his mind, you would find a very decided disbelief in most of the fables taught by the majority of the dogmatists a few decades back.

Why does the average person, even in this day of enlightenment, shy away from denying his belief in fables? The answer is, "because of the fear of criticism." Men and women have been burned at the stake for daring to express disbelief in ghosts. It is no wonder we have inherited a consciousness which makes us fear criticism. The time was, and not so far in the past, when criticism carried severe punishments—it still does in some countries.

The fear of criticism robs man of his initiative, destroys his power of imagination, limits his individuality, takes away his self-reliance, and does him damage in a hundred other ways. Parents often do their children irreparable injury by criticizing them. The mother of one of my boyhood chums used to punish him with a switch almost daily, always completing the job with the statement, "You'll land in the penitentiary before you are twenty." He was sent to a reformatory at the age of seventeen.

Criticism is the one form of service of which everyone has too much. Everyone has a stock of it which is handed out, gratis, whether called for or not. One's nearest relatives often are the worst offenders. It should be recognized as a crime (in reality it is a crime of the worst nature) for any parent to build inferiority complexes in the mind of a child through unnecessary criticism. Employers who understand human nature get the best there is in men, not by criticism, but by constructive suggestion. Parents may accomplish the same results with their children. Criticism will plant fear in the human heart, or resentment, but it will not build love or affection.

Seven Symptoms that Show Fear of Criticism

This fear is almost as universal as the fear of poverty, and its effects are just as fatal to personal achievement, mainly because this fear destroys initiative, and discourages the use of imagination. The major symptoms of the fear are:

1. *Self-consciousness:* Generally expressed through nervousness, timidity in conversation and in meeting strangers, awkward movement of the hands and limbs, shifting of the eyes.
2. *Lack of poise:* Expressed through lack of voice control, nervousness in the presence of others, poor posture of body, poor memory.
3. *Weak Personality:* Lacking in firmness of decision, personal charm, and ability to express opinions definitely. The habit of side-stepping issues instead of meeting them squarely. Agreeing with others without careful examination of their opinions.

4. *Inferiority complex:* The habit of expressing self-approval by word of mouth and by actions as a means of covering up a feeling of inferiority; using "big words" to impress others (often without knowing the real meaning of the words), imitating others in dress, speech and manners, boasting of imaginary achievements. This sometimes gives a surface appearance of a feeling of superiority.

5. *Extravagance:* The habit of trying to "keep up with the Joneses," spending beyond one's income.

6. *Lack of initiative:* Failure to embrace opportunities for self-advancement, fear to express opinions, lack of confidence in one's own ideas, giving evasive answers to questions asked by superiors, hesitancy of manner and speech, deceit in both words and deeds.

7. *Lack of ambition:* Mental and physical laziness, lack of self-assertion, slowness in reaching decisions, being too easily influenced; the habit of criticizing others behind their backs and flattering them to their faces, the habit of accepting defeat without protest or quitting an undertaking when opposed by others; suspicion of other people without cause, lack of tactfulness of manner and speech, unwillingness to accept the blame for mistakes.

Do You Fear Ill Health?

This fear may be traced to both physical and social heredity. It is closely associated, as to its origin, with the causes of fear of old age and the fear of death because it leads one closely to the border of "terrible worlds" of which man knows not, but concerning which he has been taught some discomforting stories. The opinion is somewhat general, also, that certain unethical people have engaged in the business of "selling health" by keeping alive the fear of ill health.

In the main, man fears ill health because of the terrible pictures which have been planted in his mind of what may happen if death should overtake him. He also fears it because of the economic toll which it may claim.

A reputable physician estimated that 75% of all people who visit physicians for professional service are suffering with hypochondria (imaginary illness). It has been shown most convincingly that the fear of disease, even where there is not the slightest cause for fear, often produces the physical symptoms of the disease feared.

Powerful and mighty is the human mind! It builds or it destroys.

Playing upon this common weakness of fear of ill health, dispensers of patent medicines have reaped fortunes. This form of imposition upon credulous humanity became so prevalent some decades ago that a popular magazine conducted a bitter campaign against some of the worst offenders in the patent medicine business.

Through a series of experiments conducted some years ago, it was proved that people may be made ill by suggestion. We conducted this experiment by causing three acquaintances to visit the "victims," each of whom asked the question, "What ails you? You look terribly ill." The first questioner usually provoked a grin, and a nonchalant "Oh, nothing, I'm all right," from the victim. The second questioner usually was answered with the statement, "I don't know exactly, but I do feel badly." The third questioner was usually met with the frank admission that the victim was actually feeling ill.

Try this on an acquaintance if you doubt that it will make him uncomfortable, but do not carry the experiment too far. There is a certain religious sect whose members take vengeance upon their enemies by the "hexing" method. They call it "placing a spell" on the victim.

There is overwhelming evidence that disease sometimes begins in the form of negative thought impulse. Such an impulse may be passed from one mind to another by suggestion, or created by an individual in his own mind.

A man who was blessed with more wisdom than this incident might indicate, once said, "When anyone asks me how I feel, I always want to answer by knocking him down."

Doctors send patients into new climates for their health, because a change of "mental attitude" is necessary. The seed of fear of ill health lives in every human mind. Worry, fear, discouragement, disappointment in love and business affairs cause this seed to germinate and grow.

Disappointments in business and in love stand at the head of the list of causes of fear of ill health. A young man suffered a disappointment in love which sent him to a hospital. For months he hovered between life and death. A specialist in psychotherapy was called in. The specialist changed nurses, placing him in charge of a very *charming young woman* who began (by prearrangement with the doctor) to make love to him the first day of her arrival on the job. Within three weeks the patient was discharged from the hospital, still suffering, but with an entirely different malady. He was in love again. The remedy was a hoax, but the patient and the nurse were later married.

Seven Symptoms that Show Fear of Ill Health

The symptoms of this almost universal fear are:

1. *Autosuggestion:* The habit of negative use of self-suggestion by looking for, and expecting to find, the

symptoms of all kinds of disease; "enjoying" imaginary illness and speaking of it as being real; the habit of trying all "fads" and "isms" recommended by others as having therapeutic value; talking to others of operations, accidents and other forms of illness; experimenting with diets, physical exercises, reducing systems, without professional guidance; trying home remedies, patent medicines and "quack" remedies.

2. *Hypochondria:* The habit of talking of illness, concentrating the mind upon disease, and expecting its appearance until a nervous break occurs. Nothing that comes in bottles can cure this condition. It is brought on by negative thinking and nothing but positive thought can affect a cure. Hypochondria (a medical term for imaginary disease) is said to do as much damage on occasion as the disease one fears might do. Most so-called cases of "nerves" come from imaginary illness.

3. *Indolence:* Fear of ill health often interferes with proper physical exercise, and results in overweight, by causing one to avoid outdoor life.

4. *Susceptibility:* Fear of ill health breaks down nature's body resistance and creates a favorable condition for any form of disease one may contact.
    The fear of ill health is often related to the fear of poverty, especially in the case of the hypochondriac, who constantly worries about the possibility of having to pay doctors' bills, hospital bills, etc. This type of person spends much time preparing for sickness, talking about death, saving money for cemetery lots and burial expenses, etc.

5. *Self-coddling:* The habit of making a bid for sympathy, using imaginary illness as the lure (people often resort to this trick to avoid work); the habit of feigning illness to cover plain laziness, or to serve as an alibi for lack of ambition.

6. *Intemperance:* The habit of using alcohol or narcotics to destroy pains such as headaches, neuralgia, etc., instead of eliminating the cause.

7. *Worry:* The habit of reading about illness and worrying over the possibility of being stricken by it, also the habit of reading patent medicine advertisements.

Do You Fear Loss of Love?

The original source of this inherent fear obviously grew out of man's polygamous habit of stealing his fellow man's mate, and his habit of taking liberties with her whenever he could.

Jealousy and other similar forms of neurosis grow out of man's inherited fear of the loss of love. This fear is the most painful of all the six basic fears. It probably plays more havoc with the body and mind than any of the other basic fears.

The fear of the loss of love probably dates back to the stone age, when men stole women by brute force. They continue to steal females, but their technique has changed. Instead of force, they now use persuasion, the promise of pretty clothes, fine cars, and other "bait" much more effective than physical force. Man's habits are the same as they were at the dawn of civilization, but he expresses them differently.

Careful analysis has shown that women are more susceptible to this fear than men. This fact is easily explained. Women have learned from experience that men are polygamous by nature, that they are not to be trusted in the hands of rivals.

Three Symptoms that Show Fear of Loss of Love

The distinguishing symptoms of this fear are:

1. *Jealousy:* The habit of being suspicious of friends
    and loved ones without any reasonable evidence of
    sufficient grounds; the habit of accusing a wife or
    husband of infidelity without grounds; general sus-
    picion of everyone, absolute faith in no one.
2. *Fault finding:* The habit of finding fault with friends,
    relatives, business associates and loved ones upon
    the slightest provocation, or without any cause what-
    soever.
3. *Gambling:* The habit of gambling, stealing, cheating,
    and otherwise taking hazardous chances to provide
    money for loved ones, with the belief that love can
    be bought; the habit of spending beyond one's means
    or incurring debts to provide gifts for loved ones,
    with the object of making a favorable showing; in-
    somnia, nervousness, lack of persistence, weakness
    of will, lack of self-control, lack of self-reliance, bad
    temper.

Do You Fear Old Age?

In the main, this fear grows out of two sources. First, the
thought that old age may bring with it poverty. Second, and
by far the most common source, from false and cruel teachings
of the past which have been too well mixed with "fire and
brimstone" and other bogies cunningly designed to enslave
man through fear.

In the basic fear of old age, man has two very sound reasons
for his apprehension—one growing out of his distrust of his

fellow man, who may seize whatever worldly goods he may possess, and the other arising from the terrible pictures in his mind of the world beyond.

The possibility of ill health, which is more common as people grow older, is also a contributing cause of this common fear of old age. Eroticism also enters into the cause of the fear of old age, as no man cherishes the thought of diminishing sex attraction.

The most common cause of fear of old age is associated with the possibility of poverty. "Poorhouse" is not a pretty word. It throws a chill into the mind of every person who faces the possibility of having to spend his declining years on a poor farm.

Another contributing cause of the fear of old age is the possibility of loss of freedom and independence, as old age may bring with it the loss of both physical and economic freedom.

Three Symptoms that Show Fear of Old Age

The commonest symptoms of this fear are:

1. *Premature slowdown:* The tendency to slow down around the age of forty—the age of mental maturity —and to develop an inferiority complex, falsely believing one's self to be slipping because of age.

2. *Apology for one's age:* The habit of speaking apologetically of one's self as being old merely because one has reached the age of forty or fifty. Instead, one should express gratitude for having reached the age of wisdom and understanding.

3. *Killing off initiative:* Initiative, imagination and self-

reliance are lost when one falsely believes one's self too old to exercise these qualities.

4. *Masquerading as a younger person:* The habit of affecting the dress and mannerisms of younger people, which only inspires ridicule from both friends and strangers is all too common.

Do You Fear Death?

To some this is the cruelest of all the basic fears. The reason is obvious. The terrible pangs of fear associated with the thought of death, in the majority of cases, may be charged to religious fanaticism. So-called "heathen" are less afraid of death than the more "civilized." For thousands of years man has been asking the still unanswered questions, "whence" and "whither." Where did I come from, and where am I going?

During the darker ages of the past, the more cunning and crafty were not slow to offer the answer to these questions, for a price.

"Come into my tent, embrace my faith, accept my dogmas, and I will give you a ticket that will admit you straightaway into heaven when you die," cries a leader of sectarianism. "Remain out of my tent," says the same leader, "and may the devil take you and burn you throughout eternity."

The thought of eternal punishment destroys interest in life and makes happiness impossible.

While the religious leader may not be able to provide safe conduct into heaven, nor, by lack of such provision, allow the unfortunate to descend into hell, the possibility of the latter seems so terrible that the very thought of it lays hold of the imagination in such a realistic way that it paralyzes reason and sets up the fear of death.

The fear of death is not as common now as it was during

the age when there were no great colleges and universities. Men of science have turned the spotlight of truth upon the world, and this truth is rapidly freeing men and women from this terrible fear of death. The young men and young women who attend the colleges and universities are not easily impressed by fire and brimstone. Through the aid of biology, astronomy, geology, and other related sciences, the fears of the dark ages which gripped the minds of men have been dispelled.

The entire world is made up of only two things, energy and matter. In elementary physics we learn that neither matter nor energy (the only two realities known to man) can be created or destroyed. Both matter and energy can be transformed, but neither can be destroyed.

Life is energy, if it is anything. If neither energy nor matter can be destroyed, of course life cannot be destroyed. Life, like other forms of energy, may be passed through various processes of transition, or change, but it cannot be destroyed. Death is mere transition.

If death is not mere change or transition, then nothing comes after death except a long, eternal, peaceful sleep, and sleep is nothing to be feared. Thus you may wipe out forever the fear of death.

Three Symptoms that Show Fear of Death

1. *Thinking about dying:* This habit is more prevalent among the aged, but even the more youthful often think of dying instead of making the most of life. Often this is due to a lack of purpose or inability to find—perhaps because of a lack of purpose—a suitable occupation. The greatest remedy for a fear of death is a burning desire for achievement, backed

by useful service to others. A busy person does not
think about dying.

2. *Association with fear of poverty:* One may fear the
    onset of poverty in one's own life; or one may fear
    that one's death will inflict poverty upon one's loved
    ones.

3. *Association with illness or imbalance:* Physical ill-
    ness may lead to mental depression. Disappointment
    in love, religious fanaticism, a high state of neurosis
    or actual insanity are other causes of the death fear.

Worry Is Fear

Worry is a state of mind based upon fear. It works slowly
but persistently. It is insidious and subtle. Step by step it "digs
itself in" until it paralyzes one's reasoning faculty, destroys
self-confidence and initiative. Worry is a form of sustained
fear caused by indecision: therefore it is a state of mind which
can be controlled.

An unsettled mind is helpless. Indecision makes an unsettled
mind. Most individuals lack the will power to reach decisions
promptly and to stand by them after they have been made.

We do not worry over conditions once we have reached a
decision to follow a definite line of action. I once interviewed
a man who was to be electrocuted two hours later. The condemned man was the calmest of some eight men who were in
the death cell with him. His calmness prompted me to ask him
how it felt to know that he was going into eternity in a short
while. With a smile of confidence on his face, he said, "It feels
fine. Just think, brother, my troubles will soon be over. I have
had nothing but trouble all my life. It has been a hardship to
get food and clothing. Soon I will not need these things. I
have felt fine ever since I learned for certain that I must die.

I made up my mind then, to accept my fate in good spirit."

As he spoke he devoured a dinner of proportions sufficient for three men, eating every mouthful of the food brought to him, and apparently enjoying it as much as if no disaster awaited him. Decision gave this man resignation to his fate! Decision can also prevent one's acceptance of undesired circumstances.

The six basic fears become translated into a state of worry through indecision. Relieve yourself forever of the fear of death by reaching a decision to accept death as an inescapable event. Whip the fear of poverty by reaching a decision to get along with whatever wealth you can accumulate without worry. Put your foot upon the neck of the fear of criticism by reaching a decision *not to worry* about what other people think, do, or say. Eliminate the fear of old age by reaching a decision to accept it, not as a handicap, but as a great blessing which carries with it wisdom, self-control, and understanding not known to youth. Acquit yourself of the fear of ill health by the decision to forget symptoms. Master the fear of loss of love by reaching a decision to get along without love, if that is necessary.

Kill the habit of worry, in all its forms, by reaching a general, blanket decision that nothing which life has to offer is worth the price of worry. With this decision will come poise, peace of mind, and calmness of thought which will bring happiness.

A man whose mind is filled with fear not only destroys his own chances of intelligent action, but he transmits these destructive vibrations to the minds of all who come into contact with him and also destroys their chances.

Even a dog or a horse knows when its master lacks courage; moreover, a dog or a horse will pick up the vibrations of fear thrown off by its master, and behave accordingly. Lower

down the line of intelligence in the animal kingdom one finds
this same capacity to pick up the vibrations of fear.

Thought that Destroys

The vibrations of fear pass from one mind to another just
as quickly and as surely as the sound of the human voice
passes from the broadcasting station to the receiving set of
a radio.

The person who gives expression by word of mouth to negative or destructive thoughts is practically certain to experience
the results of those words in the form of a destructive "kick-
back." The release of destructive thought impulses alone, without the aid of words, also produces a "kick-back" in more ways
than one. First of all, and perhaps most important to be remembered, the person who releases thoughts of a destructive
nature must suffer damage through the breaking down of the
faculty of creative imagination. Secondly, the presence in the
mind of any destructive emotion develops a negative personality which repels people, and often converts them into
antagonists. The third source of damage to the person who
entertains or releases negative thoughts lies in this significant
fact—these thought impulses are not only damaging to others,
but they imbed themselves in the subconscious mind of the
person releasing them, and there become a part of his character.

Your business in life is, presumably, to achieve success. To
be successful, you must find peace of mind, acquire the material needs of life, and above all, attain happiness. All of these
evidences of success begin in the form of thought impulses.

You may control your own mind, you have the power to
feed it whatever thought impulses you choose. With this privilege goes also the responsibility of using it constructively. You

are the master of your own earthly destiny just as surely as you have the power to control your own thoughts. You may influence, direct, and eventually control your own environment, making your life what you want it to be—or you may neglect to exercise the privilege which is yours, to make your life to order, thus casting yourself upon the broad sea of "circumstance," where you will be tossed hither and yon, like a chip on the waves of the ocean.

Are You Too Susceptible?

In addition to the Six Basic Fears, there is another evil by which people suffer. It constitutes a rich soil in which the seeds of failure grow abundantly. It is so subtle that its presence often is not detected. This affliction cannot properly be classed as a fear. It is more deeply seated and more often fatal than all of the six fears. For want of a better name, let us call his evil *susceptibility to negative influences*.

Men who accumulate great riches always protect themselves against this evil! The poverty-stricken never do! Those who succeed in any calling must prepare their minds to resist the evil. If you are reading this philosophy for the purpose of accumulating riches, you should examine yourself very carefully to determine whether you are susceptible to negative influences. If you neglect this self-analysis, you will forfeit your right to attain the object of your desires.

Make the analysis searching. After you read the questions prepared for this self-analysis, hold yourself to a strict accounting in your answers. Go at the task as carefully as you would search for any other enemy you knew to be awaiting you in ambush and deal with your own faults as you would with a more tangible enemy.

You can easily protect yourself against highway robbers,

because the law provides organized cooperation for your benefit but this "seventh basic evil" is more difficult to master because it strikes when you are not aware of its presence, when you are asleep and while you are awake. Moreover its weapon is intangible, because it consists of merely a state of mind. This evil is also dangerous because it strikes in as many different forms as there are human experiences. Sometimes it enters the mind through the well-meant words of one's own relatives. At other times it bores from within, through one's own mental attitude. Always it is as deadly as poison, even though it may not kill as quickly.

Protect Yourself!

To protect yourself against negative influences, whether of your own making or the result of the activities of negative people around you, recognize that you have a will power, and put it into constant use until it builds a wall of immunity against influences in your own mind.

Recognize the fact that you and every other human being are, by nature, lazy, indifferent, and susceptible to all suggestions which harmonize with your weaknesses.

Recognize that you are by nature susceptible to all the six basic fears, and set up habits for the purpose of counteracting all these fears.

Recognize that negative influences often work on you through your subconscious mind, therefore they are difficult to detect, and keep your mind closed against all people who depress or discourage you in any way.

Clean out your medicine chest, throw away all pill bottles, and stop pandering to colds, aches, pains and imaginary illness.

Deliberately seek the company of people who influence you to think and act for yourself.

Do not expect troubles as they have a tendency not to disappoint.

Without doubt, the most common weakness of all human beings is the habit of leaving their minds open to the negative influence of other people. This weakness is all the more damaging, because most people do not recognize that they are cursed by it, and many who acknowledge it, neglect or refuse to correct the evil until it becomes an uncontrollable part of their daily habits.

To aid those who wish to see themselves as they really are, the following list of questions has been prepared. Read the questions and state your answers aloud, so you can hear your own voice. This will make it easier for you to be truthful with yourself.

Think Before You Answer

Do you complain often of "feeling bad," and if so, what is the cause?

Do you find fault with other people at the slightest provocation?

Do you frequently make mistakes in your work, and if so, why?

Are you sarcastic and offensive in your conversation?

Do you deliberately avoid the association of anyone, and if so, why?

Do you suffer frequently with indigestion? If so, what is the cause?

Does life seem futile and the future hopeless to you?

Do you like your occupation? If not, why?

Do you often feel self-pity, and if so, why?

Are you envious of those who excel you?

To which do you devote most time, thinking of success, or of failure?

Are you gaining or losing self-confidence as you grow older?

Do you learn something of value from all mistakes?

Are you permitting some relative or acquaintance to worry you? If so, why?

Are you sometimes "in the clouds" and at other times in the depths of despondency?

Who has the most inspiring influence upon you? What is the cause?

Do you tolerate negative or discouraging influences which you can avoid?

Are you careless of your personal appearance? If so, when and why?

Have you learned how to "drown your troubles" by being too busy to be annoyed by them?

Would you call yourself a "spineless weakling" if you permitted others to do your thinking for you?

How many preventable disturbances annoy you, and why do you tolerate them?

Do you resort to liquor, narcotics, or cigarettes to "quiet your nerves?" If so, why do you not try will power instead?

Does anyone "nag" you, and if so, for what reason?

Do you have a definite major purpose, and if so, what is it, and what plan have you for achieving it?

Do you suffer from any of the six basic fears? If so, which ones?

Have you a method by which you can shield yourself against the negative influence of others?

Do you make deliberate use of autosuggestion to make your mind positive?

Which do you value most, your material possessions, or your privilege of controlling your own thoughts?

Are you easily influenced by others against your own judgment?

Has today added anything of value to your stock of knowledge or state of mind?

Do you face squarely the circumstances which make you unhappy, or side-step the responsibility?

Do you analyze all mistakes and failures and try to profit by them or, do you take the attitude that this is not your duty?

Can you name three of your most damaging weaknesses? What are you doing to correct them?

Do you encourage other people to bring their worries to you for sympathy?

Do you choose, from your daily experiences, lessons or influences which aid in your personal advancement?

Does your presence have a negative influence on other people as a rule?

What habits of other people annoy you most?

Do you form your own opinions or permit yourself to be influenced by other people?

Have you learned how to create a mental state of mind with which you can shield yourself against all discouraging influences?

Does your occupation inspire you with faith and hope?

Are you conscious of possessing spiritual forces of sufficient power to enable you to keep your mind free from all forms of fear?

Does your religion help to keep your mind positive?

Do you feel it your duty to share other people's worries? If so, why?

If you believe that "birds of a feather flock together," what have you learned about yourself by studying the friends whom you attract?

What connection, if any, do you see between the people with whom you associate most closely, and any unhappiness you may experience?

Could it be possible that some person whom you consider to be a friend is, in reality, your worst enemy, because of his negative influence on your mind?

By what rules do you judge who is helpful and who is damaging to you?

Are your intimate associates mentally superior or inferior to you?

How much time out of every twenty-four hours do you devote to:

    a.   your occupation
    b.   sleep
    c.   play and relaxation
    d.   acquiring useful knowledge
    e.   plain waste?

Who among your acquaintances:

    a.   encourages you most
    b.   cautions you most
    c.   discourages you most?

What is your greatest worry? Why do you tolerate it?

When others offer you free, unsolicited advice, do you accept it without question or analyze their motive?

What, above all else, do you most desire? Do you intend to acquire it? Are you willing to subordinate all other desires for this one? How much time daily do you devote to acquiring it?

Do you change your mind often? If so, why?

Do you usually finish everything you begin?

Are you easily impressed by other people's business or professional titles, college degrees, or wealth?

Are you easily influenced by what other people think or say of you?

Do you cater to people because of their social or financial status?

Whom do you believe to be the greatest person living? In what respect is this person superior to yourself?

How much time have you devoted to studying and answering these questions? (At least one day is necessary for the analysis and the answering of the entire list.)

If you have answered all these questions truthfully, you know more about yourself than the majority of people. Study the questions carefully, come back to them once each week for several months, and be astounded at the amount of additional knowledge of great value to yourself you will have gained by the simple method of answering the questions truthfully. If you are not certain concerning the answers to some of the questions, seek the counsel of those who know you well, especially those who have no motive in flattering you, and see yourself through their eyes. The experience will be astonishing.

The Difference Mind Control Makes

You have absolute control over but one thing, and that is your thoughts. This is the most significant and inspiring of all facts known to man! It reflects man's divine nature. This divine prerogative is the sole means by which you may control your own destiny. If you fail to control your own mind, you may be sure you will control nothing else. If you must be careless with your possessions, let it be in connection with material things. *Your mind is your spiritual estate!* Protect and use it with the care to which divine royalty is entitled. You were given a will power for this purpose.

Unfortunately, there is no legal protection against those who, either by design or ignorance, poison the minds of others by negative suggestion. This form of destruction should be punishable by heavy legal penalties, because it may and often does destroy one's chances of acquiring material things which are protected by law.

Men with negative minds tried to convince Thomas A. Edison that he could not build a machine that would record and reproduce the human voice, "because," they said, "no one else had ever produced such a machine." Edison did not believe them. He knew that the mind could produce anything the mind could conceive and believe, and that knowledge was the thing that lifted the great Edison above the common herd.

Men with negative minds told F. W. Woolworth he would go broke trying to run a store on five- and ten-cent sales. He did not believe them. He knew that he could do anything within reason if he backed his plans with faith. Exercising his right to keep other men's negative suggestions out of his mind, he piled up a fortune of more than a hundred million dollars.

Doubting Thomases scoffed scornfully when Henry Ford tried out his first crudely built automobile on the streets of Detroit. Some said the thing never would become practical. Others said no one would pay money for such a contraption. Ford said, "I'll belt the earth with dependable motor cars," and he did! For the benefit of those seeking vast riches, let it be remembered that practically the sole difference between Henry Ford and a majority of workers is this—Ford had a mind and controlled it. The others have minds which they do not try to control.

Mind control is the result of self-discipline and habit. You either control your mind or it controls you. There is no halfway compromise. The most practical of all methods for controlling the mind is the habit of keeping it busy with a definite purpose backed by a definite plan. Study the record of any man who achieves noteworthy success, and you will observe that he has control over his own mind, moreover, that he exercises that control and directs it toward the attainment of definite objectives. Without this control, success is not possible.

Do You Use These Alibis?

People who do not succeed have one distinguishing trait in common. They know *all the reasons for failure* and have what they believe to be air-tight alibis to explain away their own lack of achievement.

Some of these alibis are clever, and a few of them are justifiable by the facts. But alibis cannot be used for money. The world wants to know only one thing—have you achieved success?

A character analyst compiled a list of the most commonly used alibis. As you read the list, examine yourself carefully, and determine how many of these alibis, if any, are your own property. Remember too that the philosophy presented in this book makes every one of these alibis obsolete.

IF I didn't have a wife and family . . .
IF I had enough "pull" . . .
IF I had money . . .
IF I had a good education . . .
IF I could get a job . . .
IF I had good health . . .
IF I only had time . . .
IF times were better . . .
IF other people understood me . . .

IF conditions around me were only different . . .

IF I could live my life over again . . .

IF I did not fear what "they" would say . . .

IF I had been given a chance . . .

IF I now had a chance . . .

IF other people didn't "have it in for me" . . .

IF nothing happens to stop me . . .

IF I were only younger . . .

IF I could only do what I want . . .

IF I had been born rich . . .

IF I could meet "the right people" . . .

IF I had the talent that some people have . . .

IF I dared assert myself . . .

IF I only had embraced past opportunities . . .

IF people didn't get on my nerves . . .

IF I didn't have to keep house and look after the children . . .

IF I could save some money . . .

IF the boss only appreciated me . . .

IF I only had somebody to help me . . .

IF my family understood me . . .

IF I lived in a big city . . .

IF I could just get started . . .

IF I were only free . . .

IF I had the personality of some people . . .

IF I were not so fat . . .

IF my talents were known . . .

IF I could just get a "break" . . .

IF I could only get out of debt . . .

IF I hadn't failed . . .

IF I only knew how . . .

IF everybody didn't oppose me . . .

IF I didn't have so many worries . . .

IF I could marry the right person . . .

IF people weren't so dumb . . .

IF my family were not so extravagant . . .

IF I were sure of myself . . .

IF luck were not against me . . .

IF I had not been born under the wrong star . . .

IF it were not true that "what is to be will be" . . .

IF I did not have to work so hard . . .

IF I hadn't lost my money . . .

IF I lived in a different neighborhood . . .

IF I didn't have a "past" . . .

IF I only had a business of my own . . .

IF other people would only listen to me . . .

IF * * * and this is the greatest of them all . . . *if* I had the courage to see myself as I really am, I would *find out what is wrong with me, and correct it.* Then I might have a chance to profit by my mistakes and learn something from the experience of others, for I know that there is something wrong with me, or I would now be where I would have been if I had spent more time analyzing my weaknesses, and less time building alibis to cover them.

The Habit Fatal to Success

Building alibis with which to explain away failure is a national pastime. The habit is as old as the human race, and is *fatal to success!* Why do people cling to their pet alibis? The answer is obvious. They defend their alibis because they create them! A man's alibi is the child of his own imagination. It is human nature to defend one's own brainchild.

Building alibis is a deeply rooted habit. Habits are difficult to break, especially when they provide justification for something we do. Plato had this truth in mind when he said, "The first and best victory is to conquer self. To be conquered by self is, of all things, the most shameful and vile."

Another philosopher had the same thought in mind when he said, "It was a great surprise to me when I discovered that most of the ugliness I saw in others, was but a reflection of my own nature."

"It has always been a mystery to me," said Elbert Hubbard, "why people spend so much time deliberately fooling themselves by creating alibis to cover their weaknesses. If used differently, this same time would be sufficient to cure the weakness, then no alibis would be needed."

In parting, I would remind you that "Life is a checkerboard, and the player opposite you is time. If you hesitate before moving or neglect to move promptly, your men will be wiped off the board by time. You are playing against a partner who will not tolerate indecision!"

Previously you may have had a logical excuse for not having forced life to come through with whatever you asked, but that alibi is now obsolete, because you are in possession of the master key that unlocks the door to life's bountiful riches.

The Master Key is intangible, but it is powerful! It is the privilege of creating, *in your own mind,* a burning desire for a definite form of riches. There is no penalty for the use of the key, but there is a price you must pay if you do not use it. The price is failure. There is a reward of stupendous proportions if you put the key to use. It is the satisfaction that comes to all who *conquer self and force life to pay whatever is asked.*

The reward is worthy of your effort. Will you make the start and be convinced?

"If we are related," said the immortal Emerson, "we shall meet." In closing, may I borrow his thought, and say, "If we are related, we have, through these pages, met."

POINTS TO PIN DOWN:

Fears are common and some of them are justified. But others can take root and grow without your knowing it—unless you get rid of the indecision and doubt which sow the seeds of fear.

The alibis you use tell a great deal about you. No more alibis need hold you back as you THINK AND GROW RICH.

You gather riches in money and you gather riches which cannot be measured in money—although your money helps you find happiness, long life, enjoyment, peace of mind.

The most valuable treasure of all—good health—can be yours when you conquer fear and get rid of all the illness it can bring. The mightiest treasures of life are waiting for you to reach out and take them!

A fearless man thrives on far horizons.

THINK
AND
GROW RICH
ACTION MANUAL

WELCOME!—TO A GREAT NEW WORLD OF ACHIEVEMENT, wealth and happiness! You are going into action—action that makes big money—action that leads from success to success, onward and upward to the golden goal of your dearest dreams!

First of all, you are going to read *THINK AND GROW RICH,* one of the best-selling books of all time. You are going to see why more than seven million men and women have read this amazing, inspiring book. You are going to discover why W. Clement Stone, President of Combined Insurance Company of America, has this to say about THINK AND GROW RICH: "More men and women have been motivated to achieve success because of reading THINK AND GROW RICH than by any other book written by a living author." And you will see why letters have poured in from all over the world to thank and bless its author, Dr. Napoleon Hill, for revealing a method that can pour riches into any life as though from a bottomless treasure chest.

Or, if you already have read *THINK AND GROW RICH,* you are going to reread this great book with a new technique that displays riches you did not see before!

Also, while you explore Napoleon Hill's straightforward method for getting rich by applying the powers of your mind, you will be making this method *personally* yours. You see, the book itself—*THINK AND GROW RICH*—is a sure guide to great riches for *any* man who believes in his own ability. But the *ACTION MANUAL* you now hold in your hand makes the book into a *personal* guide for *you.* Every step of the way, this *ACTION*

MANUAL keys Napoleon Hill's great method to YOUR hopes, YOUR dreams, YOUR fortune, YOUR far-reaching ambitions.

The *ACTION MANUAL* is keyed page by page to *THINK AND GROW RICH*.

Some Reminders Before We Begin

Your success is based on your *motivation for success.*

All the reading in the world will not make you successful unless you *want* success and *think* success. Above all, it is necessary to *think.* No one else can think about *your* success as well as you can. *No one else can think for YOU!*

Specifically, you must question, consider and reflect on what you read . . . you must make inferences and use your judgment . . . you must use your imagination and your visualizing power, and see *yourself* when you are reading about great success that came to another man.

You, and only you, must conceive ideas and make plans as you read and think . . . must seek the means to win specific ends . . . and never forget that the improbable is always possible, and more and more possible as you wish to make it so!

Also remember: you don't act on the basis of reason alone . . . you have feelings, emotions, instincts, habits and other personal forces that you take in hand, direct and control with mighty power when all your motivations are working *for* you and never against you.

As Napoleon Hill says: "Riches begin with a state of mind." Are you ready for riches? Then we are ready to begin. Your steady progress toward a richer life, a happier life, a far more successful life begins right now.

First of all, equip yourself for this grand adventure into your own mind and this grand unfolding of your own mighty hidden success forces. In addition to the book itself, *THINK AND GROW RICH*, and this *ACTION MANUAL*, be sure you always have a pen or pencil ready at hand, and a package of 3 x 5 file cards.

Make sure you have a quiet spot where you can sit alone with *THINK AND GROW RICH* and this *ACTION MANUAL at the same time every day*. Half an hour a day will do it. Four or five days a week will suffice—but make it the same time every day. Let your family know this is your time for applying yourself to building the sturdy foundations of your success—for your own sake and for theirs. And do not merely tell them; show them you mean it as well. Everyone who shares your life must realize that you take this matter seriously, that you aren't "kidding around" in your drive toward success.

Each day, before you begin work on a new success principle, take a few minutes to review and inspect the points you have already covered to make sure you have completely absorbed and understood what has gone before. In other words, you must not only *expect* to make progress toward achieving desired results, you must also *inspect* to make sure you are on the right road to that achievement.

As W. Clement Stone has said, using this method you can " . . . work yourself into a white heat of desire for the achievement of the goals that will help you attain wealth and the true riches of life." When this happens to you, then, quickly and surely, watch your desires and dreams turn into solid reality.

Your First ACTION

You want to give yourself a kind of mental road map—a preview of where you are going and a firm indication of the "landmarks" on your journey.

Turn to the *THINK AND GROW RICH* Table of Contents, beginning on page 1. (All page numbers and similar references are keyed to the INSTANT-AID edition.)

Pick up your pen or pencil, and go through the entire Table of Contents. Underline any word or phrase that seems to touch you "where you live." This not only helps to set a "mental road map" of the book in your mind, but also it begins to give you priceless insight into *yourself*. No two men will be equally attracted or challenged by the same words or phrases.

Here is how one man underlined the first section of the Contents —*Thoughts Are Things*:

> *Edison Looked into His Face* . . . *Opportunity Came by the Back Door* . . . *The Man Who Quit Too Soon* . . . *Success with One Step Beyond Defeat* . . . *The Child Who Mastered a Man* . . . *The "Yes" Behind the "No"* . . . *With One Sound Idea You Achieve Success* . . . *"I Want It and I'll Have It"* . . . *A Poet Saw the Truth* . . . *A Young Man Sees His Destiny*

Here is how another man underlined his own choice in the same section.

Edison Looked into His Face . . . Opportunity Came by the Back Door . . . The Man Who Quit Too Soon . . . Success with One Step Beyond Defeat . . . The Child Who Mastered a Man . . . The "Yes" Behind the "No" . . . With One Sound Idea You Achieve Success . . . "I Want It and I'll Have It" . . . A Poet Saw the Truth . . . A Young Man Sees His Destiny

After you have done this, go through the book, just flipping pages. Read the chapter titles and the subheads (in bold-face type). If you feel impelled to check or underline any chapter title or any subhead, do so without hesitation. Many of us have been brought up with the idea that one should not make marks in books—but this is no ordinary book! It is strongly and personally *yours* to keep as a lifelong guide, and the more marks you make in it, the more notes you make in the margins, the more powerfully will it do its great work for you.

Your Second ACTION

Read "A Word from the Publisher" on page 6 and the Preface on page 9. Keep your pen in your hand and keep on underlining and checking.

Now Pause and Think

Already you know a good deal about *THINK AND GROW RICH*. You know why its title fits it so well. You understand that *THINK AND GROW RICH* is based on one great idea—a secret that will seem to jump from the pages and stand boldly before you when you are ready for it.

You saw clearly that Napoleon Hill presents 13 steps toward riches and that every one of these steps is connected with every other . . . *just as every part of a man's life is connected with every other part.*

And you realize that the cost of *THINK AND GROW RICH* and this *ACTION MANUAL* together may be a thousandth or a ten-thousandth part of the extra riches they can bring you within the space of one year!

Your Third ACTION

Read *THINK AND GROW RICH*. This, however, will be a very special kind of reading.

Chapter by chapter, this *ACTION MANUAL* is to be your guide. It will give you tested directions—directions that have proved over and over they bring *results*.

Chapter by chapter, then, read according to the directions in this *ACTION MANUAL*. And take specific action, here and there, according to the directions in the *ACTION MANUAL*.

Underline

All through the book, underline (or check) any words or sentences or passages that are especially significant to you.

Many men add extra slips of paper to the book, taped or stapled in at the pages where they apply. Thus you are able to add your own extended comments, your own stories that prove a point, anything that YOU know is useful to YOU.

At the same time, you will be making notes in the *ACTION MANUAL* itself. Space has been left at the back of the Manual for your notes, and you will find suggestions as to the kind of personalized (and confidential) notes to make.

Now you are ready to dig in. Take as much time as necessary. Think as you read. Read as you think.

Read **Thoughts Are Things,** beginning on page 16 in **THINK AND GROW RICH.**

READ THE CHAPTER UP THROUGH THE TWO PARAGRAPHS AT THE top of page 31, but do not read "Points to Pin Down" on that page—we'll come back to it. Underline, check, annotate as you read, and add extra sheets of notes if you wish. Don't "let the book do all the talking." You can and should set down, right in the book, what *you* think, how *you* react to this material.

As you read, you notice the several subheads you underlined before, in your pre-reading. Now, as you see these subheads a second time around, you may change your mind about the ones you wish to emphasize. Change your mind if you wish. It is really your *point of view* that is changing. You may want to use a red pencil for the second-time-around underlining. And you are now also underlining within the text itself—any word, any phrase, any section that hits home to YOU.

Now you know that "thoughts are things" in that they are inseparably connected with definite, constructive action; and thought must precede action. You saw how the thought of success—success in a very special area that appealed to him—took hold of Edwin C. Barnes, so that even his lack of money and his tramplike appearance did not stop him. You saw how the opposite kind of thought—a thought of failure—made a man named Darby lose untold riches in solid gold. And again, you now understand and appreciate that great little story about the child who conquered a man and got her fifty cents. You are beginning to understand what it really means to concentrate on a single goal.

You stopped reading partway down page 31. Good. Before you read the rest of page 31—right now—use one of the note pages in this manual and write a short summary of the main points in the chapter. Don't try to outguess the book's author. Write what YOU consider to be the main points in this chapter, but be brief; do it in a hundred words or so. Do it neatly, and label it plainly: *My Points to Pin Down—See Page 31.*

Bear in mind that there is no *right* and no *wrong* to be considered when you underline parts of *THINK AND GROW RICH,* when you add your own notes, or when you write your own Points to Pin Down. For example, one man wrote in regard to the Darby story: *Mining is a risky venture.* Another wrote: *When you need expert advice, get it, so that any decision you make can be based on expert knowledge.* Both are right. To compare the different points of view, however, is very interesting. To compare your own interpretation with these other interpretations of the Darby story (if you included it as a main point) also should be very interesting.

When you have finished your own Points to Pin Down, and only then, read Dr. Hill's Points on page 31. Notice where you agreed with him and where you disagreed. Notice what you put in that he left out, and vice versa. If you disagreed flatly with any statement, think about it. Do not consider that you are wrong, but think about it.

Now set aside your own Points to Pin Down and take up Dr. Hill's Points. Basing yourself on those points, go through a very interesting and rewarding procedure: turn each point into a question addressed to yourself.

In order to do this, make full use of those ancient servants of the inquiring mind, the question-words WHO, WHAT, WHEN, WHERE, WHY, and HOW. For example, you could ask yourself:

WHEN and WHERE did *I* overcome a great obstacle because I had a burning desire to reach a goal?

HOW did it turn out? WHAT was the eventual outcome?

Or—

WHO has benefited from my ability to transmit my faith to others?

These may not be the right questions for you. Find your own. As you search for questions to ask, questions keyed to specific points of success, *you search within yourself* and stir up old memories of success, reward, coordinated effort.

Most of us win more victories in our lives than we generally remember. That is because the victories are often scattered, and they may have no long-term effects to help us remember them. But when you search back in your life, you begin to stir up all kinds of success-memories. You realize there have been many times when you exerted power over yourself, over your career, over events, over the minds and hearts of other people. Well, sir, you are still the same person! You are now proceeding to *focus* the forces that make men rich.

Now take special notice of Napoleon Hill's key thought: *When you begin to think and grow rich, you will observe that riches themselves begin with the feeling that barriers have been swept aside, the **inward** surety that you are ON YOUR WAY toward being rich.*

When you are ready to go back to the book. . . .

Read **Step 1 Toward Riches: Desire,** page 32.

READ THROUGH THE TOP LINES OF PAGE 49, BUT DO NOT READ THE Points to Pin Down section for the time being. Underline as you read, and make copious notes in the margins or separate sheets you attach to the book.

Again, as you read, you will notice the subheads you underlined in your pre-reading, and you may change some of the points you now wish to emphasize.

You have read that Edwin C. Barnes gave himself no way to retreat, so he had to go forward. You have read six steps that turn desires into gold, and you have read of many men who put *desire* behind their dreams and made those dreams magnificently come true. You realize that many who succeed get off to a bad start, but they keep going.

You have read a twelve-line poem that it will pay you to read again, and yet again, and think about. And you have read the story of Napoleon Hill's son, who "could not hear," until desire and persistence broke through the barrier.

Now, without looking back at the book, take this little test on Dr. Hill's famous Six Steps That Turn Desire into Gold. The test requires you to fill in the missing letters so that you complete the missing word or words. Fill it in right here:

SIX STEPS THAT TURN DESIRE INTO GOLD

1. Fix in your mind the e --- t a ---- t of money you desire.
2. Determine exactly what you intend to g --- in return for the m ---- you desire.
3. Establish a definite d --- by which you intend to possess that amount of m ----.
4. Create a definite p --- for carrying out your desire, and begin a - o ---.
5. Write out a st ------ t of the amount of m ---- you intend to acquire, name the t --- l ----, state what you intend to g --- in return for the money, and describe clearly the p --- through which you intend to accumulate the m ----.
6. Read your written statement aloud t --- e d --- y, once just before retiring at night, and once after arising in the morning. As you read, s -- and f --- yourself already in possession of the m ----.

The sixth point brings up a question: What should you do when you are given instructions in the book itself, in *THINK AND GROW RICH* rather than in the *ACTION MANUAL*?

In such a case, follow Dr. Hill's instructions *unless the ACTION MANUAL says otherwise*. So, by all means, follow the instructions given at step 6, page 36 in *THINK AND GROW RICH*. *The instructions given at step 6, page 36, lead you to perform one of the most important actions of your life.*

Here again is the poem you read on page 41.

> I bargained with Life for a penny,
> And Life would pay no more,
> However I begged at evening
> When I counted my scanty store.

For Life is a just employer,
  He gives you what you ask,
But once you have set the wages,
  Why, you must bear the task.

I worked for a menial's hire,
  Only to learn, dismayed,
That any wage I had asked of Life,
  Life would have willingly paid.

The next step is to prepare your own Points to Pin Down for this chapter, as you did for the chapter before. Be brief. See how much "meat" you can crowd into a few words. It is good practice! Remember, do not attempt to choose important points as you believe Dr. Hill would choose them. Choose points that are important to YOU. Say them in your own words. Write your Points to Pin Down on the note pages.

When you are finished with your own Points, read Dr. Hill's Points for the same chapter on page 49. Consider, as you did before, where you agreed, where you disagreed, what you left out as compared with what Dr. Hill put in. *Think* about this.

Then take those useful words that lead you into questions, WHO, WHY, WHAT, WHEN, WHERE, and HOW. Transform the points on page 49 into questions you ask of yourself; questions that you will try your darndest to answer. You will notice some overlap with points made in the previous chapter; this is purposely done to reinforce your knowledge and to help you search all the more strongly and confidently within the maze of memories and abilities and submerged talents that is YOU.

Make at least two questions bear on the Six Steps. Make at least one question bear on the twelve-line poem that has stirred many a man to set a high price upon his services, deliver what he promises and live joyously, handsomely.

"Tune yourself in" to that poem. Many times in your life, however briefly, you have acted as though you expected life to treat you like a prince. Remember those times. Know that was YOU and this still is the same YOU. The feeling will return, and with it, first in flashes, then in periods of hours, then continuing through weeks and years, will return the *confidence* that goes with the feeling.

Take special notice of this key thought: *Nobody is ready to receive wealth until he BELIEVES he can acquire it and he IS acquiring it. The state of mind must be BELIEF, not mere hope or wishful thinking.*

When you have done justice to this chapter, when you know you have its mighty lesson well in hand, go back to the book. . . .

Read **Step 2 Toward Riches: Faith,** page 50.

READ AT YOUR OWN PACE, READ WITH ATTENTION, READ WITH A pencil in your hand to the end of page 70. Do not yet read "Points to Pin Down" on page 71. Underline words, phrases. Bracket whole paragraphs boldly when you feel they are talking to YOU. Change any emphasis you applied in your pre-reading, if you take a different viewpoint now.

You have read about faith, the head chemist of the mind that blends your thoughts with a powerful spiritual catalyst that gives them many times their former power. Faith merely waits for you to find it; it is not a gift that is available only to a fortunate few. A method of giving orders to your subconscious mind, which you will learn soon, is a tested way to develop faith, and a way to use faith to translate your thoughts into their physical counterparts.

To transform thoughts of wealth into solid wealth—to transform thoughts of a fully rewarding life into the actual thrill of living that life—cast aside any belief in luck. Do not believe in "good" luck— it is only the manifestation of rewards well earned. Do not believe in "bad" luck—it is poverty and failure attracted by negative belief, attracted often because the subconscious mind really wants it.

In this chapter you went on to discover the magnetic force of the emotions; how they attract similar or related thoughts (of vast aid in making plans and forming campaigns of action). You read five steps to self-confidence, and I am sure you noted how the fourth step reminds you again of the importance of *writing* your description of *your definite chief aim in life.*

Now head a Note Page: *Five Steps to Self-confidence, told in my own words.* Go through Dr. Hill's five steps, beginning on page 56 in *THINK AND GROW RICH.* Write each point in your own words. Write for yourself; nobody else ever has to see this *ACTION MANUAL*—nor your own personalized, annotated copy of *THINK AND GROW RICH.*

This chapter contains another short poem you should have in your *ACTION MANUAL.* Here it is:

If you *think* you are beaten, you are.
If you *think* you dare not, you don't.
If you like to win, but you *think* you can't,
It is almost certain you won't.

If you *think* you'll lose, you're lost,
For out of the world we find,
Success begins with a fellow's will—
It's all in the *state of mind*.

If you *think* you are outclassed, you are,
You've got to *think* high to rise,
You've got to *be sure of yourself* before
You can ever win a prize.

Life's battles don't always go
To the stronger or faster man,
But soon or late the man who wins
Is the man WHO THINKS HE CAN!

Also in this chapter you read the great story of Abraham Lincoln, who was "a failure at everything he tried," yet gloriously succeeded. Yes, in this book about *riches,* you read about the power of *love* . . . and I hope you realized there is a strong connection. And finally there was the story of Charles M. Schwab, and the far-reaching results of an after-dinner speech, to show you that a man's riches begin *inside the man.*

Now write your own Points to Pin Down for this chapter. You need not choose any points from the Charles Schwab story. Take time to be brief!

When you have written your own Points, compare them to Dr. Hill's on page 71.

Compare. Think.

Use WHO, WHY, WHEN, WHERE, WHAT and HOW to turn Dr. Hill's Points into questions. Pin at least two pointed, personal questions on the Five Steps to Self-confidence. Self-confidence with WHOM, self-confidence WHY, self-confidence WHERE and WHEN and HOW.

Take note of this key statement: *Whatever one repeats to one's self, whether it be true or false, is what you come to believe and what you come to be.* Also remember it in Ralph Waldo Emerson's words: *A man is what he thinks of all day.*

When you understand Step 2 Toward Riches, go back to the book. . . .

Read **Step 3 Toward Riches: Autosuggestion,** page 72.

READ THIS CHAPTER THROUGH TO THE END OF PAGE 80, AND SAVE "Points to Pin Down," on page 81, till later. You know the processes by which you stir up your own hidden powers while you make the book *yours*:

> underline
> check
> bracket
> add your own notes

Any or all of these! And change any emphasis that seems to need changing.

As you have read, the subconscious mind resembles a fertile garden. But weeds will grow in a fertile garden unless you take care to sow the seeds of more desirable crops. You sow thought-seeds through the power of autosuggestion.

The subconscious mind takes any orders given it in a spirit of absolute faith and acts upon those orders. But the orders must be made to sink in—to take root—by being repeated over and over.

Make your subconscious mind believe that you must have the amount of money you have visualized, that this money is already awaiting your claim. Soon you get rid of all self-consciousness. (Some men don't get rich because they never form the subconscious belief that money *belongs* in their pockets.) See yourself making money, rendering the service or delivering the merchandise that gets you the money.

You read the three steps of autosuggestion that help you give invincible orders to your own subconscious mind. You see how they blend with the six steps given in the second chapter. Without looking back at the three steps of autosuggestion, take this short quiz; check Yes or No for each question.

Should your written statement give you an "out,"
that is, should it say you will have the amount
of money you desire only if "all goes well" or
something of the sort?   ( )Yes ( )No

Should your written statement include a definite date by which you are going to have your money? ( )Yes ( )No

In order to obtain the money you want, will you depend on winning a lottery? ( )Yes ( )No

Will you obtain your sum of money by giving service or merchandise to your fellowmen? ( )Yes ( )No

Should you refrain from writing down your statement if you are sure you can memorize it? ( )Yes ( )No

The correct answers are, in order: No—Yes—No—Yes—No. If you had any answer wrong, read this chapter and Chapter Two once more.

Now write your own Points to Pin Down for this short but significant chapter. Then read Dr. Hill's Points on page 81, and compare yours with his. Take time to think. Take time to read back if necessary.

Ask WHAT? WHERE? WHY? WHEN? WHO? HOW? Most especially, think back on times you missed opportunities because you waited too long to get going. And—MUCH MORE IMPORTANT—think back on times when you got going without a quibble and achieved a breakthrough.

Read carefully, understand, remember this main point: *Nature has so built man that he has absolute control over the commands which reach his subconscious mind.*

When you have given this chapter its full due, go back to the book. . . .

Read Step 4   Toward Riches: Specialized Knowledge, page 82.

READ WITH A PENCIL IN YOUR HAND, ANNOTATING AND CHECKING with an eye toward what seems significant to YOU. The process should be clear by now. Also you should be aware of certain patterns in your choice of what is significant. Of course there are patterns; the pattern is part of YOU.

In this chapter you master a point that many men miss; *all knowledge is potential power* but *general* knowledge has to be organized, backed up with *specialized* knowledge and definite plans of action.

You see once and for all that school learning is only one source of education. Probably you got a chuckle out of Dr. Hill's own story of the lesson he learned when he wanted to drop a correspondence course he had begun. You have an idea of the pains that can be taken in finding the right job.

Answer Yes or No:

Will a self-made man, who has had little formal
education, always make more money than a well-
educated man?   ( )Yes ( )No

If you answered Yes, read the chapter again. The point of this chapter is not that it is better to be educated nor that it is better not to be educated. The point is that you should get the knowledge you need and use it with definite direction.

Long after a man has stopped going to school as a part of compulsory public education, he can educate himself privately and effectively. The self-discipline one receives from a definite program of specialized study makes up to some extent for the knowledge you did not appreciate when you got it without cost. You may be better off in the end because you are learning as an adult and you are learning exactly what you want to learn—as part of your written plan to make a definite amount of money in a definite way.

Read again the five sources of knowledge listed by Dr. Hill on page 86. Ask yourself how many you have used, or are using. *The blueprint given in this chapter can start you ten years ahead in any job.*

Write your own brief Points to Pin Down.

Compare your Points with Dr. Hill's, page 99. And think.

Ask yourself insistent questions based on page 99. Now you can branch out from the strictly personal question. For example, instead of asking only: *WHEN did I profit from education I gained from experience,* you may ask: *WHO among my friends has profited by education gained from experience, and HOW?* You branch out from your own life-experience and look for lessons in the lives of others.

Bear strongly in mind this key statement: *The "missing link" in education often is the failure of teachers to show students how to organize and use their knowledge.*

When you feel you are ready, go back to the book. . . .

Read **Step 5   Toward Riches: Imagination,** page 100.

WITH YOUR PENCIL IN YOUR HAND, READ THIS CHAPTER THROUGH to the middle of page 113.

Imagination, you now understand, can be synthetic or it can be creative. Both kinds work for you, each in its own way. Man's only limitation, within reason, lies in his development and use of his imagination. And through our imagination, through our thought-impulses sparked with imagination, we connect our own minds with the energy that moves the universe; we make it possible for ourselves to go right along with universal, immutable laws that are of incalculable aid in building a worthy life and a fortune.

The story of Coca-Cola—from a mixture stirred in an iron kettle to a vast world-ranging enterprise—showed you what can happen when Idea meets Desire and a man goes into action. The story of the philosopher-preacher who asked for—and got—a million dollars is further proof of the mighty power of visualization. You see in this chapter and in many other places in *THINK AND GROW RICH* that behind every "good break" lies something more; and that the mind of every man is capable of commanding that same ineluctable force; that omnipresent *something*.

When you have read this chapter—when you have emphasized parts of it that seem to *you* to stand out above the others—write your own Points to Pin Down.

Compare your Points with Dr. Hill's on page 113.

Have you any serious conflict with Dr. Hill's opinion? Always pause to think about this, and to *know* the conflict, if any—which involves knowing yourself.

Use Dr. Hill's Points to spark questions. Let your questions range widely, let them be anything that the points suggest, as long as you find an answer for each question.

Hold this thought: *All the "breaks" you need in life wait within your imagination.*

When you have absorbed all the ideas in this chapter—it's a short chapter packed with ideas—and have taken note of the important directions it gives, you are ready for the next chapter. Go back to the book. . . .

Read **Step 6 Toward Riches: Organized Planning,** page 114.

THIS IS A LONG CHAPTER. IT WAS PLANNED THAT WAY, TO NAIL down much that has been discussed so far. We will proceed somewhat differently in learning the vital lessons of this chapter on Organized Planning.

Again with a pencil in your hand, underlining and checking and annotating as you go, read to the beginning of the quiz on page 144. You glanced at this in pre-reading; do not read the quiz now, but skip it and continue to the bottom of page 154. Stop there.

The chapter began by explaining the principle of the Master-Mind alliance. This highly important principle will be dealt with again when you reach **Step 9 Toward Riches.** Meanwhile you are assured that "No individual has sufficient experience, education, native ability, and knowledge to assure the accumulation of a great fortune without the cooperation of other people."

This statement takes nothing away from the essential independence of the individual in finding his own best way toward wealth. But it does recognize that we all share the world.

Defeat? What is it? Make it a means of becoming stronger. Defeat is a signal to try again, not to give up. If your conception of defeat is that of a signal that says The End, you are not making correct use of experience. A quitter never wins. A winner never quits.

On page 119 you read the "Eleven Secrets of Leadership." Pause at this page, read each secret again, carefully. Think. Then rate yourself right here on each of those eleven vital factors that make a man a leader. Rate yourself from 1 to 5. If you rated yourself "1" on self-control, for example, that would mean you have practically no self-control. A rating of "5" would mean your self-control is just about perfect. Make each rating carefully; remember, you are building here a very personal picture of yourself and a very personal guide toward YOUR success. Remember that in future years you will be checking back on your notes and ratings again and again.

	1	2	3	4	5
UNWAVERING COURAGE					
SELF-CONTROL					
A KEEN SENSE OF JUSTICE					
DEFINITENESS OF DECISION					
DEFINITENESS OF PLANS					
THE HABIT OF DOING MORE THAN PAID FOR					
A PLEASING PERSONALITY					
SYMPATHY AND UNDERSTANDING					
MASTERY OF DETAIL					
WILLINGNESS TO ASSUME FULL RESPONSIBILITY					
COOPERATION					

You also read the remarks listed under ten categories beginning on page 121: "Why Leaders Fail." Now go through each of those items again, reading both the item (such as Inability to Organize Details) and the comments made by Dr. Hill. Then, in each case, stop and think. Ask yourself: *Does this apply to me?* Get an answer before you read the next item. Get a coldly honest answer—personal, private, confidential—drawn from your deepest being.

Then, when you have finished the list, come back to the first item again. This time, item by item, *change every negative into a positive.* Thus, inability to organize details becomes—firmly stated in your own mind—"I can and I do take the time and effort needed in order to classify and arrange duties or objects or time or whatever else needs to be organized."

Use your own words; speak for YOURSELF.

The material beginning on page 125, "Five Ways to Get a Good Job," may not apply to you. Scan it nevertheless, since a man who has qualities of leadership often helps others find jobs. For the same reason, the directions on preparing a resumé should be read with care.

The same applies to the seven steps outlined on page 131, on finding a job you like to do. You may have the job you like to do, but you always can help someone else find his own best job. Or you can see—by applying the criteria of those seven points—that someone you work with needs the advice—or someone you work *for* is making it impossible for you to make your job the right job. The right job for YOU is a vastly important factor in your life. Everyone who works, everyone who employs others should take special note of item 5: Concentrate on what you can *give*. This factor alone has been a major key to success for many a man.

Tie this in with the "QQS" formula, page 134. Note, just below it, the mention of Andrew Carnegie's insistence on working with men who worked in a spirit of harmony. Henry Ford also—among many other successful men who employed thousands of others—saw the value of harmonious personal relations. He said he would pay more for the ability to handle men than he would pay for any other ability. Charles M. Schwab was famous for his ability to command.

Beginning on page 136, you read Dr. Hill's list of Thirty-one Ways to Fail. Dr. Hill recommends: "As you go over the list, check yourself by it point by point for the purpose of discovering how many of these causes of failure stand between you and success." Do this. And do more: Take each of those headings—Unfavorable Hereditary Background, Lack of a Well-Defined Purpose in Life, and so forth—and write it where it belongs, under one of the two following headings. Make two lists. Do it here.

Applies to me   *Does not apply to me*

Applies to me	*Does not apply to me*

Do this thoughtfully. When you have finished, take each of the items you wrote under *Applies to me,* and break down that list into two smaller lists, as follows:

I can do something about it	*I cannot do anything about it*

But—before you set down any item under *I cannot do anything about it*, challenge yourself. Say: "Now, I've simply got to do something about this," and your former resignation can change in that moment to resolution. As with many another man, when you are about to write a feature of YOURSELF under *I cannot do anything about it,* the statement "sticks in your craw." And suddenly you bang your fist on the table and say, "Who says I can't!" As Dr. Hill points out, there are very, very few insurmountable obstacles. Life is filled with roads to success that bypass obstacles, rise and soar over obstacles, crash through obstacles.

Page 144 begins a list of Twenty-eight Very Personal Questions. Some of them can be answered with a Yes or a No. Number 28 takes a bit of work—but every minute you spend in answering that question rightly may be worth a thousand dollars to you. (This question was purposely made rather broad; for example, it forces you to isolate the fundamental principles of success, and you may even go through the entire volume again in order to make sure you know them.)

Answer every one of the twenty-eight questions. Jot your short answers right there in the margins. Where you may have a long answer, write it out separately and staple or tape it into the book.

Make sure you read and digest the text of this chapter as well as its lists and its questionnaire. Since in "processing" this chapter you certainly dwelt on its main points, you need not, in this case, write any Points to Pin Down. Read Dr. Hill's on page 155 and make sure you see their significance.

Hold hard to this key thought: *Money cannot move, think or talk; but it can "hear" when a man who desires it calls it to come!*

Now go back to the book. . . .

Read **Step 7 Toward Riches: Decision,** page 156.

SINCE WE ARE NOW MIDWAY THROUGH THE 13 STEPS TOWARD riches, you know the process used in finding the key points of any chapter in *THINK AND GROW RICH* and burning those points into your own mind. From now on I shall only remind you to *process* a chapter, and shall use other brief instructions you have learned how to extend.

The heart of this short chapter is the story of the Declaration of Independence. Read this story with care. It is a far more deep-reaching, psychologically significant true story than many men ever know.

Note especially, on page 167, how this story reflects at least six of the principles you master in *THINK AND GROW RICH.*

What does *Decision* mean to you? Can you recognize *decision* in yourself? Can you recognize it in others? Can you see and re-member the lessons you learn in observing others as well as your-self?

Make a list down the left-hand side of this page, of ten people you know who are *either* notably decisive *or* notably indecisive.

1.

2.

3.

4.

5.

6.

7.

8.

9.

10.

After you have made the list, go back and check each person as being either successful or unsuccessful. Apply the terms within their particularized context; that is, a successful housewife is a successful person, whereas an unsuccessful man who may handle more money in a day than she does in a year is still unsuccessful.

You will certainly see how often DECISIVE coincides with SUCCESSFUL. You can't help but find it. That is the way it is!

Now process the Points to Pin Down—your own—Dr. Hill's—questions you yourself create—as you have done before.

Bear firmly and vividly in mind this key thought: *Every powerful man has within himself his own power.*

When you are ready, go back to the book. . . .

Read **Step 8   Toward Riches: Persistence,** page 170.

PROCESS THE MAIN POINTS IN THIS CHAPTER, AS FAR AS THE TOP paragraph on page 189.

You can see that persistence and decision go hand in hand; the decision is inherently weak if the decider does not persist, follow through, even to the extent of finding out absolutely he is wrong; but even then the mind has been strong and the ways of decision remain clear and firm, to be found again.

Several times in *THINK AND GROW RICH* you come back to a consideration of *money consciousness*. Note that poverty is attracted to the one whose mind is favorable for it, as money is attracted to him whose mind has been deliberately prepared to attract it. And: *Poverty consciousness will develop without conscious application of habits favorable to it.* And remember always; you are governed by your SUBconscious; your conscious is only the effectuating agent for your subconscious "boss," but, consciously, you can send commands down to your subconscious mind till they take hold and "feed back."

The story of Fannie Hurst and the story of Kate Smith are grand lessons in persistence. On page 177, you must have noted eight major attitudes that stand behind persistence. Read them again, then come back to this page and fill in the missing words or letters in the short quiz below:

Persistence is based largely upon:

De_____s of p____se

S_f-r_____e

A____te k_____e

W___-p___r

Ha___

D____e

De_____ of ____ns

C_____on

The Persistence Inventory, which begins on page 178, should present you with nothing you have not read before. Read it carefully, again. If any point does seem new or unfamiliar, go back and re-read Chapters One, Two, Six, and Seven. Make sure you have absorbed every item in *THINK AND GROW RICH*; let the checklist help you.

Read the story of Mohammed carefully. Like the story of the Declaration of Independence, it is filled with hidden meanings. Take hold of its mystical elements and reduce them to practical terms; find parallels in your own life, if possible, although those parallels may have to do with workaday problems, the opposition of businessmen, and suchlike familiar events. Then go back and ask yourself: *Where has FAITH entered MY life?* Don't think of religion as such; think of FAITH in its overall meaning.

Then take note of the content of the third paragraph on page 186: "As one makes an impartial study of the prophets, philosophers, miracle men, and religious leaders of the past, one is drawn to the inevitable conclusion that persistence, concentration of effort, and definiteness of purpose were the major sources of their achievements."

Now write out at least five instances in which you have shown money consciousness; or, if you can find none, write out instances of money consciousness in people you know. And in doing this, hold hard to a definition of money consciousness that is rooted in *faith in one's self.*

You see, the term "money consciousness" is easily misunderstood. You are not looking for miserliness—an overwhelming consciousness of little more than hoarded money. You are not looking, either, for the kind of outlook that measures everything, every value of human existence, in terms of money. You are looking for —and, I hope, finding—money consciousness of a kind that bespeaks your inward faith in yourself as a man who can earn substantial amounts of money, who *will* earn that money, who *is earning* that money.

Take care of Points to Pin Down. Do it well. You may consider your instances of money consciousness as part of your Points.

Remember: *Weak desires bring weak results,* and *Anyone can learn persistence.*

When you have done all this well and truly, go back to the book. . . .

Read **Step 9 Toward Riches: Power of the Master Mind,** page 190.

WITH YOUR PENCIL IN HAND (AS THOUGH I HAVE TO REMIND YOU!) process this chapter through page 198.

This chapter refreshes and strengthens your knowledge as to the wonderful ways in which one mind can help another. Now you see the almost-limitless extension of this principle that has been so profitable for so many.

You see that a man in Andrew Carnegie's position had a consulting staff of about fifty. You yourself may work wonders of transformation in your own life with the aid of half a dozen friends, or even just three or four.

We have planned the *ACTION MANUAL* to include further details of using the Master-Mind principle. Here is your blueprint:

1. Begin with just two or three others whom you know well. Make sure of their harmony with you and with each other. Agree all around that the major purpose of the alliance is mutual growth in mind and in spirit.

2. Stay clear of such matters as politics, religion, and any other topic that is "touchy." You aim to aid each other with knowledge based on your collected experience. Each of you naturally will have had experiences the others have not had. Do not introduce any controversial matters that may weaken the cordial, cooperative spirit of the entire enterprise.

3. Your group acts as one mind in *holding its tongue.* Everything you say to each other must be treated as a confidence. Freedom of expression must always be encouraged, never discouraged.

4. Upon the unanimous consent of all members, another member may from time to time be invited to join the group. Do not let the group grow so big as to be unwieldy. Also, offer new members a trial membership for some short period, to make sure they are in harmony with the others.

5. While each member of the Master-Mind group may take a different approach, depending on his own experience and his own personality, you all should agree on *general* principles of life-success. The principles in *THINK AND GROW RICH* have served so rewardingly for so many men that they can be recommended without reservation.

6. Give each member a chance to serve as chairman, rotating the chairmanship from time to time. One of the chairman's major duties will be to enforce a time limit on speaking, to keep the more talkative members in line. He also should encourage each member to say what he really thinks.

7. Some successful Master-Mind groups have been formed within the personnel employed by a single business. In such a case it should include members of management; this plan has resulted in cooperation and profit all around.

8. Every Master-Mind group should have a purpose outside

its immediate purpose. It should aim to bring specific benefit to persons outside the group. You may, for example, run a Problem Clinic, or sponsor some youth club or similar organization.

A Master-Mind group both reminds you and constantly proves to you how well it pays to use brains other than your own—while, of course, you offer the "lend" of your own mind to the others.

Again, in this chapter, we came back to that very important point: *Poverty needs no plan.* See in your mind's eye the great "stream of power." Realize how a PLAN backed with FAITH IN YOURSELF, a faith that includes firm MONEY CONSCIOUSNESS, can swing you to the side of the unseen river that flows upward toward achievement and enjoyment and bountiful wealth.

Process Points to Pin Down. I hope you are continuing to put all matters of this kind very carefully into the notes pages.

In asking questions of yourself, hinge them on Dr. Hill's statement: *Staying poor is very easy; poverty needs no plan.*

Take note of people who prove this point. You will see that an inward *willingness to stay poor* often takes hold of a man when he has lifted himself a little, so that with a great flurry of so-called effort he lets himself sink down again. Then he can turn to everyone he knows and say: "See? It's no use."

Remember: *You can use more brains than your own.*

When you have done full justice to this important chapter, go on to the next one. . . .

Read **Step 10   Toward Riches: The Mystery of Sex Transmutation,** page 200.

READ THIS CHAPTER AND PROCESS IT FOR IMPORTANT POINTS. Read to the bottom of page 224.

Do you agree with this chapter's general premise?

Have you noticed the sex magnetism of successful men? Can you think of a successful man in public life, right now, who radiates sex magnetism?

You have seen that the emotion of sex has three purposes in our lives. The obvious one is the perpetuation of mankind. But there are two others of great importance. Without looking back into the chapter, name them here; then check.

1._____

2._____

Sexual emotion, when properly harnessed and redirected, is a motivating force that maintains all its attributes of keenness of imagination, courage, persistence, and creative ability. All the powerful forces that accompany the sex drive now are available for tremendous creation in literature, in art, in business, in political affairs, in any profession or calling. Men who accumulate great fortunes and achieve outstanding recognition are invariably motivated by the influence of a woman.

Sex expression stands foremost on any list of the stimuli to which the mind responds. Here is a double list of such stimuli. Cross out the one you believe is not a stimulus; when you are finished, check your answers with the list beginning on page 203 in *THINK AND GROW RICH*.

Mind Stimuli—Good and Bad

Sex frustration	Sex expression
A burning desire to reach your goal	A "don't care" attitude
Friendship	Friendless lonesomeness
Complete absence of any mental or physical distress	Mutual suffering, such as that experienced by a persecuted group
Fear	Courage
Abstinence	Narcotics and alcohol
No attempt to reach the subconscious	Autosuggestion
Never asking advice	Using a Master-Mind alliance
Music	No appreciation of music
Hatred	Love

Take note that some mind stimuli may be harmful in the end. And take special note of how many mind stimuli are available that are wholesome and sustaining.

The stimulated mind is lifted above the horizon of ordinary thought. Working along with creative imagination—the Sixth Sense —this source of genius is available to anyone. And behind this limitless reservoir of directed energy lies the magic of sex transmutation.

Does sex transmutation mean sex starvation? Never. It means only the correct use of sex as opposed to its abuse. Consider why most men enter their greatest period of achievement after they are forty. Experience has much to do with it; but also, and unknown to most men, the control of the physical side of sex expands the mind and the imagination, lends mighty power to the creative faculties. Admit, and be glad, that man's greatest motivating force is his desire to please women!

Where may hunches come from? Read and ponder the four sources detailed on page 205. In considering the Points to Pin Down in this chapter, question yourself as to any pattern you may find in your hunches. Do you tend to have hunches before you retire? When you awaken? While you shave? Pinning down *that* point may be of great value. The time when you get your hunches is probably the time when you are best "in tune" for making important decisions.

Question yourself, too, as to what happened when you followed hunches. Try to see, in your experiences, the difference between following a real hunch and following the dictates of wishful thinking—some mind-picture of what you would *like* to happen.

Having built this advance questioning, proceed to Points to Pin Down.

The key thought is: *The source of all genius is available to YOU*.

When you have mastered this chapter, go ahead to the next Step. . . .

Read **Step 11 Toward Riches: The Subconscious Mind,** page 226.

PROCESS FOR THOUGHTS THAT MAKE YOU THINK.

You read—and I hope you underlined—a vital statement on page 226: *You may voluntarily plant in your subconscious mind any plan, thought or purpose which you desire to transplant into its physical or monetary equivalent*.

This is not intended to be a novel thought. Its purpose is to remind you of this great universal truth, now to be emphasized to a strong degree.

The subconscious mind works day and night. If you fail to plant desires within it, it will feed upon the negative thoughts that reach it as a result of your neglect.

Everything begins with an impulse of thought. The subconscious mind is especially susceptible to influence by thought mixed with emotion. Your emotions may be among the seven positive emotions. (Fill in the missing letters.)

D____e

L__e

En_____m

H__e   (See page 231.)

F____h

__x

R_____ce

Or you may victimize yourself by falling prey to impulses fed into the subconscious by the seven major negative emotions. (Fill in the missing letters.)

J_____y

Re_____e

Su_____n

A____r   (See page 232.)

F__r

G__d

H_____d

Positive and negative emotions cannot occupy the mind at the same time. Let the positive predominate; the effect will be felt in your subconscious too, and fed back into all your affairs. You also will find your subconscious mind is the intermediary that translates one's prayers into terms which Infinite Intelligence can recognize, and through which you may be supplied with plans and ideas that truly answer your prayers.

Repeat the key thought: *You may voluntarily plant in your subconscious mind any plan, thought or purpose which you desire to translate into its physical or monetary equivalent.*

Now go through the highly important Points to Pin Down procedure.

Stay with every chapter till you have made it part of you. When you are ready—when you really KNOW this chapter—go on reading. . . .

Read **Step 12 Toward Riches: The Brain,**
page 236.

PROCESS THROUGH PAGE 244.

This "pin down" chapter gives you some idea of the magnitude of the forces at work within your brain, where some ten billion to fourteen billion nerve cells are capable of almost infinite combination into circuits. Your brain has a potential capacity for thought, memory, conditioning and self-improvement vastly beyond that of any computer, which, after all, only remembers and processes what it is told. Do not forget: A computer cannot, as you can, add creative imagination to the data in its memory banks. It cannot soar into undiscovered realms of thought and achievement. This privilege belongs to man.

The subconscious mind is the "sending station" of the brain. It broadcasts vibrations of thought to the "receiving set" of the creative imagination. From careful scientific tests at Duke University, it seems enormously probable that telepathy and clairvoyance do exist, providing a natural means with which one brain may communicate directly with another. All of us appear to be controlled by forces that are unseen and intangible; yet these are perfectly *natural* forces.

This chapter may seem at first to have little to do with getting rich—in everything that "getting rich" means. Read it carefully, process it carefully, and your attention will be drawn to its focal thought on page 239: . . . *the intangible force (and intelligence) wrapped up in the soil of the earth—the force which provides him with every morsel of food he eats, every article of clothing he wears, every dollar he carries in his pockets.*

You may then connect this thought with the key thought, the great motif of *THINK AND GROW RICH.* Surely you have noticed it, though you may have expressed it inwardly in your own words. This is the key thought and golden core of the entire book:

WHAT THE MIND CAN CONCEIVE, THE MIND CAN ACHIEVE.

Thus your success, your happiness, your health, your life in its entirety is not merely a matter of work, play, and sleep. It is always a matter of *mind*; and the concept of *mind* includes realms far beyond ordinary, conscious thinking.

In handling Points to Pin Down for this chapter, do not formalize them. Simply try to rephrase the chapter. Tell the heart of the chapter back to yourself in one or two hundred words.

Move on, when you are ready, to the 13th Step toward riches. . . .

Step 13 Toward Riches: The Sixth Sense, page 246.

READ THIS CLIMACTIC CHAPTER UP TO THE TOP OF PAGE 255. Underline as you go, but only to the bottom of page 248. Read, but do not underline, Dr. Hill's much-discussed account of his "invisible counselors." Begin again to underline at the top of page 253—*"How to Inspire the Sixth Sense."*

Note that Dr. Hill's "imaginary cabinet" is purely the creation of creative imagination. Yet, as he says, the imagined members of that cabinet have led him into glorious paths of adventure, rekindled an appreciation of true greatness, encouraged creative endeavor, and emboldened the expression of honest thought.

The difficulty has been that people of small imagination tend to misunderstand such an experience. Anyone who really reads and thinks about *THINK AND GROW RICH,* however, will understand how the creative imagination can reach out to form a partnership even with minds long dead. The partnership is not literal, but it is vastly effective just the same. Long-dead minds help to move our present world with the thoughts they left behind (in words) and the vast, overall impression of their personalities, let alone their accomplishments that always will affect us.

Do you want to form your own imaginary cabinet of great minds who visit you? Not every man can do it. It involves first of all—as mentioned early in this *ACTION MANUAL*—your inner ability to take yourself seriously as a person who can improve his inward *self*. The man who can and does summon his own imaginary cabinet puts himself several long steps ahead of his fellows. Choose your own cabinet members. They may be statesmen. They may be masters of finance or industry or invention or art. Choose them carefully. Your continued searching of yourself, your new vision of your goals and deep desires, will help you choose "cabinet members" who can aid you most.

The Sixth Sense cannot be pinned down as we can pin down and limit the other five senses—sight, taste, touch, smell and hearing. With practice and with faith, the Sixth Sense becomes a kind of guardian angel who opens the door to the temple of wisdom.

The key thought of this chapter appears in Dr. Hill's Points to Pin Down: *Now you are in touch with the unknown "something" which has stood steadfast for all great men of all time.*

In forming your own Points to Pin Down, concentrate on the principle of *guidance*. Find instances in your life when you have felt an invisible guidance; a hunch, a Sixth Sense. You did this before. Your subconscious has been working on it meanwhile, so that now, when you seek again for such instances, dozens more will come thronging.

When you have seen the great root-power of your own Sixth Sense, you have finished reading and annotating the 13 Steps Toward Riches. The final chapter will present important, all-embracing information about FEAR and how to get rid of it. In this final chapter you also will take several short tests in preparation for the Examination Section which completes this booklet. Are you ready?

Read **The Six Ghosts of Fear,** page 256.

READING AND UNDERLINING, PROCEED TO THE BOTTOM OF PAGE 292, but do not answer the questionnaire beginning on page 283.

You took inventory of yourself, saw that fears are nothing more than states of mind which, of course, are subject to your own direction and control. Nature has endowed man with absolute control over but one thing: *thought.* Few men exercise this control, but with practice and faith behind it, it is vastly effective.

What are the six *basic* **fears?** Write them here, with no hints:

1.

2.

3.

4.

5.

6.

Now check on page 258 to see if you remembered them correctly.

In analyzing your own fears, you may discover you hold a fear of POVERTY, a highly destructive fear. We tend to "eat" each other financially, so that the fear feeds upon itself. What are the characteristic symptoms that show fear of poverty? Fill in the missing letters:

Ind_____e

In_____on

D__t

W____y

Ov_____n

Pr_____n

Check the symptoms in the book, beginning on page 262. You read the short discussions of the symptoms a little while ago. Now read them again.

Do you fear CRITICISM? This one fear can rob a man of his initiative, destroy his power of imagination, do him damage in a hundred ways. It is really a crime for any parent to build inferiority into a child's mind through unnecessary criticism. You may be suffering from childhood influences, *but you can overcome them*. Set down the seven symptoms that show fear of criticism. As you fill in the missing letters, look these fears in the face:

S__-co_____s

L__k of p____

W__k p_____y

In_____y c_____x

Ex_____e

L____ of in____e

L____ of am_____n

Check these inward-eating fears on page 268. Go ahead immediately (when you have reread the comments) to see how well you remember the seven symptoms that show fear of ILL HEALTH:

Negative au_____n

Hy_____a

In_____e

Sus_____y

S____-co_____g

In_____e

W____y

Check, beginning on page 271. By now you see how certain symptoms overlap; how one such symptom as *worry* can rear its ugly head in half a dozen different areas of life.

What are the three major symptoms that show fear of LOSS OF LOVE?

J_____y

F__t f____g

Ga_____g

Check these on page 274. Proceeding: What four symptoms show FEAR OF OLD AGE?

Pr_____e sl____n

A————y for —— ——

Ki____g off in_____

Ma____g as a y____r p____n

Check on page 275. Proceeding: What three symptoms show FEAR OF DEATH?

Th____g about d____g

Asso_____ with ____ of _____y

Asso_____ with i____s or im_____e

Check the list beginning on page 277. Now take six of your 3x5 file cards and copy the lists onto the cards, one to each card. Put those cards on a table, push them around in varying relation to each other. Once again notice the patterns of fear that can run through a life and how certain fears overlap each other. You will notice that a basic fear can have more than one name, or more than one approach. See this for yourself. Look at the lists till you see it. Tape or staple those six cards into your notebook.

Worry is fear—a state of mind based on fear. Once you reach a decision, you free yourself of worry. You also can reach a general, blanket decision that nothing life has to offer you is worth the price of worry.

Another great evil is *susceptibility to negative influences*. You should make careful analysis to see if you are too susceptible. The material in the Examination Section will aid you in this. As Dr. Hill says: "Without doubt, the most common weakness of all human beings is the habit of leaving their minds open to the negative influence of other people."

Before you answer the questionnaire on page 283, write your own Points to Pin Down. Go to Dr. Hill's points. Create half a dozen questions, all based on the list of alibis that begins on page 289. *Guide yourself especially by the alibis you underlined.*

Now sit down with the questionnaire that begins on page 283. Handle this very important questionnaire in a very special way. Answer it first in the book. Wait three days; then answer it here, in the *ACTION MANUAL,* where it is reprinted. Then compare your answers with the answers you gave in the book. Probably some will be different. Ask yourself why. Ask yourself what *mood,* or state of mind, has in varying degree affected your answers.

So, for the time being, skip the questionnaire as it is printed below. Answer it first in the book; come back to this one in three days.

Think Before You Answer

Do you complain often of "feeling bad," and if so, what is the cause?

Do you find fault with other people at the slightest provocation?

Do you frequently make mistakes in your work, and if so, why?

Are you sarcastic and offensive in your conversation?

Do you deliberately avoid the association of anyone, and if so, why?

Do you suffer frequently with indigestion? If so, what is the cause?

Does life seem futile and the future hopeless to you?

Do you like your occupation? If not, why?

Do you often feel self-pity, and if so, why?

Are you envious of those who excel you?

To which do you devote most time, thinking of success, or of failure?

Are you gaining or losing self-confidence as you grow older?

Do you learn something of value from all mistakes?

Are you permitting some relative or acquaintance to worry you? If so, why?

Are you sometimes "in the clouds" and at other times in the depths of despondency?

Who has the most inspiring influence upon you? What is the cause?

Do you tolerate negative or discouraging influences which you can avoid?

Are you careless of your personal appearance? If so, when and why?

Have you learned how to "drown your troubles" by being too busy to be annoyed by them?

Would you call yourself a "spineless weakling" if you permitted others to do your thinking for you?

How many preventable disturbances annoy you, and why do you tolerate them?

Do you resort to liquor, narcotics, or cigarettes to "quiet your nerves"? If so, why do you not try will-power instead?

Does anyone "nag" you, and if so, for what reason?

Do you have a definite major purpose, and if so, what is it, and what plan have you for achieving it?

Do you suffer from any of the six basic fears? If so, which ones?

Have you a method by which you can shield yourself against the negative influence of others?

Do you make deliberate use of autosuggestion to make your mind positive?

Which do you value most, your material possessions, or your privilege of controlling your own thoughts?

Are you easily influenced by others against your own judgment?

Has today added anything of value to your stock of knowledge or state of mind?

Do you face squarely the circumstances which make you unhappy, or side-step the responsibility?

Do you analyze all mistakes and failures and try to profit by them, or do you take the attitude that this is not your duty?

Can you name three of your most damaging weaknesses? What are you doing to correct them?

Do you encourage other people to bring their worries to you for sympathy?

Do you choose, from your daily experiences, lessons or influences which aid in your personal advancement?

Does your presence have a negative influence on other people as a rule?

What habits of other people annoy you most?

Do you form your own opinions or permit yourself to be influenced by other people?

Have you learned how to create a mental state of mind with which you can shield yourself against all discouraging influences?

Does your occupation inspire you with faith and hope?

Are you conscious of possessing spiritual forces of sufficient power to enable you to keep your mind free from all forms of fear?

Does your religion help to keep your mind positive?

Do you feel it your duty to share other people's worries? If so, why?

If you believe that "birds of a feather flock together," what have you learned about yourself by studying the friends whom you attract?

What connection, if any, do you see between the people with whom you associate most closely, and any unhappiness you may experience?

Could it be possible that some person whom you consider to be a friend is, in reality, your worst enemy, because of his negative influence on your mind?

By what rules do you judge who is helpful and who is damaging to you?

Are your intimate associates mentally superior or inferior to you?

How much time out of every twenty-four hours do you devote to:

    a. your occupation

    b. sleep

    c. play and relaxation

    d. acquiring useful knowledge

    e. plain waste?

Who among your acquaintances:
   a. encourages you most
   b. cautions you most
   c. discourages you most?

What is your greatest worry? Why do you tolerate it?

When others offer you free, unsolicited advice, do you accept it without question or analyze their motive?

What, above all else, do you most desire? Do you intend to acquire it? Are you willing to subordinate all other desires for this one? How much time daily do you devote to acquiring it?

Do you change your mind often? If so, why?

Do you usually finish everything you begin?

Are you easily impressed by other people's business or professional titles, college degrees, or wealth?

Are you easily influenced by what other people think or say of you?

Do you cater to people because of their social or financial status?

Whom do you believe to be the greatest person living? In what respect is this person superior to yourself?

How much time have you devoted to studying and answering these questions? (At least one day is necessary for the analysis and the answering of the entire list.)

If you have answered all these questions truthfully, you know more about yourself than the majority of people. Study the questions carefully, come back to them once each week for several months, and be astounded at the amount of additional knowledge of great value to yourself you will have gained by the simple method of answering the questions truthfully. If you are not certain concerning the answers to some of the questions, seek the counsel of those who know you well, especially those who have no motive in flattering you, and see yourself through their eyes. The experience will be astonishing.

EXAMINATION SECTION
Score your own get-rich power

THE TESTS AND PROCEDURES YOU FIND IN THIS SECTION ARE TO be undertaken *when you are well prepared*. This involves:

   1. *Pre-reading THINK AND GROW RICH,* as explained in this *ACTION MANUAL,* then

2. *Reading,* annotating and otherwise "processing" *THINK AND GROW RICH*, as explained in this *ACTION MANUAL.*

When you have done this conscientiously, you are ready to proceed with this section.

Take the questionnaires and other material in order, as they are given. In some cases you will see the material draws upon *THINK AND GROW RICH* or closely parallels material in the book. This is done deliberately, and follows proved learning patterns. Answer each question as though you never had seen it before. Follow all directions. Rate yourself as instructed.

Examination One

Go through every page of *THINK AND GROW RICH.* Wherever you underlined a subhead, write that subhead separately on a file card.

Lay out the cards on a table. Inspect them, and look for patterns you may have shown in your choice. Other men have found patterns toward instant action, patterns toward inward-looking thought, patterns toward planning, and others. Do not be guided or influenced by anyone else. Look for a pattern that YOU show. If, after an hour, you can find no discernible pattern, put away the cards and try again three days later.

If you find no discernible pattern, search through the many underlinings you made in the body of the text. You are almost certain to find a pattern.

When you find a pattern, write it carefully into your notes. Keep the cards for future reference.

Examination Two

The table below lists ten general causes of fear. Do not stop to consider whether you can be "blamed" for having any of these fears; only ask if they may apply to you. Rate yourself on each, from 1 to 3 as indicated. If you sincerely feel your rating falls in-between any two of the given ratings, give yourself a fractional rating —either 1½ or 2½. Note your rating in the last column on the right. When you are finished, total your score at the bottom of the column.

ROOTS OF FEAR	RATE YOUR FEAR			SCORE
	1	2	3	
1. Childhood fear of parents	I generally was in fear of my mother, father, or both.	I feared my parents now and then.	I do not recall ever fearing my parents.	
2. Feelings of inadequacy	I feel deeply inadequate when I face problems.	Sometimes, when I face problems, I feel inadequate.	Almost always I feel adequate to handle my problems.	
3. Apprehension about job	I live in fear of losing my job (or other income).	Now and then I worry about my job security.	I never falter in my confidence that I can earn a living.	
4. What others think of you	I'm always concerned about other people's opinions.	Other people's opinions worry me sometimes.	I am not at all disturbed by what others think of me.	
5. Aggressive people in your life	Aggressors always scare and bother me.	I steer clear of such people.	Nobody scares me.	
6. Harmless animals; dogs, etc.	I can't help being frightened of dogs and cats.	Dogs and cats makes me feel a bit uneasy.	Domesticated animals never cause me any fear.	
7. Insecurity in love	I constantly fear losing the love of my beloved.	Sometimes I brood about losing love.	I am quietly confident in my love relation.	
8. Health	I always feel I am heading for serious illness.	Every once in a while I find a health sign to worry about.	I don't fuss about my health.	
9. Decisions	It costs me a lot of mental agony to make any decision.	I get fussed about a few decisions I have to make.	I have no trouble in making up my mind.	
10. Responsibility	I won't take on responsibility if I can help it.	I take on responsibility if I see it's up to me.	I naturally accept responsibility, even seek it out.	

Examination Three

The table below lists ten significant causes of guilt. Do not stop to consider your "blame," if any, for a type of guilt; only ask if it applies to you. Rate yourself from 1 to 3 as indicated; or rate yourself at the 1½ or 2½ point if you honestly feel that is your nearest-correct rating. Note your rating in the last column on the right. When you are finished, note your score at the bottom of the column.

ROOTS OF GUILT	RATE YOUR GUILT			SCORE
	1	2	3	
1. You tend to slander others	I go right on hurting other people's reputations.	I used to slander others, but I have stopped doing this.	I never have injured anyone by slander or gossip.	
2. You don't keep promises	It seems inevitable that I must break promises.	That was in the past; my promises mean something today.	I always have been careful to keep my promises.	
3. You steal	So what? It gives me a little "break" I badly need.	My thefts were minor and mean; I've stopped any theft, now.	I do not steal—not even someone's time.	
4. You never "feel right" about sex	Never have and never will; sex and guilt go together.	Now and then I feel as though sex is wrong, but not always.	I see sex as healthful, natural and enjoyable.	
5. You live in a graveyard of plans	Nothing ever seems to come out the way I plan it.	I achieve some of my ambitions.	Seeing clear goals ahead, I almost always reach them.	
6. You feel you have failed others	Obviously, others are disappointed in me quite consistently.	Now and again I know I let someone down.	Invariably I exceed anyone's expectations.	
7. You neglect your family	I'm ashamed, but I know I neglect those loved ones.	I slip up now and then in my duty toward my family.	My family finds me always cooperative and loving.	
8. Work opportunities? Wasted!	Good openings? I let them slip through my fingers.	I try for some good jobs, at least.	I seek higher, better jobs all the time.	
9. You lie in word and deed	Can't help it—I say.	I may lie or cheat sometimes.	I simply do not lie or cheat, no matter what happens.	
10. You let education pass you by	I refused to face the fact that education *pays*.	I made some small efforts toward attaining knowledge.	I have acquired a full measure of book learning and other learning.	

336

Examination Four

The table lists ten common causes of antagonism. Viewing yourself as objectively as possible, rate yourself from 1 to 3 on each cause; or rate yourself at 1½ or 2½ if you feel these in-between ratings are correct. Note your rating in the last column on the right. Note your score at the bottom of the column.

ROOTS OF ANTAGONISM	RATE YOUR ANTAGONISM			SCORE
	1	2	3	
1. Envy of others	I simply hate people who have something I don't own.	There are some people I envy.	I hardly ever envy anybody.	
2. Jealousy	When I care about someone, I am very jealous about that person.	I am learning to put aside the smallness of jealousy.	Why be jealous? It never enters my mind.	
3. Brooding resentment	I'm invariably bitter about someone or something.	Now and then I give way to resentment.	Rarely if ever am I resentful.	
4. Hair-trigger rage	Look out! I am always ready to roar.	I lose my temper now and then.	It takes a great deal to get me riled.	
5. Intolerance	Either you believe as I do, or I will have nothing to do with you.	Some people who disagree with me may be right, in their own way.	Differences of opinion and appearance add zest to life.	
6. Distrust	Everyone is out to "do" me; I trust nobody.	Some people can't be trusted.	If anything, I am too trusting.	
7. Backbiting slander	I like to talk damagingly about others behind their backs.	Sometimes I spread gossip and rumors.	This kind of action has no part in my life.	
8. Antagonistic tone and words	I prefer to be blunt no matter how others don't like it.	My tone and words occasionally show my shaky temper.	I keep my words kindly and my tone quiet.	
9. Lack of patience	I am known as an impatient person and I don't care.	I do get impatient from time to time.	People can count on me to be patient.	
10. Sarcastic attitude	I "put myself over" very often by being sarcastic.	Now and then I feel sarcastic and I show it.	Rarely, and only for emphasis, am I sarcastic.	

Examination Five

The table lists ten common factors that affect self-confidence. Carefully and candidly rate yourself on each. Score yourself, with fractional scoring (1½ or 2½) if you see fit. Note your rating for each item in the right-hand column, and your score at the bottom of the column. (By now you must have noticed "overlaps" in these examinations, themed to the interdependence of every factor of your personality.)

ROOTS OF SELF-CONFIDENCE	RATE YOUR SELF-CONFIDENCE			SCORE
	1	2	3	
1. A good income	Something keeps me from earning enough.	I do pretty well, though I should do much better.	I earn a good sum and enjoy spending it.	
2. A wide acquaintanceship	I don't remember people and I don't need them anyway.	I have a few friends.	I have more friends than I can handily count.	
3. Your face and bearing	Call me ugly; I know it.	I rate about average in appearance.	They tell me I make a very good appearance.	
4. General intelligence	I don't seem to "have it"—upstairs.	I'd say I'm medium-smart.	I know I have a high level of intelligence.	
5. Acceptance in others' eyes	I am sure that people avoid me.	I get along more or less.	People want to share their hours with me.	
6. Courage	I'm a mouse.	When I must, I'll face up to people or situations.	Nothing frightens me.	
7. Speaking up in public	Not I!	I don't like it, but I will speak up on occasion.	I like to speak up and to indulge in public speaking.	
8. Physical condition	My health is poor; I drag around.	I'm sick occasionally.	I feel robust and rarely have a day of illness.	
9. Faith in the infinite	What's faith? Who needs it?	Sometimes I feel faith; other times I shrug it off.	I feel I am "tuned in" to vast forces that aid me.	
10. Stable attitudes	Emergencies make me go to pieces.	I may crack up under heavy pressure.	I can meet almost any situation calmly.	

Examination Six

The table lists ten *negative* factors that prevent people from becoming truly mature. Rate yourself as before, including the fractional ratings 1½ or 2½ if necessary. Note ratings in the right-hand column, and score yourself at the bottom of that column.

| ROOTS OF IMMATURITY | RATE YOUR MATURITY | | | SCORE |
	1	2	3	
1. A false front	I am always putting up a bluff.	At times I hide behind a false front.	As people see me, so I am.	
2. Selfish attitudes	Of course I am out for myself all the time.	Yes, I see I am selfish now and then.	I do have self-interest, but stop short of selfishness.	
3. Persecution complex	I know that many people are out to "get" me.	Here and there I meet someone who wants to hurt me.	I have no enemies and no reason to have enemies.	
4. Lack of self-control	Any little thing gets me into a tizzy.	There are occasions when I lose my self-control.	I am my own master always.	
5. Putting things off	That's me—the world's most confirmed procrastinator.	In some things I put off action when I should act.	I get things done, and do them promptly.	
6. Belittling	I love to "run down" others.	While I rarely belittle, I rarely praise, either.	I never belittle and prefer to build up and praise.	
7. Boastfulness	Hear me blow my own horn!	If I've done something worth bragging about, I brag.	I let my actions speak for themselves.	
8. Cruelty	I get in a nasty remark with great joy.	I let somebody have it if it's coming to him.	Almost always, I spare others any cruel remarks.	
9. A closed mind	Bigoted? I know my viewpoint is right, and that's it.	On certain subjects I don't want any argument.	I may "know my own mind" but will change an opinion if shown good reason.	
10. Excusing one's self	The list of alibis in *Think and Grow Rich* was for me.	I use an alibi when it's handy.	Any alibi I may use is very valid—and very rare.	

339

You have just completed five examinations of ten items each. How did you score? Maximum score for any examination is 50; total maximum is 250; average for any examination is 25; total average is 125.

While your total score is significant, it is more important to note and consider your score on each examination. Then correlate the score with your rating (sometimes informal) in any similar quiz in *THINK AND GROW RICH*. Do not mark yourself *Passed* or *Failed*. It is far more important to SEE YOURSELF.

Graph for Significance

In Step 6 Toward Riches you took a short examination on your qualities of leadership, rating yourself from 1 to 5 on various qualities. Go back to this table and draw lines connecting the check marks you made so that you form a vertical graph. Here is an example:

	1	2	3	4	5
UNWAVERING COURAGE		●			
SELF-CONTROL			●		
A KEEN SENSE OF JUSTICE			●		
DEFINITENESS OF DECISION				●	
DEFINITENESS OF PLANS			●		
THE HABIT OF DOING MORE THAN PAID FOR					●
A PLEASING PERSONALITY		●			
SYMPATHY AND UNDERSTANDING			●		
MASTERY OF DETAIL			●		
WILLINGNESS TO ASSUME FULL RESPONSIBILITY				●	
COOPERATION					●

Now draw a similar graph for each of the five examinations you just completed. If you rated yourself on the 1½ or 2½ lines in any instance, put a dot on the line. For a rating of 1, 2 or 3, put a dot in the middle of the column. Draw lines connecting the dots. You will come out with very jagged, dramatic graphs—and if you tended to rate yourself right down the middle, the very lack of drama in your graph will be significant. Question it! To call one's self average in just about everything is to indicate an unwillingness to know one's self.

Come back to all six graphs at intervals of a month, for six months. Reexamine yourself in each case. Undoubtedly you will change some ratings. Draw a new graph each time. Use different-colored pens or pencils; or, if you run out of colors, use dotted lines, dashed lines or dashed-and-dotted lines. Six graphs is about all you should make on one page. Also make a key to show you the date of each graph. Many men are so fascinated by this process, and feel so much aid in building their own ability to get rich, that they duplicate the examinations and go on graphing after the six months are up.

You need not score yourself formally after giving yourself the first, "familiarization" score. Rely on the graphs. They are *pictures of you.*

How Will You Shift Each Graph Toward the Right?

You certainly noticed that the positive, profitable, healthful, wealth-building indications for each graph lie toward the right. As you redraw each graph, month by month, you will see your progress by the swings of your lines toward the right.

What will you be doing meanwhile to assure those swings toward the right—those definite indications that you are mastering the SELF who alone is responsible for bringing you riches?

The following list, culled from hundreds of items, is purposely not keyed to any particular trait of character, physical aspect or ability. It is intended to make you think, with each item: *Is this for me? Why?*

For any item you check, *make half a check,* just the downward stroke, like this: /. Later, after you have definitely embarked on the indicated course of action, complete the check, like this: √. Thus, in referring back to the list (as you should, every time you refer back to your progress graphs), any incomplete check mark will catch your eye.

Now go through the list carefully and thoughtfully, making only half-checks:

Graph-Swinging Actions
I will analyze my fears.

I will enlist aid from someone who can handle situations that trouble me, and learn from him.

I will go to a wise counselor.

I will stop brooding and go into action.

I will accept the possibility of things going wrong and plan beyond that point.

I will insist to myself that I be patient.

I will stop all gossip, backbiting and slander.

I will make friends among those with whom I disagree.

I will control my temper; laugh at it.

I will get rid of resentful brooding.

I will no longer covet what others have.

I will overcome jealousy.

I will stop hating and try to substitute love, or at least understanding, for hatred.

I will learn how to relax.

I will practice forgiveness.

I will indulge in enough physical activity to keep my body in good condition.

I will pray in the way set forth in *THINK AND GROW RICH*.

I will get periodic medical examinations.

I will not exaggerate any physical faults, and will remember how many have overcome these faults and worse.

I will read in my field, and also read for pleasure.

I will take courses to fill in gaps in my education toward success and my education toward enjoyment.

I will also take any special course of general value that I may need; say a course in public speaking.

I will pay more attention to my dress and grooming.

I will participate in discussion groups and in other group activities.

I will, in such activities, make sure I speak up.

I will look for (and I know I will find, as have so many others) energies and abilities that come from a cosmic source.

I will develop my imagination and use it further as a tuning-in power toward other minds.

I will get things done when they should be done.

I will get things well done.

I will put up no bluffs, and thus find no further reasons to be ashamed of my bluffs.

I will aid rather can afflict others, avoid cruelty in word or deed or attitude.

I will not boast, no matter how tempted I may be.

I will not browbeat anyone else with my own opinion.

I will finish what I start.
I will respect myself.
I will respect others.
I will have firm goals and firm plans for reaching those goals.
I will get rid of guilt feelings about sex.
I will get rid of all unwarranted guilt feelings.
I will consistently see myself as worthy of the best in life.

A Special Checklist: General Skills That Wait to Aid You

Many a man stops far short of the top because he lacks some skill he could have acquired. One of the items in the foregoing list called your attention to general skills you may need. Among such skills is the ability to *read rapidly* and *retain what you read*. This skill is of inestimable value because *knowledge is power*. As with all the general skills to be mentioned shortly, rapid reading may have no immediate application. You never know when it will go to work for you and provide a significant, indispensable *lift*.

Here are hints on rapid reading. They represent core methods taken from several different rapid-reading courses; but you may also wish to take such a course.

Pre-read: You already have had some instruction in pre-reading. It amounts to looking for the signposts an author sets up in his book—table of contents, foreword, subheads, index, and so forth.

Annotate: Underlinings and similar devices help you come back and pick up needed information very quickly. You also fix facts in your mind when you underline them.

Do not move your head, fingers or lips when you read: Move only your eyes. Let your eyes scan each line, not your head and not your finger. Your eyes can move as rapidly as you can think, but your head, fingers and lips cannot, so they will slow your reading if you let them go into motion.

Scan down the middle: Depending on how thoroughly you wish to absorb what you are reading, you can read down the middle of any printed column, not really looking at the inch of print to the right and to the left. Try this; you'll be surprised at how well you understand.

Read in phrases: This takes practice. You will find, however, that a great deal of what you read is made up of familiar phrases such as *this takes practice*. You don't have to *read* such phrases; you *know* them. Extend the phrase-flashing process gradually and you soon pick up four or five words as a unit.

Read "firsts and lasts": Use your judgment. Realize, however, that the first paragraph and the last paragraph of a letter or report often tell you what you really need to know. The first paragraph or the first two paragraphs of the average newspaper story contain the "meat" of that story, and answer the questions raised by our old friends WHO, WHY, WHAT, WHEN, WHERE and HOW. The first paragraph of a newspaper editorial states what it is about; the last paragraph gives the stand the editor takes.

Ask questions; look for the answers: When you have pre-read a book, or have read the first paragraph and last of a newspaper story or a report or magazine article, your mind will come up with questions. Then, scanning in the body of the printed matter, look for the answer to those questions. You need not actually skip anything if you do not wish to; but you will not really *read* till you come to a part that answers one of your questions.

Naturally, rapid reading takes practice. As with many another skill, it responds quickly to your *knowing* you can do it.

Other skills that can "come in handy"—sometimes to the tune of a million dollars worth of handiness—are:

Typewriting	Some knowledge of music
Basic accounting	Knowledge of trade customs and
Basic psychology	papers
Basic finance and banking	Technical trends and processes
Current news	knowledge
Knowledge of government	Memory training
Public speaking	Knowing how to use reference
Foreign language ability	works and libraries
Some knowledge of art	

One Last Instruction: REVIEW

You have read *THINK AND GROW RICH* according to directions given in this *ACTION MANUAL*. You have followed all directions conscientiously. You have taken all the examinations. Now—review!

It is in review that the great lessons of success take hold of the deep, inner self and become a part of the personality.

Some men will neglect to review, will not check back on their questionnaires, will not refresh their memories by going through the examinations again. Such men do not give a wonder-working process a chance to work its full wonders. Other men *will* review, and count every hour of review in thousands of dollars and every other form of life-reward.

You Are the Master of Your Fate.
YOUR Motivations Must Move YOU Forward.

Nobody can think for you, nobody can act for you, nobody can succeed for you—but yourself. Be glad of that!

Remember: What the mind can believe, the mind can achieve.

THINK AND GROW RICH has motivated more men and women to achieve success than any other book written by a living author.

Every secret you need in order to *THINK AND GROW RICH* is now abundantly in your hands.

FREE!

SUCCESS PROFILE

Find out your personal success profile!

75 vital questions give you a complete analysis of your own personal potential.

Find out the personal information you need to truly maximize your own abilities—and discover facts about yourself that will amaze you!

There's no cost and no obligation. The Napoleon Hill Foundation has developed this Success Profile Questionnaire to help you **Think and Grow Rich**—so send for this vital success tool today!

YES! *Send my FREE Success Profile Questionnaire to:*

NAME _____

ADDRESS _____

CITY _____ STATE _____ ZIP _____

DAY PHONE NO. ( ) _____ NIGHT PHONE NO. ( ) _____

Discover how to achieve *true* success

Order today and get this powerful step-by-step 8-cassette program. You'll also receive the 254-page HARDCOVER EDITION of the BEST-SELLING BOOK and a 72-page study guide with tests and summaries for each chapter.

You'll learn:
- 13 practical principles to create success on all levels of your life
- How to turn ideas into fortunes — six definite, practical steps
- How to overcome the 6-primary fears
- 4 steps to persistence
- How to harness your subconscious mind
- 5 steps to self-confidence
- The 8-point formula for setting — and *achieving* — your goals

Learn how to achieve financial security and true happiness with Dr. Hill's powerful step-by-step program — for enduring riches throughout your life.

UNCONDITIONALLY GUARANTEED

☐ **YES!** Please send me Dr. Napoleon Hill's NEW *Think and Grow Rich* 8-cassette program plus the book and study guide. I understand that if I'm not completely satisfied within 30 days I may return the program. Napoleon Hill Foundation will refund the full purchase price of **$89.95.**

☐ Check ☐ Visa ☐ Mastercard ☐ American Express

Card Number _____ Exp ___

Signature _____

Name _____

Title _____

Company _____

Address _____

City _____ State ____ Zip _____

Daytime Phone (_____) _____

CA Residents add 6% tax   SU 4/87

THE NAPOLEON HILL FOUNDATION
1440 Paddock Drive
Northbrook, Illinois 60062